Education and Constructions of Childhood

Other titles in the *Contemporary Issues in Education Studies* series

Changing Urban Education, Simon Pratt-Adams, Meg Maguire and
   Elizabeth Burn
Multiculturalism and Education, Richard Race
Young People, Popular Culture and Education, Chris Richards

Also available from Continuum

Ethnicity, Race and Education, Sue Walters
Rethinking Children's Rights, Phil Jones and Sue Welch

Education and Constructions of Childhood

Contemporary Issues in Education Studies

David Blundell

continuum

Continuum International Publishing Group

The Tower Building   80 Maiden Lane
11 York Road   Suite 704
London SE1 7NX   New York, NY 10038

www.continuumbooks.com

British Library Cataloguing-in-Publication Data
A catalogue record for this book is available from the British Library.

ISBN: 978-1-8470-6025-9 (paperback)
        978-1-4411-7884-8 (hardcover)

Library of Congress Cataloging-in-Publication Data
Blundell, David.
Education and constructions of childhood / David Blundell.
   p. cm. — (Contemporary issues in education studies)
Includes bibliographical references and index.
ISBN 978-1-8470-6025-9 — ISBN 978-1-4411-7884-8 1. Early childhood education—Social aspects. 2. Popular culture. 3. Critical pedagogy. 4. Curriculum planning. 5. Child development. 6. Educational anthropology. I. Title.

HQ767.9.B59 2011
306.43—dc22

                                                   2011007243

Typeset by Newgen Imaging Systems Pvt Ltd, Chennai, India
Printed and bound in India

To Charlotte Gordon Barrie (Blundell) on becoming an octogenarian, and for Imogen, Ted, Alex and Laurence, with love and in hope.

He picked up a pebble
and threw it into the sea.
And another, and another.
He couldn't stop.
He wasn't trying to fill the sea.
He wasn't trying to empty the beach.
He was just throwing away,
nothing else but.
Like a kitten playing
he was practicing for the future
when there'll be so many things
he'll want to throw away
if only his fingers will unclench
and let them go.

Small boy by Norman MacCaig from *Collected Poems* (1990)
Reproduced with permission from Polygon, an imprint of Birlinn Ltd.

Contents

viii Contents

Series Editors' Preface

The series *Contemporary Issues in Education Studies* is timely for its critical exploration of education in this period of accelerating change. Responding to this challenge, the books in the series have titles which correspond closely to the needs of students taking a wide range of courses and modules within Education Studies and related fields such as teacher education. Education Studies is an important subject area that should be at the heart of many faculties of education. There is a need for relevant, core texts within Education Studies, which explore and critique contemporary issues across the discipline and challenge prevailing discourses of what education is about. We also need to provide students with strong theoretical perspectives and frameworks, focusing on relevant literature in an accessible and readable format.

We set the authors of this series a number of challenges in terms of what to include in their text. Therefore, each book addresses a contemporary issue in education and has an international rather than just an English focus. The texts are structured to provide a clear grasp of the topic and to provide an overview of research, current debates and perspectives. Contextualized extracts from important primary texts ensure readers' exposure to dominant contemporary theories in the field of education, by demystifying essential vocabulary and educational discourse, enabling the education student to engage with these texts in a meaningful way. The extensive and appropriate literature review in each text gives a firm base for contextualizing the subject and promoting understanding at multiple levels.

This series is grounded in a strong conceptual, theoretical framework and is presented in an accessible way. Each book uses features such as case studies, reflective exercises and activities that encourage and support student learning. Key relevant and contemporary questions are inserted throughout each chapter to extend the readers' thinking and understanding. Furthermore, additional material is also provided in the companion website to each book.

Education and Constructions of Childhood is authored by David Blundell, who is Principal Lecturer and Programme Director of Undergraduate and Postgraduate Studies, in the Faculty of Humanities, Arts, Languages and Education at London Metropolitan University. He writes from extensive experience as a primary school teacher and Deputy Head, as well as a Lecturer and Senior Lecturer in Further and Higher Education, including a spell as course leader for the BA Education Studies degree. His research interests include teaching and learning, mathematics and environmental education.

Drawing on his current role as Strand Leader for Children and Young People at London Met, David Blundell's text analyses the continuing influence of debates concerning education and the construction of the child. This is both a timely, important and welcome addition to the literature in this subject area following recent Human Rights legislation and the introduction of the education policy document Every Child Matters and its aspirations towards notions of accountability and integration that have been introduced. This legislation has the potential to change the ways the State and adults perceive children and childhood in contemporary Western societies.

David Blundell highlights the evolution of the construction of the child by placing these constructions within historical, social and cultural contexts. Through analyses of meanings and ideas of the child that draw on the works of theorists including Rousseau, Pestalozzi, and Froebel the author underlines the international perspectives which have shaped notions of childhood. The introduction of mass schooling in the modern era intersects with economic, political and religious discourses that have institutionalized childhood and that have influenced the evolution of the English system of education from the nineteenth century.

The author examines how such developments have continued into the twentieth century – the 'Century of the Child' with the emergence of child-centred methods of pedagogy and practice, finally captured by English education policy makers in the Plowden Report of 1967. The notion of progressivism and discourses of difference are highlighted as significant developments in child-centred approaches to the curriculum, teaching and learning. The author also encourages the reader to consider critically more recent approaches that have focused on education as preparation for work and the implications of this for childhood, children's well-being and child-centred pedagogy; furthermore for the reader to reflect upon where this places 'child-centred' discourses as articulated in international and national government policy that will continue to impact on the relationship between children and teachers and the implication for the quality of life of children in the twenty-first century.

Education and Constructions of Childhood underlines the continuing focus on how we perceive children and the condition of childhood across academia and in everyday life. The book is crucial not only for students across a broad range of subject areas but also education and social policy makers and for all professional practitioners situated in the various institutions of childhood. As in other books in the Series, we challenge and encourage the reader to think critically and differently about education, in this instance about the meanings attached to the child and childhood in educational settings. One of the many challenges in this book focuses on the need not only to recognize the importance of the child, but to promote a construction of childhood and the child that encourages an approach to education that is not constrained by adult-led expectations but that involves children and young people in decision making about their lives.

Simon Pratt-Adams and Richard Race
April 2011
London

Preface

All the indications are that we are rather obsessed with the quality of childhood. It is almost impossible to turn on the television news or open a newspaper without encountering a story about children that questions whether childhood is being fatally compromised in our early twenty-first century world. If we go to any University library and look for books on children and childhood, we find them scattered through education, psychology, social science and social care, medicine and health studies, cultural and media studies and history, as well as some in the sections for law, sport science, architecture, art and design. In short, there is no lack of people who have children and childhood in their sights and we might think that in consequence, we know more about them and that the condition of childhood is as secure as it has ever been. Moreover, many of these disciplinary areas claiming an interest in childhood are linked to professional roles tasked with providing for children and meeting their needs and entitlements; these include teachers and teaching assistants, educational psychologists, educational welfare officers, mentors, careers' advisors, social workers, probation officers, health visitors, paediatricians and paediatric nurses, play and youth workers, road safety officers, sport coaches, software designers and any number of others. In turn, these professional roles are frequently situated within, and reinforced by, institutions of childhood, such as schools, nurseries, one o'clock clubs, playgroups, clinics, libraries, junior sport clubs, children's hospitals, toy shops and children's centres; the list is long and growing as educational and social policy widens its focus.

The message is clear; accompanying our broad range of knowledge and expertise concerning children and childhood are huge social capital resources dedicated to their upbringing, safety, entertainment and care. However, there is evidence that this huge effort is proving insufficient to ensure the well-being, optimism and quality of life of our children, and that we have cause to be worried about it. This book attempts to contribute to contemporary debates about the condition of childhood and the state our children find themselves in by examining how we have come to think about children in the way we do, the meanings we attach to our working ideas of the *Child* and the childhoods children experience in and through educational settings.

Acknowledgements

I am greatly indebted to the interest, support and encouragement offered by my colleagues and students during the preparation of this book. Thanks to Simon, Richard and Ally for their patience over missed deadlines and delays. I am especially grateful to Cécile Tschirhart and Dr Robin Shields for making time and headspace available; to my colleague Tom Burns for reading an early draft and likewise to Friederike Größe – each offering excellent suggestions for improvement; to Dr Trevor Welland for sources on childhood and Original Sin; and, to Andrea Mian, Jessie Bustillos, Jenny Lange and all my brilliant Education and Early Childhood Studies students and colleagues at London Metropolitan University for their interest, enthusiastic questioning and forbearance during difficult times! Above all, thanks to Mandy Maidment, my resident natural scientist, whose love, encouragement and scepticism about *social* science sustain and challenge me in equal measure, and who understands more about children and young people than any book could tell!

David Blundell
London Metropolitan University

Introduction

Despite the very obvious prominence given to children and their childhood in our homes, high streets and popular media and the preciousness afforded them, there is evidence that growing up in the United Kingdom is far from easy; indeed that young people in Britain seem to be among the unhappiest, least confident and optimistic children in the developed world. A series of reports that have appeared throughout the first ten years of the new millennium seem to confirm this view, with the demands imposed by schooling cited among a range of explanatory factors for this state of unease.

UNICEF (2007) surveyed the condition of childhood in 21 industrialized countries using 40 key indicators that included poverty, family relationships and children's health and well-being. Although the Scandinavian States (to little surprise) came high in the rankings, The Netherlands and the United Kingdom, as ostensibly similar countries and societies separated by little other than the North Sea, found themselves top and bottom of the league respectively. Similarly, the Children's Society (2009), a UK charity, published findings from their Good Childhood Inquiry suggesting that children's lives are being curtailed by fears over their safety and given largely unrealizable materialistic desires through the consumerist culture surrounding them. This reinforced the view of an earlier report published by the Compass policy think tank in 2008, that childhood was being excessively commercialized and mediated through an unhealthy fixation with aggressively marketed gadgetry and brand names – a theme addressed earlier by *The Daily Telegraph* (2006) under the telling headline 'Childhood "Dying in Spend, Spend Britain"'.

The dystopian gloom surrounding childhood in the United Kingdom found a rallying point with the publication of *Toxic Childhood: How the Modern World Is Damaging Our Children and What We Can Do About It* (Palmer, 2006), and the toxicity metaphor seemed to take hold of the popular imagination. In the book the author takes stock of the impact of technological change over the past 30 years, arguing that this period has seen unprecedented shifts that have put children and childhood under pressure by promoting consumption as the root of happiness, squeezing out opportunities and places to play from children's lives – frequently replacing them with adult-organized play and sport – placing ever more stress on exam results and levels of attainment with growing piles of homework as their corollary and increased surveillance that induces rather than allays anxiety and fear.

It is instructive to see how these tensions have become focused on education. In a web-based discussion forum hosted by the government's Department of Schools, Children and Families, a parent identified as 'Julie L' posted the following observation:

> A child spends on average 8 hours a day preparing for or attending school, why then should they be expected to do more school work when they get home?...I therefore have taken the step of informing the school that I was not going to allow my children to do homework any more...School buildings and grounds are maintained for the purpose of education and teachers are trained accordingly, the home is a place for family life. If I wanted my home turned into a school I would home educate. My children now have time for play and bike rides, in other words a childhood. (DCSF, 2006, website now unavailable)

That said there have been more sober contributors to the debate. The recent *Cambridge Primary Review* (Alexander, 2009) expressed the view that as a generality, 'the "crisis" of contemporary childhood may have been overstated' and that through the process of gathering their evidence, 'children themselves were the review's most upbeat witnesses'. However, as for 'Julie L', the review (Alexander, 2009) was perhaps less sanguine about the increasingly totalizing influence of schooling in children's lives and felt 'that childhood's rich potential should be protected from a system apparently bent on pressing children into a uniform mould at an ever younger age'. It is, however, salutary to reflect on just how thoroughly intertwined with schooling and education childhood and children's lives have become over the 140 years since the passage of The Elementary Education (Forster) Act in 1870 (Board of Education, 1870; see also MacLure, 1986). Indeed, the title of the *Cambridge Primary Review* 'Children, their World, their Education' reveals this, even if the authors are critical of the influence that the imperatives of schooling exert.

Increasingly it appears to many that it is not merely the environment or context for childhood that is at fault, but perhaps the very ideas of the *Child* and of *childhood* that inform so much of our thinking, shape our institutions and direct practice, may not be conducive to children's happiness. Indeed, the Enlightenment vision for the Child is in the dock and, in particular, the belief that the Child can be the means to redeem our failed dreams and transform society for good, places too great a burden on our children (Prout and James, 1997; Jenks, 2005; Kehily, 2009; Stainton Rogers, 2009). It is arguable that what Moss and Petrie (2002, pp. 58–60) describe as the discourse of 'the Child as Redemptive Vehicle' – embodying on the one hand, the latency of unfulfilled potential, and on the other, our best hope for our future – places too great a burden upon actual children and has produced institutions that constrict and constrain the lives of young people in ways that would rarely be acceptable for people who are older. The notion that children are our future is a commonplace (if at times trite) truism; however, the sense in which children and young people are being burdened with the responsibility not just to replace and reproduce the population but also to assure the survival of the species is unhelpful, and may do long-term harm to those young people who become targeted as candidates for concern – consider ways in which certain children become stigmatized as pathological liabilities when the media speaks of an 'obesity timebomb' (Evans, 2010, pp. 21–38).

The corollary to constructing children as the embodiment of hope is that they should also be virtuous and devoid of the moral ambiguities that characterize adulthood; moreover, that childhood should be facilitated and arranged so as to ensure that children's moral virtue flourishes. Thus, modern childhood and the Enlightenment Child emerge from a state of being uninteresting to the mediaeval world – as suggested by Aries (1962) – through their construction as strictly *other* to adults and characterized as being in a state of innocence and vulnerability, the loss of which marks the point of entry to adulthood (Jenks, 2005). Though this view of childhood as oppositionally other to adulthood may have shielded children from what De Mause (1974) termed the 'long nightmare' of exploitation, abuse and (even) infanticide, it raises a number of difficult questions and, ironically, may have made some children more vulnerable to abuse (Kitzinger, 1997). Recent cases involving children's brutality towards other children have reprised the intense reactions that surfaced following James Bulger's murder in 1993 at the hands of two 10-year-old boys (Scraton, 1997) – where notions of childhood innocence did nothing to dispel the sense of moral confusion. Besides the specific issues of each (fortunately rare) case, children who murder expose our ambiguity about the moral status of children in their middle years and familiar discourses of childhood, founded on notions of needs and rights, innocence and vulnerability, rapidly break down under the strain of media scrutiny. A recent, short television film made by the children's charity Barnardo's entitled 'Hunting' highlighted the widespread vilification of children. Its script was entirely based on negative verbatim comments about children posted by adults on the charity's website. The advertisement is shocking and suggests how conflicted and brutally ambivalent UK society can be about children (Barnardos, 2010).

School and education find themselves at the centre of these anxieties about children and childhood. In part this is because, outside of the family, school is the institution that most defines and shapes our children's childhoods. Moreover school is a point where wider social tensions, as well as anxieties about national economic competitiveness and underperformance impinge upon children's lives. The purpose of this book is to explore how this came to be and to suggest that understanding the ideas about children and childhood that have grown up in the Western world over the past 400 or so years, might help us to explain why many of our children seem to be far from happy, secure and confident about their lives.

This book seeks to contribute to our understanding of the childhoods our children experience and trains its sights on two different things. First, the book charts the intellectual history of ideas around which the objectified idea of the Child has been constructed. Further, it examines the way in which these ideas have become translated into the imperatives, practices, professional identities and the educational institutions that confirm what a normatively conceived childhood should look like. It also notes that these ideas of the Child have frequently not solely been concerned with children per se, but that the Child has been deployed as an avatar, or object to think with, about philosophical, moral and religious questions concerning human nature – that is, what we think people are like. The second strand within the book explores the historical construction of mass schooling as a response to industrialization and as a means to regulate societies in which the traditional social hierarchies and Church authority were, and are still, crumbling. Children's youth, and therefore their implicit status as humans in the process of *becoming*, has meant that childhood has been institutionalized as a site within which, at best, the good society of the future can be assured and, at least, the status quo maintained as the populace becomes disciplined or socialized to economic imperatives and cultural mores.

Although proposed as distinct strands, the ideas of the Child fostered by an intellectual elite and the *childhoods* constructed by mass schooling have historically fed off each other, if only as a means to assert their distinctiveness and difference. The book explores this braiding of the two strands as well as their relationship to the actuality of real children's lives. It argues that this process culminated in the attempt to construct a mass system of child-centred, progressive schooling in the 1960s and the 1970s. However, it goes on to suggest that this had within it the seeds of its own downfall, namely, placing real children centre stage began to undermine the idea of the universal Child that had been its central intellectual construct.

The book is committed to the idea that childhood is not a fixed, natural phenomenon rooted in biology and genetics, but is socially constructed (Prout and James, 1997; James et al., 1998; Mills and Mills, 2000; Burr, 2003; Jones, P., 2008; Kehily, 2009). This does not undermine its significance or importance, but suggests that we turn our gaze away from a search for truths about children and their childhoods, and rather look at the socially produced meanings and ideas we attach to them. There is no new theory of children or childhood per se proposed in the book, nor does it seek to finesse or develop theories we already have. However, it does concern itself with how these theories came about, why we think about children the way we do and whether this could or should be the only way to imagine them and, in turn, construct institutions for them to live and learn within.

Central to this enquiry will be a discussion of *discourses* of childhood and their various roles in constructing the social realities within which we make sense of what childhood means, but also through which our practices are justified as the right things to do (Burr, 2003). However, our enquiry will reveal that these discourses are frequently far from straightforward and are shot through with contradictions that emerge as what social scientists refer to as *dualisms*. For example, consider the way in which we use ideas about how children behave as metaphors for adults' conduct. To describe someone as *childlike* is very different from being *childish*, whereas the former suggests rather endearing qualities, the latter's connotations are wholly negative. What we might infer from this is that our ideas about children embody a deep moral ambiguity. Jenks (2005, pp. 62–70) identifies these as, respectively, the Apollonian (sweetness and light) and Dionysian (chaos and disorder) discourses of the Child and we shall see that they surface throughout the course of our explorations.

Other structurally important, but oppositional ideas concern childhood as conceived as a state in and of itself, and childhood as a preparation for adulthood – this has been dualistically characterized as the distinction between childhood as 'being' and childhood as 'becoming', otherwise described as a state of 'futurity'. Prout and James (1997, p. 239) suggest that this notion of futurity is widespread and conceives childhood as an elaborately designed 'moonshot', whose trajectory and purpose is to attain adulthood. Moreover, as we have seen from comments posted by Julie L. on the DCSF (2006) parents' forum website, this stubborn dualism continues to shape arguments over curriculum and pedagogy as well as the overall objectives of education and their relation to a proper childhood.

Whether children are seen as the embodiment of pure virtue or evil, the social constructionist position proposes that 'they' have no intrinsic essence beyond the meanings that these discourses bestow upon them. To paraphrase Wittgenstein, the idea that there is something concrete for which 'they' stands, is a trick that words play on us or 'a bewitchment of our intelligence by language' (Wittgenstein, 1952, p. 109; see also Burr, 2003, chapter 4 for a full discussion of discourse). Moreover, historical study suggests that meanings change, which leads us to ask whether meanings *can be changed*? But beyond academic or philosophical debates about whether things can change, it is proposed here that our approach to children and childhood *needs* to change because something quite fundamental is going wrong. Report after report suggests that our children are far from happy with their lives and there is evidence that many adults see themselves at war against youth (see the Barnardos' advert and Chapter 9).

Further, in a global age in which societies are marked by cultural plurality, it seems that many of our most influential and cherished ideas about children and childhood, together with the institutions and educational practices founded on those ideas, stem from a particular moment in the emergence of the Western world view. In consequence, they have become unhelpful to many real children and young people in pluralistic, globalized societies and can lead to underachievement, alienation and social tensions.

A guide to reading this book

There are six lines of enquiry running through the book:

- Why should it be that our ways of thinking and theorizing about children and childhood invariably tap a deep vein of moralization and that the idea of the *Child* became a lens through which human nature could be scrutinized? (See Chapters 2–6 and 9.)

- Second, and linked to the inclination towards moralization: what roles have theological notions and the influence of Christian doctrine played in the historical construction of Western childhood institutions and does this continue to be the case in a broadly secular society? (See Chapters 2, 3, 5 and 6.)
- Third, to what degree have the progressive ideals in childhood and children's education championed by the intellectual and social elite served philanthropic goals or the self-interest of that elite? (See Chapter 9; see also Chapters 5, 7 and 8.)
- Fourth, the contemporary connection between education, health and social care found in the Every Child Matters initiative is not new, but this aspiration to holism runs as a golden thread through ideas of modern childhood; so how new is modern childhood? (See Chapters 3–6 and 9.)
- Fifth, can the requirements of mass schooling, that exercised nineteenth-century politicians and educationists, be reconciled both with universal ideals of childhood and the pluralistic reality presented by real children in contemporary multicultural and globalized Western societies? (See Chapters 6, 8 and 9.)
- Sixth, and finally, does an emphasis on discourses of 'childhood as futurity' – or as primarily concerned with what is to come – overburden children with an excess of adult-inspired hope and expectation so that education becomes a panacea for all social ills and childhood is constructed as a time of redemption not merely for the nation, but also the human race and planet? (See Chapters 5, 6, 8 and 9)

Further reading

Burr, V. (2003), *Social Constructionism*, London: Routledge.

Corsaro, W. (1997), *The Sociology of Childhood*, Thousand Oaks, CA: Pine Forge.

James, A. and James, A. L. (2004), *Constructing Childhood: Theory, Policy and Social Practice*, Basingstoke: Palgrave Macmillan.

James, A. and James, A. L. (2008), *Key Concepts in Childhood Studies*, London: Sage.

James, A., Jenks, C. and Prout, A. (1998), *Theorizing Childhood*, Cambridge: Polity Press.

Jenks, C. (2005), *Childhood*, London: Routledge.

Kehily, M. J. (2009), *An Introduction to Childhood Studies*, Maidenhead, UK: Open University Press.

McDowell Clark, R. (2010), *Childhood in Society for Early Childhood Studies*, Exeter: Learning Matters.

Mills, R. and Mills, J. (eds) (2000), *Childhood Studies: A Reader in Perspectives of Childhood*, London: Routledge Falmer.

Palmer, S. (2006), *Toxic Childhood: How the Modern World Is Damaging Our Children and What We Can Do About It*, London: Orion.

Websites

Barnardos: www.barnardos.org.uk/, last accessed 17 December 2010.

The Children's Society: www.childrenssociety.org.uk/, last accessed 17 December 2010.

UNICEF: www.unicef.org.uk/, last accessed 17 December 2010.

Victoria and Albert Museum of Childhood: www.vam.ac.uk/moc/, last accessed 17 December 2010.

The Women's Library: www.londonmet.ac.uk/thewomenslibrary/, last accessed 17 December 2010.

Part 1
Education and the Construction of the Child

1

Lightening Our Darkness: Renaissance, Reformation and Enlightenment

Introduction

The rebirth, or Renaissance, that brought the Mediaeval period to an end and was precursor to the Age of Enlightenment and the Modern era, also generated a new interest in children and produced ideas about the Child and childhood that continue to shape educational provision. This chapter explores the proposition that many of the meanings we attach to childhood have their origins in this era, and that childhood should be seen as a socially constructed phenomenon rooted in historical and cultural circumstance.

Phillipe Aries and an emerging idea of childhood

An early contribution to the critical study of childhood was made by Phillipe Aries, a French polymath and cultural historian, who published the seminal *L'Enfant et laFamiliale Sous l'Ancien Regime* in 1960 (translated as *Centuries of Childhood* in 1962). Aries made the provocative proposal that in the mediaeval era the idea of childhood neither existed nor made any sense because it had no use. A large part of the evidence for this came from Aries' study of mediaeval paintings:

> Mediaeval art until about the twelfth century did not know childhood or did not attempt to portray it. It is hard to believe that this neglect was due to incompetence or incapacity; it seems more probable that there was no place for childhood in the mediaeval world. (Aries, 1962, p. 31)

Aries goes on to chart how we get from this period where childhood was not depicted or recognized to the near ubiquitous images of children found in our twenty-first century family albums, advertisements and televisions (see Holland, 2004, for full treatment of this).

Despite the absence of childhood as a theme in early Mediaeval painting, Aries' survey recognizes that around the thirteenth century three new and distinct types of representation appear embodying childlike figures. These were: the clergeons (or little priests) who made responses during mass and were depicted as youthful angels, the infant Jesus depicted as a child rather than as a shrunken adult and, the depiction of a man at the point of death, whose soul is exhaled from his body as a small child. The depiction of the young Christ as a little man in early Mediaeval painting seems to confirm Aries' (1962) assertion that childhood went unrecognized. However, despite the frequency with which Aries' claim has been repeated, Pollock (1983) sounded a note of caution, stating that the saviour of the world is hardly any ordinary child and His conscious depiction as a little man, may be more expressive of the stress placed on His divinity than of contemporary attitudes to children.

It should be said that other historians challenge the claims made by Aries, feeling that they make better headlines than scholarly history. Among them are Pollock (1983), Heywood (2001) and Cunningham (1995 and 2006). Rosenthal et al. (2007), published the outcomes of an influential colloquium on mediaeval childhood, including a paper by Barron demonstrating that children were highly visible if court records from London concerning their deaths, derelict status as orphans and disputes around apprenticeship are to be believed. It is also worth noting that the popular culture of the time seemed to have clear notions about children and young people and their moral status. Here is a proverb from 1303 (Apperson, 1993):

> Gyue thy chylde when he wyl kraue,
> And they whelpe whyl hyt wyl haue,
> Than mayst thou make you a stounde
> A foule chylde and a feyre hounde. (1303)

Translated as:

> Give a child all he shall crave,
> And a dog while his tail doth wave;
> And you'll have
> A fair dog and a foul knave.

To understand this apparent change in the visibility of children, or at least, their emergent portrayal as *children* in late Mediaeval art, it is important to understand seismic shifts in philosophical, doctrinal and scientific outlook that were simultaneously underway, owing in large part to the writings of St Thomas Aquinas (1225–74). Aquinas was a philosopher–priest who was instrumental in rediscovering the work of the ancient pre-Christian Greek philosophers, especially Aristotle (see Russell, 1979), and reconciling their writings with Christian doctrine (Hankins, 2007). The medieval world was aware that there had once been a great civilization in antiquity, but the works produced by it were largely unknown in Europe. However, they were in wide circulation among scholars throughout the Muslim world and were a cornerstone upon which Arabic mathematics, science and cosmology were constructed. When the Muslim scholar Ibn-Rushd (1126–98), who went by the *nom de plume* 'Averroes', deferentially claimed in the preface to his own work on physics that 'The author of this book is Aristotle', we are given some indication of the esteem in which these works were held outside Europe (Lewis,

1982; Tarnas, 1991; see also Braudel and Mayne, 1993, pp. 80–3 and 366;). As trade expanded between the Christian and the Arabic Muslim worlds across the Mediterranean, so ideas were also exchanged and Italy became focal for the European Renaissance (or rebirth) of learning. A rediscovery of Aristotle and his works on science and scientific methods was central to this rebirth and, in particular, a rekindled interest in examining the external natural world. Until Aquinas, Church doctrine had been dominated by the work of St Augustine of Hippo (who as we shall see later was central to the promulgation of a doctrine of Original Sin that was so significant in forming attitudes to human nature and particularly the moral status of children). Augustine saw the world of nature as 'fallen' and full of sinful distractions for those who earnestly sought spiritual understanding (Tarnas, 1991). Undoubtedly this view chimed with a world where everyday life was precarious and nature capriciously manifested itself in dangers, disasters and destruction. However, with increasing trade and wealth through the thirteenth century, outlooks were changing. Aquinas' contribution was to suggest that far from being in opposition to understanding spiritual truth, nature demonstrated God's providence and in its everyday beauties we could glimpse something of divine beauty (Tarnas, 1991). This redirected gaze, from the contemplative internal world of prayer and meditation to the external world, encouraged closer scrutiny of that world and this is undoubtedly evidenced in the increasingly lifelike depiction of flowers, trees, animals and landscapes found in contemporary painting and as decoration to the great gothic cathedrals that were rebuilt across Europe at this time (Rice, 2009). But more significantly here, whereas the infant Christ is depicted as a little man in early thirteenth century paintings of Madonna and child, he becomes a bouncing baby when Raphael paints him 200 years later. Aquinas was not alone in expressing a new reading of nature; others, including a little-known theologian and mystic named Meister Eckhart (c. 1260–1328) went further and risked trial for heresy when he claimed that nature was not a source of sinful distraction, but was an 'original blessing' from God, being intrinsically virtuous rather than marred by sin (Keen, 1989). These assertions – that there are sermons about God's providence to be found in nature – represent a first step towards our contemporary, secularized Western world view underpinned by a faith in empirical science and where human experience becomes the measure of all things. However, more directly, they led to the suggestion that if nature was not fallen, then children might also not be born burdened by Original Sin, indeed that they might possess original virtue and be morally blameless – a point that finds full expression 400 years later in Rousseau's *Emile*.

The gradual appearance of children *as children* rather than as shrunken, stylized adults in paintings is, therefore, suggestive of changes both in their visibility and moral status. But for Aries it is education (and particularly the establishment of institutions at the University of Paris expressly intended for young people) that begins to consolidate the idea that children and young people are fundamentally different from adults and require organization and regulation in and through quite specific institutional spaces and provision (Aries, 1962, pp. 151–70).

Reflection:

Can you think of any examples where age is important in shaping the day-to-day organizational practices or the spatial arrangements of educational institutions? Could this be different?

This growing recognition of the importance of a good childhood finds expression in the work of the humanist Dutch scholar Desiderius Erasmus who, again, made the connection with education in his *De pueris institudiendis* (*The Liberal Education of Children*) published in 1529, where he championed education as the medium through which the young could be moulded and peaceful dispositions could be developed. As a humanist scholar, Erasmus was also at the centre of fierce debates around individual reason, authority and faith raging between Protestant reformers and Church traditionalists that crystallized in the Reformation and the displacement of the Catholic faith across much of northern Europe. Protestant values and beliefs would, in turn, reinforce the centrality of children and proper Christian education to debates concerning human nature, redemption and divine authority.

The Protestant Revolution: Calvinism, childhood and redemption through learning

The outward facing view on the world that accompanied the rediscovery of classical Greek scholars and ushered in the Renaissance, generated not just wealth through trade, but with it a new, non-aristocratic class of landowners and merchants eager to secure their own interests. Furthermore, the exercise of reason proposed by secular scholars such as Erasmus was consistent with a growing intolerance of established Church authority and the arbitrary exercise of its powers. Therefore, in renouncing his priesthood and nailing a written challenge to Church authority to the church door at Wittenberg on 31 October 1517 a hitherto unknown priest named Martin Luther catalysed a revolution that would transform Europe and continue to challenge the monopoly of the Catholic Church in Western spiritual and political life (MacCulloch, 2009).

Besides the global significance of the Protestant revolution, there were very specific implications for children and their education. Central to this were continuing discussions and disparities in interpretation of the doctrine of Original Sin that had been promulgated by the Catholic Church since the time of St Augustine, and especially, how children could be redeemed from it. In Judaeo-Christian doctrine the moment of the Fall from Grace occasioned by Adam and Eve's disobedience in eating the fruit of the 'Tree of the Knowledge of Good and Evil' and their subsequent expulsion from the Garden of Eden on account of it, represents the 'hinge-point' in the moral evolution of humankind. For this was when the whole of creation, including humankind, became 'fallen'; and according to St Augustine (354–430 AD), all humankind became inheritors of this 'original sin' at birth. In his 'Confessions', Augustine illustrates this inherent propensity for sinfulness through 'the abominable things I did' and 'sins of the flesh which defiled my soul' during his own childhood and youth (Book 2) and challenges the presumption of childhood innocence (Book 1) (transl. Pine-Coffin, 1961). However, while Christianity taught that redemption from both this fallen state and subsequent damnation, was possible through the death and resurrection of Jesus Christ, Protestants and Catholics disputed how this redemption and release from the burden of Original Sin could be achieved (Ford, 1999).

Catholic doctrine taught that the new-born child could be released from the burden of Original Sin by the sacrament of infant baptism – a symbolic burial and resurrection with Christ that matches his own death and resurrection. However, the Protestant reformers of the sixteenth and seventeenth centuries saw things differently. Protestants placed emphasis on redemption as a personal transaction with God. For them salvation followed a personal realization of sinfulness; moreover, that as a gift from God, no earthly actions, ecclesiastical authority or ritual could in themselves achieve the salvation sought by the repentant sinner. In the allegorical 'A Pilgrim's Progress' (published in 1678), the puritan dissenter John Bunyan (Bunyan, 1678 and Owens (ed.), 2008) shows how salvation for the main character, named Christian, is preceded by a personal realization deriving from his direct reading of the Bible: *as he read, he wept and trembled: and not being able longer to contain, he brake out with a lamentable cry; saying, what shall I do?* (Bunyan, 1678). Christian sees that his sins are literally and figuratively a heavy burden on his back and are responsible for the misery he feels.

The power ascribed to the written word and its capacity to deliver self-knowledge as a first step to redemption is vital to understanding the place of education and literacy in the Protestant imagination and the role that a proper Christian childhood plays in the production of the complete human subject. For Protestants, redemption came through knowledge and understanding, not through the sacraments of the Church per se. This knowledge and understanding was specifically inscribed in 'The Catechism', which:

> . . . was a question-and-answer way of instilling Christian doctrine. For Protestants it was not enough that a child could repeat the words of the Lord's Prayer or the Creed. The child needed to have an inward understanding that would lead to a realization of the need for salvation. (Cunningham, 2006, p. 65)

Thus, Catechism and the learning by heart that followed from it became the vital route to saving the child's soul and a central condition for a Christian childhood:

> In religious families, exercises in godliness loomed large, driven by the parental urgency to bring the child to a sense of its sin and of the necessity of faith. With child death all too common, there could be no delay in starting the teaching. (Cunningham, 2006, p. 66)

The acquisition of divine knowledge therefore became a central responsibility placed upon parents and in turn a requirement of the child of God; thus infant baptism – as the point of redemption – is replaced by an extended period of education, realization and then redemption and thus Protestant childhood is invented. Moreover, this childhood is affirmed within the protestant imagination as preparation for *what is to come* and as the foundation for proper Christian life, and through this a discursive stress on *childhood as futurity* was set to flourish.

The following extract from the 'Short Catechism of 1553' gives a sense of how the material was set out as dialogue, to be inscribed in the memory or, more appropriately perhaps, *learnt by heart*:

> Master: What is the use of the Lord's Supper?

Scholar[:] Even in the very same, that was ordained by the Lord himself, Jesus Christ: which (as S. Paul saith) the same night, that he was betrayed, took bread: and when he had given thanks, brake it: and said, This is my body, which is broken for you: Do this in remembrance of me. In like manner, when the supper was ended, he gave them the cup, saying: This cup is the new testament in my blood. Do this, as oft as ye shall drink thereof, in remembrance of me. This was the manner and the order of the Lord's supper: which we ought to hold and keep; that the remembrance of so great a benefit, the passion and death of Christ, be always kept in mind; that, after that the world is ended, he may come, and make us to sit with him at his own board. (Calvin College, 2005)

Thus, a set of moral imperatives demanding the sound education of the young protestant child emerge; but, importantly, these imperatives lend purpose and direction to a modern childhood, conceived as the stage for education towards redemption. At this point the philosopher John Locke (1632–1704), as a somewhat unlikely figure, steps in to make a major contribution. Locke is best known for 'An Essay Concerning Human Understanding' (published in 1689) (see Russell, 1979; Dunn, 1984 and 2003; or Magee, 1988), but was also a regular and copious correspondent on matters concerning the wellbeing and upbringing of children that he brought together in 'Some Thoughts Concerning Education' in 1693 (see later in this chapter; Dunn, 1984 and 2003; Stainton Rogers, 2001, p. 202).

Descartes and Newton – the individual in a mechanical universe

Besides the growth of religious dissent and the personal imperatives placed on the believer by Protestantism there were also other philosophical and scientific currents ushering in new ways of seeing not just what it meant to be a person, but also, the nature of the world. Moreover, these new ways of seeing would provide the foundation stone for the ensuing Age of Enlightenment and a recognizably Western world view. Of central importance here was on the one hand, the invention of the modern individual by the philosopher Rene Descartes, and on the other, what became known as the mechanical view of the Universe stemming from the physics of Sir Isaac Newton (Tarnas, 1991, pp. 282-3 and 366-7; Porter, 2001).

The Protestant emphasis on a reasoned, informed faith embraced as a conscious, agentic and individual choice by the believer is lent support by the work of Descartes, of whom Bertrand Russell could say:

> Rene Descartes (1596–1650) is usually regarded as the founder of modern philosophy, and, I think, rightly. (Russell, 1979)

Although neither a Protestant nor concerned in his writing with children, Descartes established the capacity to exercise reason as the defining characteristic of being human and the basis for reliable knowledge of the world. After rejecting empirical experience as unreliable, he expresses his doctrine thus:

> While I wanted to think everything false, it must necessarily be that I who thought was something; and remarking that this truth, **I think, therefore I am**, was so solid and so certain that all the most extravagant suppositions of the sceptics were incapable of upsetting it, I judged that I could receive it without scruple as the first principle of the philosophy that I sought. (From Descartes' Discourse on Method (1637), Latin: **Cogito ergo sum**.) (see Russell, 1979, p. 547)

Armed with Descartes' rational individual as its core construct, the Enlightenment's convictions concerning the power of reason were combined with the transformative power of science, commerce, warfare and education to change the political, economic and cultural character not just of Europe, but the whole world. Furthermore, the 'Cartesian mind' with its prime emphasis on the capacity to exercise reason, became the primary preoccupation of Western education and it followed that curricula, pedagogy and its core educational values would be constructed around it.

Reflection:

Consider the status that school subjects are widely perceived to have. Where does Physical Education (PE) stand in relation to, say, mathematics or classical languages, higher or lower? Do the ideas of Descartes suggest any reasons why these subjects seem to be given the status they have?

This emphasis on the *cogito*, or reasoning mind, continues to shape the understanding of children and their development as primarily an internal, individualized process; indeed, Descartes' rational self looms large in the work of the Swiss genetic epistemologist Jean Piaget, (e.g. Piaget, 1952; see also Phillips, 1975 and Boden, 1980) for whom the whole character of the developing child can be mapped against a genetically determined, stage-by-stage unfolding of mental capabilities that culminate in what he describes as a capacity for *formal operational* thinking, whose qualities bear a close resemblance to those of the Cartesian mind. Critics, notably feminists, post-colonial theorists and exponents of the new sociology of childhood (Walkerdine, 1984 and 2009; Burman, 1994; Jenks, 2009) have challenged the implicit masculinity and Eurocentrism of the Cartesian self or subject and more specifically, the capacity of rationalistic theorists such as Jean Piaget to inform us about the diverse lives of real children (see Chapter 8).

If Descartes appeared to have established the capacity to exercise reason as the foundation upon which an understanding of human nature could be built, then Sir Isaac Newton's work on forces, gravity and matter in his *Philosophiæ Naturalis Principia Mathematica* (completed in 1687) established a view of the Universe as transparent and comprehensible through scientific enquiry. In his scheme the physical world could be understood in terms of forces causing attractive and repulsive interactions between atoms imagined much like billiard balls. Thus, science seemed to be able to unlock the mysteries of a universe that, like a pocket watch, had been set in motion by God, but then regulated and ran itself. Enlightenment science and philosophy suggested that God was not required to intervene further, indeed, as secularism gained a hold, that there might be no need for God at all.

This view of the world was not limited to the science of physics, but shaped other areas of learning and scholarship:

> ...the mechanical philosophy achieved towering prestige in the early Enlightenment, and not just in the physical science. 'Clockwork' thinking, for example, invaded physiology and medicine; 'iatromechanism'...cast the human body as a system of pulleys, springs and levers, pipes and vessels, its fluids being governed by the laws of hydraulics. Life itself was potentially explicable within the new mechanical paradigm. (Porter, 2001, p. 139)

These new ways of knowing were given added impetus by a moral imperative placed on humankind as the custodian of scientific rationality and centre of the human-scale universe that God had created and set in motion. As Porter has it:

> The mechanical philosophy fostered belief that man was permitted, indeed duty bound, to apply himself to Nature for (in Bacon's words) the 'glory of God and the relief of man's estate'. Since Nature was not, after all sacred or 'ensouled', there could be nothing impious about utilizing and dominating it. (Porter, 2001, p. 142)

We might, however, reflect that the idea that the reproductive power of nature could and should be harnessed, controlled and improved to meet human goals and interests may not now appear so attractive as the atmosphere warms, oil spills threaten to despoil remaining wilderness areas and mass drought and famine may be around the corner.

Reflection:

On balance, has science enhanced or diminished the quality of life for humankind? Can you think of any recent topical examples that support your argument?

This injunction to 'relieve man's estate' (Porter, 2001, p. 142) and harness reproductive power in pursuit of human progress, extended to children and their education as fundamental to the improvement of human nature. However, a prerequisite for the formulation of rational systems of education that were congruent with scientific knowledge of the world, was a correspondingly rational, scientifically informed model for the child that would be at the heart of those systems.

Locke on children and their education

Descartes and Newton were architects of Enlightenment thought; however, neither wrote anything of real significance about children and childhood. No less a giant of the Enlightenment was the English philosopher John Locke best known for 'A Treatise on Human Understanding' of 1689. Nonetheless

Locke was also a copious correspondent with his landed gentleman friend, Edward Clarke, on matters concerning children and childhood. Such was the quality of the philosopher's advice and the attention Locke gave to the welfare and education of young children, that the letters began to circulate and were gathered together in 1693 to become the first modern treatise on children and their upbringing. Through the advice we see fascinating congruencies with the commitment to empiricism found in his philosophical work, for example, 'children should be trained to use their powers of observation in getting to know the world at first hand' (Porter, 2001, p. 341) or that children should be 'hardened up' through direct, sensory engagement with outdoor life. Accordingly, when discussing the qualities of appropriate footwear for children, he suggested that children's feet should not be so protected that they were unable to feel the roughness of the ground or have the sensation of moist feet in the rain – underlining perhaps the value of lessons learnt through direct empirical experience. Locke was a Puritan and there is undoubtedly a self-denying 'hair-shirt' mentality underlying these strictures – 'It seems plain to me, that the Principle of all Vertue and Excellency lies in the power of denying our selves the satisfaction of our own Desires, where Reason does not authorize them.' (Locke, 1693, in Cunningham, 2006, p. 111).

Locke's views are often seen to epitomize the view of childhood as 'futurity', that is, as concerned with what the child is to become, with childhood as an apprenticeship to adulthood. The dualistic tension between childhood as *being* and childhood as *becoming* continues to surface in educational debates on weighty and routine matters – such as whether homework denies them time to enjoy their childhood (see Chapters 8 and 9).

Reflection:

Is the principle of denying or deferring the gratification of our immediate desires still considered important in becoming educated and qualified? What do you hope to gain by being a student and is it worth the sacrifices involved?

However, Locke's tendency to moralize in his ruminations on childhood should not deflect us from recognizing the high value he placed upon the exercise of reason both about children and with children. Nor did his moral convictions endorse the physically brutal approach that was frequently the norm and still is for so many children. He was clear that when offering guidance to children, adults should appeal to reason not force; moreover, that the child's nature as a rational being required that it be thus.

The general point may seem obvious to us, but Locke's work makes sense because it is now assumed by his correspondents that children matter and their upbringing is worthy of serious scrutiny – we have, apparently, come a long way from Phillipe Aries' assertion that childhood did not exist in a meaningful form in Mediaeval times.

Schooling and children's lives in early Modern England

If we are witnessing the emergence of a coherent ideal of childhood during this period, it did not translate into the daily lives of many children. Schooling was patchy and generally limited in its scope; however, whereas it was not exclusively the preserve of the very wealthy or powerful it was usually only available to those who were financially and socially 'secure'. Gentry, professionals, farmers, merchants, better-off tradesmen and artisans and shopkeepers were likely to send children to schools, including the relatively new 'King's Schools' and charitable or guild institutions. The former came into being after the dissolution of the monasteries by Henry VIII in the 1540s. Typical of the charitable and guild schools were Christ's Hospital (founded in 1552 at Greyfriars in London) or the Merchant Taylor's boys schools (founded in 1561 at Northwood, Hertfordshire). However, *boys* from lower social ranks could not aspire to them:

> Colchester Free Grammar School in the mid-seventeenth century was typical: nearly one third of the boys were from aristocratic backgrounds, a mere 12 per cent were the sons of yeomen, and there were no sons of husbandmen or labourers. (Cunningham, 2006, p. 85)

Because:

> If a boy remained at school until he was eight, he would probably by then have learnt to write. But it was a year earlier, at seven, that a boy became of some economic use to the family, so reading was a skill much more likely to have been acquired than writing. (Cunningham, 2006, p. 79)

These economic imperatives meant that for the great majority of boys, apprenticeship remained the most tangible aspiration but, as we shall see, even this was not for all. However, though not universal, schooling had become normalized as a form of social organization that separated people into distinct groups on the basis of age and thus was becoming a defining condition for childhood.

If opportunities for boys were curtailed by family income, then there were even fewer options for girls. Despite the fact that Elizabeth I was known as 'the learned princess' on account of her ability to read Latin and Greek (like her father Henry VIII), opportunities for girls were curtailed by what was seen as their natural destiny. As Cunningham observes:

> For the mass of girls the norm was to become servants of one kind or another in order to prepare them for the only vocation open to them: marriage. (Cunningham, 2006, p. 92)

Even the aristocracy, who increasingly assumed that their sons would go to school, had no such aspiration for their daughters. Cunningham cites Sir Justinian Isham, who in 1642 wrote to his daughters seeking to console and counsel them following the death of their mother:

> Prayers, meditations, and such like holy treatises, I rather commend unto you than knotty disputes; and although your sex is not so capable of those stronger abilities of the intellect, to make you so learned and knowing as men ought to be; yet to be sure to keep your hearts upright and your affections toward God unfeigned and there is no doubt but that will be more acceptable to him than all the wisdom of the whole world...(Cunningham, 2006, pp. 86-7)

It is clear that Sir Justinian's grief and condolences are not permitted to eclipse his duty to ensure that his daughters understand the importance of pursuing a pious femininity in preference to education. That said, the age was not without those who were more far-sighted and egalitarian; in Utopia (1515), Sir Thomas More, a great friend of the scholar Erasmus, argues for a national system of education for men *and* women.

Along with the Isham girls, many children could not dream of schooling. England's population had doubled between 1520 and 1680 and coupled with changes to both the tenure and husbandry of the land as well as inflation that ate into their capital, many people found themselves without employment or the means to shelter and maintain themselves. The corollary was a signal increase in vagrancy and begging; further, rapid population rise meant that England was a youthful country, with nearly one third of the population under the age of 15 by the end of the fifteenth century so that children were numbered among the vagrants and beggars (Cunningham, 2004, p. 95). It is salutary to note that in the following century we see concerns about purposeless and/or misdirected youth culminate in an Act of Parliament of 1547 allowing Church and State authorities to remove children from vagrants and beggars and 're-habilitate' them with masters who would take them in hand, occupy them and treat them as slaves if they dared to run away. More drastically, in 1627 a solution to the challenge of youth was found in the nascent colonial lands of the New World:

> There are many ships now going to Virginia, and with them, some 1400 or 1500 children, which they have gathered up in diverse places...imprison, punish, and dispose any of those children, upon any disorder by them committed, as cause shall require .... (Cunningham, 2006, p. 98)

Not for the last time, the new colonies would offer England a 'safety-valve' against the pressures of population growth, worklessness and disorder among the nation's youth.

> **Reflection:**
>
> Is so-called 'anti-social behaviour' a new phenomenon or might its prevalence seem more pressing because the options for dealing with it have become more limited?

Rousseau, *Emile* and the Enlightenment Child

Now we proceed to look at the work and ideas of Jean Jacques Rousseau and their importance in the construction of the *Child* as an idea that continues to shape educational institutions and their practices. Furthermore, we shall see how Rousseau provoked discussion about human nature, moral progress and the remodelling of society through what he saw as the natural mien and manners of this Child. The concerns of the revolutionary times in which Rousseau lived are summed up in his oft-quoted aphorism:

> Man is born free, and everywhere he is in chains. One man thinks himself the master of others, but remains more of a slave than they are.

Under the onslaught of Enlightenment notions of individual reason, rational progress, liberty and new scientific understandings of nature, the mediaeval theocentric world glued together by the mystical transaction of the Mass and in which religious doctrine explained everything, was crumbling. Taking its place was a self-regulating clockwork universe (see discussion of Newton) that operated at a human scale with humankind as the measure of all things and humanistic values placed at its centre. This increasingly left little room for the God of mediaeval times or the Catholic Church that claimed to represent Him on Earth. As MacCulloch observes: 'the philosophy of Locke and the mechanical universe of Newton had banished mystery from human affairs' (MacCulloch, 2009, p. 800). The rise of new monied classes frequently motivated by Protestant and non-conforming religious ideologies, stoked the flames of opposition to established political, economic and spiritual order across Europe and its North American colonies. Typical of this new thinking was a political treatise written by Tom Paine (1792) called 'The Rights of Man' that inspired the republican revolutionaries in Britain's North American colonies, as well as in France and its overseas Caribbean territories.

Besides violent political revolutions, improvements and progress in scientific, agricultural and industrial matters also exerted revolutionary effects upon society and the natural world. Taken as a whole package this era has been described as the Age of Enlightenment and marks a significant moment in the emergence of the Western world view. The Enlightenment Project (Porter, 2001) declared that progress in human affairs was possible because human nature could be perfected both through the exercise of reason and a scientific understanding of the world.

It is indicative of the confidence in Enlightenment ideals that change became virtually synonymous with positive ideas of improvement and progress. However, confidence in the capacity of science to control nature unleashed a darker side as it enabled a new entrepreneurial class to treat the earth and its peoples as components in a wealth-creating system that has gone on to engulf the whole planet – arguably we are now reaping the rewards of this cavalier approach to the earth and its reproductive power through the challenges of climate change, species extinctions and environmental degradation (Ponting, 1991). Furthermore, much of the wealth that underpinned this confidence in progress and facilitated the imperative to improve, was profit derived from a system of slavery that de-humanized and exploited the vitality, strength and reproductive capacities of huge numbers of people, reducing them to mere factors in the process of wealth creation. The Atlantic slave trade (Blackburn, 1988), in full-swing throughout the period of Rousseau's life, no doubt shaped the imagery in his aphorism concerning freedom (mentioned earlier in the chapter). However, it would be 30 years after Rousseau's death before dissenters, political radicals and progressive intellectuals, including a small but influential group of former slaves such as Olaudah Equiano (BBC, 2010a), had secured the *moral* case against slavery, that was an eventual precursor to abolition.

It is against this background that in 1762 Rousseau published *Emile: or, on Education* and declared that he believed it to be the 'best and most important of all my writings'. He was prolific at this time, having also published *The Social Contract* in the same year. The two are related, in that through *Emile* Rousseau illustrates how the proper relationship between individuals and society can be put into practice. This philosophical concern with nature and society, freedom and human progress is vital to understanding *Emile*. However, even as Rousseau consciously addresses some of the *big* philosophical concerns exercising the intellectual and political imagination of his Enlightenment times, he also establishes a perspective on the Child that has shaped institutions and pedagogic practice since then and, therefore, the ways in which many children have experienced their childhoods.

Reflection:

Is having a theory of the *Child* enough to support appropriate provision for real children? In turn, is practice without theory sufficient?

Seen as a treatise on childhood, there is much that we can learn by comparing Rousseau's *Emile* with Locke's writings; the latter principally conceives childhood as *futurity*, or as a platform for what is to come, whereas

Rousseau seeks to establish childhood as valid in its own right. Indeed, for Rousseau, Locke's concern with childhood as principally preparation for adult life and social responsibility would have been illustrative of how society makes inimical demands on children and stymies children's instincts.

If we are looking for radicalism in *Emile*, we need look no further than its denial of the doctrine of Original Sin that asserted the intrinsic evil of human nature. The Church had preached the doctrine of Original Sin since Augustine of Hippo (354–430AD) affirmed that humanity was fundamentally marred by the disobedience of Adam and Eve when they ate fruit from the 'Tree of the Knowledge of Good and Evil' and all bore the legacy of their *Fall* from grace (MacCulloch, 2009, and earlier in this chapter).

In *Emile*, Rousseau challenged the idea that children were born evil and needed to be straightened out. Thus for Rousseau, the Fall was:

> merely a wrong turning, a mistake, rather than the catastrophe which humankind had brought upon itself. The force of love and the right ordering of human affairs would put right the mistakes of the past. (MacCulloch, 2009, p. 802)

After denying the validity of the doctrine of Original Sin, Rousseau placed himself at odds with the Church and, becoming the object of its wrath, fled France while the book was burned in Paris and Geneva. However, those who burn popular books often exert a perverse effect, and *Emile* became a bestseller among European savants; indeed many booksellers found it more profitable to lend *Emile* out to readers than to sell it. Moreover, just 16 years after his death, Rousseau had become a virtual saint of the French Revolution and was ceremoniously re-interred in the Pantheon – a converted Parisian church that became a shrine to the secular heroes of those revolutionary times.

The heart of Rousseau's appeal lay in his mobilization and articulation of the idea of nature as the wellspring for the intrinsic goodness of the Child. This is how Harry Hendrick puts it:

> Rousseau captured the imagination of Europe with his validation of nature...Part of the originality of Emile's educational theory lay in the claim that from both the physiological and the psychological perspective, the educator...was to treat the child as a 'little human animal destined for the spiritual and moral life' who

developed 'according to certain laws whose natural progression must be respected above all'. (Hendrick, 1997a, p. 36)

Rousseau asserts in *Emile*, that: 'Nature wants children to be children before they are men' so that the priority is squarely placed on assuring *being* rather than *becoming* – on the imperatives of nature rather than those of society – because respect for *being* facilitates the child's *natural development*, and thereby assures the emergence of an adult who is secure, responsible, confident and at ease with him or herself. For Rousseau, society was a corrupting force and alienated humans from that true nature. However, Rousseau recognized a paradox, in that although society is corrupting, children are members of society and do not grow up as isolated islands. It is therefore imperative that while children should be enabled to grow *naturally* they should also be *social beings* with nature and society reconciled in ways that avoid the corruption of the child. For Rousseau the key to this dilemma was love and particularly an understanding of *self-love* (Hendrick, 1997a). But, the idea of self-love can be ambiguous. In everyday speech we find ourselves on the one hand exhorting friends who lack self-confidence or may be overly self-critical to 'love themselves a little more'; but on the other we say that the narcissistic person is 'far too in love with themselves', so that self-love is here regarded as a fault. Addressing this apparent contradiction, Rousseau suggests that these are not contradictory, but actually two different things, namely: *amour de soi* and *amour propre* (IEP, 2005).

Amour de soi is a natural, healthy form of self-love which is not dependent on the judgement or validation of others, whereas *amour propre* has connotations of an unhealthy, neurotically obsessive hygiene. In the latter, the self is dependent upon validation by others and easy prey both to their negative criticism and their positive approval. For Rousseau *amour propre* fails to offer security to the adult but leads to an alternating sense of superiority/inferiority that provokes tendencies towards contempt, jealousy, hostility and destructive competitiveness.

Rousseau's educational scheme

In Book III of *Emile*, Rousseau (1762 and see 2005 edition) describes his educational scheme. From the outset, Rousseau allies his conception of the *Child* as naturally and instinctually good with an assertion that he [sic] is also actively driven by curiosity and inquisitiveness (Ross, 2000, p. 135). The implicit faith placed in the agency of the Child allows Rousseau to stress learning through reason and experience rather than what is gleaned from books or by being told by the teacher. There seem to be echoes of Locke here:

> Let the senses be the only guide for the first workings of reason. No book but the world, no teaching but that of fact. The child who reads ceases to think he only reads. He is acquiring words not knowledge…Put problems before him and let him solve them himself. Let him know nothing because you have told him, but because he has learnt it for himself. Let him not be taught science, let him discover it. If ever you substitute authority for reason he will cease to reason; he will be a mere plaything of other people's thoughts. (Rousseau, 1762 and 2005, p. 376)

He goes on to illustrate through an example in which the starting point for understanding geography lies not with 'globes, spheres and maps' but with the child's observation of sunset and sunrise and the totality of an experience this offers:

> ….brief hour of enchantment which no man can resist; a sight so grand, so fair, so delicious, that none can behold it unmoved. (Rousseau, 1762 and 2005, p. 377)

Note the emphasis on the emotional response to the voluptuous experience that is the necessary precursor to more rational understanding, and this is summed up in the following maxim: 'Never tell a child what he cannot understand: no descriptions, no eloquence, no figures of speech, no poetry'. However, this is not to suggest that the teacher should be casual in shaping learning, even if it may appear that way:

> …when you and he have carefully observed the rising sun, when you have called his attention to the mountains and other objects visible from the same spot, after he has chattered freely about them, keep quiet for a few minutes as if lost in thought and then say, 'I think the sun set over there last night; it rose here this morning. How can that be?' Say no more; if he asks questions, do not answer them; talk of something else. Let him alone, and be sure he will think about it. (Rousseau, 1762 and 2005, pp. 378-9)

In this way:

> …we always advance slowly from one sensible idea to another, and as we give time enough to each for him to become really familiar with it before we go on to

another, and lastly as we never force our scholar's attention, we are still a long way from knowledge of the course of the sun or the shape of the earth; but as all the apparent movements of the celestial bodies depend on the same principle, and the first observation leads on to all the rest, less effort is needed, though more time, to proceed from the diurnal revolution to the calculation of eclipses, than to get a thorough understanding of day and night. (Rousseau, 1762 and 2005, p. 379)

It is clear that Rousseau's educational method is not founded upon random or undirected discovery, but is constructed around a carefully sequenced scheme and should not be interpreted either as a free-choice regime in which the child's interests and curiosity provide the only rudder to what is studied, or one in which the teacher is redundant, rather:

> The teacher, through a carefully engineered exploitation of experiences of every-day life, devises a highly structured, orderly and disciplined regime. The freedom Rousseau proposes is conditioned by the constant surveillance the tutor has over the child. (Ross, 2000, p. 136)

The role of the teacher as an active and decisive, yet also unobtrusive, presence is summed up by Rousseau in the following injunction:

> As a general rule – never substitute the symbol for the thing signified, unless it is impossible to show the thing itself; for the child's attention is so taken up with the symbol that he will forget what it signifies. (Rousseau, 1762 and 2005, p. 380)

Although Rousseau's attempt to bring together the skill of the teacher and the natural faculties of the learner were central to his argument, the tension between them was not easily resolved and would not only go on to motivate the work of Dewey (see Chapter 7), but also finds expression in the permissive child-centred progressivism of A. S. Neill on the one hand, and in the more rigid pedagogic strictures of Montessori on the other (see Chapters 3 and 7 respectively).

Rousseau's contemporary influence

Rousseau fixes the Enlightenment gaze firmly on the *Child* and seeks to frame a pedagogic system congruent with ideals of social, political and moral progress rooted by reason; therefore childhood becomes a vital component in the Enlightenment project to improve humankind. When the philosopher Immanuel Kant (who had read *Emile* with an almost religious fervour) posed the question 'What is Enlightenment' in a short essay from 1784, his rhetorical reply was: 'Enlightenment is mankind's exit from its self-incurred immaturity' (from Schmidt, 1996, and quoted in MacCulloch, 2009, p. 802); paradoxically, Rousseau sought to secure this 'exit' through a fresh appraisal of children and how life begins.

The idea of the Child imbued with *original innocence,* that Rousseau promoted through the avatar of *Emile* became an emblem for Romantic artists who located art and truth and beauty in opposition to the vicissitudes of industrialization and the perceived grubbiness of commerce. Those who, following Rousseau, saw the potential of the *Child* to catalyse discussions of human nature included the English poets Samuel Taylor Coleridge, William Blake and William Wordsworth. As Hendrick observes, for them:

> the child stood centrally in the search of poets and novelists to investigate the 'Self' and to express their romantic protest against 'the Experience of Society'. (Hendrick, 1997a, p. 37)

The innocence of this romantically conceived childhood is depicted by Thomas Gainsborough in a series of paintings of his own daughters that are highly expressive of an emerging sentiment about how childhood should be. In contrast to the stiffly arranged family portraits typical of a century earlier, we see his daughters holding hands and caught instantaneously in pursuit of a butterfly. The butterfly suggests a will-o'-the-wisp emblem for childhood that would still find expression 150 years later through J. M. Barrie's Peter Pan as the boy who wouldn't grow up (Hollindale, 2008).

Given the enthusiasm for Rousseau's educational scheme it was inevitable that there would be those who sought to implement it. Among these enthusiasts was a polymathic landed gentleman, inventor, educator and reformer named Richard Lovell Edgeworth (1744–1817) who, following a meeting with the great philosopher, became a devotee, describing how, 'In 1765...I formed a strong desire to educate my son according to the system of Rousseau', a task he duly attempted. However, as Roy Porter remarks:

> The experiment...proved a disaster. Little Dick proved unmanageable: 'I found myself entangled in difficulties with regard to my child's mind and temper...It

was difficult to urge him to do anything that did not suit his fancy'. (Porter, 2001
pp. 343–4)

Despite being baulked in this practical direction, Lovell Edgeworth and his
daughter Maria turned to instructing others through a monumental work
entitled *Practical Education*, published in 1798. In this they stressed an
'experimental' approach to learning through technical, scientific and practical instruction that was emblematic for the era and its new concern with the
education of the *Child* (Porter, 2001, p. 344).

However, Lovell Edgeworth's work was part of an arcane, private conversation conducted by a literary, intellectual and fiscal elite and had little or
nothing to do with the lives of the growing army of factory children at home,
or the slave populations that produced the wealth emanating from Britain's
overseas' colonies (see Diptee, 2006 and 2007; Jones, C., 2008). The size and
agility of children made them suitable for some of the most dangerous activities such as in keeping mill machinery serviced while still running and, as
a particular *cause celebre* for those who opposed child labour, in sweeping chimneys. When making the case for the abolition of child labour, the
plight of these 'climbing boys' was frequently cited and ethnocentric com-
parisons were made with the lot of children working on the plantations of
the Caribbean. However, as the historian Audra Diptee observes, there were
crucial differences:

[The]...vast majority of labourers in Jamaica were enslaved and those in Britain
were not. The slave status of Jamaican child labourers meant that they were not
subjects of the British crown but, in fact, were legally defined as the property of
subjects to the crown. (Diptee, 2007, p. 53)

Conclusion

Enslaved or free, the processes of industrialization that the Romantics
opposed through the image of the innocent *Child* had swallowed up a
multitude of child workers in long and unrelenting hard labour. Further,
the image of the idealized *Child* would become emblematic for opposition
to the demands of mass schooling through the nineteenth and twentieth
centuries among progressive educators and continues to shape a sense that

harsh, real-world imperatives still make too many demands on our children in their golden age.

Reflection:

Look back on your own education and schooling.

- Which was more important in shaping your experience, the things that interested and inspired you or the demands of employment, exams and school success?
- Are there social factors that mean that the idea of childhood as futurity and the importance of securing life chances is more important for some children than for others?

Further reading

Cunningham, H. (2001), *Children and Childhood in Western Society Since 1500*, London: Longman.

Cunningham, H. (2001), *The Invention of Childhood*, London: BBC Books.

Diptee, A. A. (2007), 'Imperial ideas, colonial realities: enslaved children in Jamaica, 1775–1834', in Marten, J. (ed.), *Children in Colonial America*, New York: New York University Press.

Porter, R. (2001), *Enlightenment: Britain and the Creation of the Modern World*, London: Penguin.

Rhodes, M. (2000), 'Uncovering the history of childhood', in Mills, J. and Mills, R. (eds), *Childhood Studies: A Reader in Perspectives of Childhood*, London: Routledge.

Robinson, D. and Groves, J. (1998), *Introducing Philosophy*, London: Icon Books.

Rosenthal, J. T. (ed.) (2007), *Essays on Mediaeval Childhood: Responses to Recent Debates*, Donington: Shaun Tyas.

Website

Internet Encyclopaedia of Philosophy (IEP): www.iep.utm.edu/, last accessed 17 December 2010.

2

A Pastoral Symphony: Pestalozzi, Froebel and Romanticism

Chapter Outline

Introduction

Despite the mixed outcomes of attempts to realize Rousseau's ideas in educational practice by enthusiasts such as Lovell Edgeworth (Porter, 2001, pp. 343–6 and Chapter 1), there were others who derived inspiration from Rousseau's work and sought to develop educational systems that resonated with its propositions.

Romanticism and the Enlightenment project

Along with the mismatch between the aspirations of the Enlightenment project and the actual lives of real people (that we saw in the last chapter), the project itself was far from uniform in its world view. Tarnas (1991) suggests that the Enlightenment position was deeply conflicted and broadly split into camps that represented two distinct cultures. He describes these two intellectual cultures, thus:

> One emerged in the Scientific Revolution and Enlightenment and stressed rationality, empirical science, and a skeptical secularism. The other was its polar complement...tending to express those aspects of human experience suppressed by the Enlightenment's overriding spirit of rationalism. First conspicuously present in Rousseau, then in Goethe, Schiller, Herder, and German Romanticism, this side of the Western sensibility fully emerged in the late eighteenth and early nineteenth centuries, and has not ceased to be a potent force in Western culture and consciousness...

Although both cultures shared a faith in humankind as the measure of all things, were iconoclastic in their relations with established order and shared an interest in the intellectual worlds of the Greeks and Romans, there were distinct and important differences between them. Tarnas continues his argument, suggesting that:

> ...the Romantic vision perceived the world as a unitary organism rather than an atomistic machine, exalted the ineffability of inspiration rather than the enlightenment of reason, affirmed the inexhaustible drama of human life rather than the calm predictability of static abstractions. (Tarnas, 1991, pp. 366–7)

This Romantic vision, stressing holism (that the world can best be understood as a complete, indivisible whole) over atomism (that the world is understood by examination of its individual and distinct parts) is vital to understanding the construction of the *Child* presented in *Emile* and the construction of progressive ideas about childhood and education that flowed from it. The Romantics' vision of the completeness of the natural world was replicated in their vision of the *Child* and in turn, set the conditions for proper and effective learning that drew strength from its alignment with the growth of a child as a unitary organism. What we are witnessing is the construction of the *Child* as an objectification of philosophical ideas that emerge in relation to changing social, economic and political conditions (Hendrick, 1997a, p. 36).

Alongside these philosophical concerns, early industrialization and technological changes in the eighteenth century were bringing about a transformation in humans' capacity to shape and control the world. This apparent increase in human power and control of nature led many to question the relationship between human beings, knowledge and the world. Therefore, we shall begin by introducing the work of Immanuel Kant, because as MacCulloch (2009, p. 803) has suggested 'he shaped the way that the West did its thinking through the nineteenth and twentieth centuries', as well as Pestalozzi and Froebel's thinking in particular.

The influence of Immanuel Kant (1724–1804)

Kant's working life was spent at the University of Konigsberg in what was then East Prussia and is now Russia. Unlike Rousseau with his capacity to court controversy, Kant was outwardly rather dull and a man of consistent habit (Russell, 1979, p. 678). Local townspeople remarked on the way that they could set their watches by the strict timekeeping that he maintained, except, that is, for a few days when curiously, his pattern was disrupted and he failed to appear for his daily constitutional walk at the usual time. It emerged that Kant had spent these days reading and re-reading *Emile*. Kant was fascinated by the work of Rousseau and approved the French Revolution. Respect for the values of liberty and freedom is found in his philosophical work (Neiman, 2009). As with Descartes however, Kant's work did not directly address children or childhood, but his influence on education and educationists has been extensive and significant.

Kant shares the concerns of Descartes and Locke to establish a sound basis for reliable knowledge. However, since the time of Descartes and Locke problems concerning the relationship between mind and matter, that were unresolved by their work, had led the sceptical David Hume to suggest that our knowledge may never be founded on anything we can really trust (Russell, 1979, p. 676). In his monumental *Kritik der reinen Vernunft* or *Critique of Pure Reason* (published in 1781 and then 1787) Kant addresses these questions, challenging Hume by proposing that reliable knowledge of the world is possible and that both mind and matter play their part in its construction. For Kant, our belief that when we witness an effect there will be an identifiable cause preceding it, as well as our assumptions about reality, such as the existence of space and time, do not come from sensory experience; rather they exist in advance of experience as innate mental faculties or what he calls *categories* of mind. Further, although experience does supply information about the world, this is always filtered through our senses so that an ultimate reality, or *noumenal* world, cannot be known. However, being furnished with innate categories, the mind is able to work on this sensory material to construct concepts that form the model of the world with which we organize and direct our lives. Kant proposes that mind and matter come together to create our knowledge as a synthetic human artefact. But this knowledge of the world is not merely instrumental or mechanistic, for Kant asserts that our sense of morality, duty and beauty are also categories of the mind. This imposes a moral dimension or *categorical imperative* upon us that Kant's followers would use both to justify political revolution, for Kant's work insists that pauper or king, all humans are subject to a requirement to behave morally (Neiman, 2009, p. 150 et seq). With regard to childhood, Kant can be interpreted as insisting that the education of the *Child* must have moral purposes in view, while possessing an active capacity to construct knowledge. Moreover, there are also important spiritual implications. For Kant the categories are given from the outset, therefore they must be beyond rational scrutiny and open up the possibility of a transcendent or spiritual reality that is beyond the grasp of reason (Korner, 1955; Russell, 1979; Davis and Hersh, 1981; Magee, 1988; Robinson and Groves, 1998). The combination of moral imperative, the *Child*'s active nature and transcendent spirituality would be at the heart of the socially and morally transformative vision for the *Child* and its education that is expressed in the works of Pestalozzi and Froebel.

Johann Heinrich Pestalozzi (1746–1827): *Emile*, Kant and schooling

The renowned Swiss educationist, Johann Heinrich Pestalozzi had read *Emile* as a young man and the book remained on his bedside table throughout his life (Heafford, 1967; Palmer, 2001). He was greatly impressed by Rousseau's stress on children's moral innocence and active curiosity about the world. For Pestalozzi, this view of children was complemented by Kant's assertion that reliable knowledge was possible and that moral progress was a duty placed upon us. For Pestalozzi, Rousseau not only affirmed the importance of childhood but also that through the pedagogical methods found in *Emile* the reliable knowledge of the world that Kant had suggested was possible could be acquired.

Thus armed and inspired, Pestalozzi set up a school for children of the poor and housed it in his farm at Neuhof, near Zurich when still in his twenties. Perhaps his idealism had run ahead of him and the school failed in part due to the hostility of parents to his scheme for their children.

Reflection:

Pestalozzi was an educational visionary who, it seems, struggled to convey his vision to the parents of the children he taught. We live in an era that champions 'parent power', but do parents know what is best for their children's education?

However, he learnt from the experiment and in *How Gertrude Teaches Her Children* (1801) he published his educational philosophy and prescriptions for a practical pedagogy. The book was highly influential and made Pestalozzi something of a celebrity; so that when in 1805 he deployed his ideas in a new experimental school in the Swiss town of Yverdon (Heafford, 1967), his work became a focus for considerable attention among intellectuals and educators throughout Europe. These included the young Froebel, for whom a visit to the school in 1805 was revelatory and formative.

Although a profound admirer of *Emile* and Rousseau's work, Pestalozzi was also critical of what he saw as a paradoxical tension arising between Rousseau's concern with the freedom of the individual and the responsibilities of citizenship (Smith, 1997). Moreover, he felt that some of Rousseau's assertions were untried and possibly suspect – a result perhaps of the novel way in which he had published his beliefs in *Emile*. In consequence, Pestalozzi proposed that Rousseau's philosophical account of childhood and education should be complemented by empirical study of real children, and thereby, pedagogic practices could be made more congruent with their nature.

Pestalozzi offers us a first coherent statement of what have become articles of faith for the 'progressive' tradition in pedagogy. For Pestalozzi, as for Rousseau, words come after experience, therefore children should learn through action and when these are internalized the words will follow. Echoing Kant, Pestalozzi asserts that children possess active mental powers of judging, reasoning and seeing and that the purpose of education is to encourage and cultivate these and with them, their participation in the world. Therefore, children should not merely be told things or given rote answers; rather, effective learning required them to explore, experiment and arrive at answers for themselves. The cultivation of these powers would enable children to make sense of the world in future, as yet unknown, situations. Pestalozzi's biographer, Kilpatrick (1951), explores his concept of *Anschaung* found at the heart of his pedagogical method; the German does not translate readily into English, however, *Anschaung* refers to what might be described as direct concrete observation, or more literally, 'sense perception' or 'object-teaching' (Adelman, 2000). Pestalozzi asserted that no word should be offered until *Anschaung* had occurred and was complete, so that a thing, a distinction between things or a process must be felt and experienced in concrete form before a verbal formulation of it should be offered. It should be noted, however, that the educator is always responsible for guiding the child's education and he emphasizes purpose and repetition in effective learning. There are direct echoes of Kant here and his insistence that the mind is active in the application of its categories to the organization of sense data, that is, children are furnished with the capacity of making sense of the material presented by the world (Heafford, 1967). We should also note that this tends to affirm the internalized, mental account of human development that is a direct product of much Enlightenment philosophy, rather than a socially founded one that stresses the role of language, interaction and a socially constructed reality (Rorty, 1980).

However, Kilpatrick (1951) continues that Pestalozzi is insistent, as a cardinal principle, that education should incorporate a child's whole being and characterized this holistic view of education as being about 'head, hands and heart' (or, the intellectual, practical and emotional) (Kilpatrick,1951). The child's personality is central and almost sacred, being the site for the 'inner dignity of each individual for the young as truly as for the adult' and its emergence is described using an organic metaphor, asserting that just as 'a little seed...contains the design of the tree', so in each child is the promise of his potentiality, thus 'The educator only takes care that no untoward influence shall disturb nature's march of developments'. Moreover, Pestalozzi follows Kant by proposing love as 'the sole and everlasting foundation' for real human progress that transcends what reason can achieve: 'Without love, neither the physical not the intellectual powers will develop naturally'. As for his predecessor Rousseau, and for Froebel who would follow him, congruency with the nature of the *Child* permitted access to a deep spiritual reality that was a vital precondition for effective education. This placed him in vehement opposition to established pedagogues who he saw as going against nature and thus doomed to failure, Pestalozzi expresses the passion behind his enterprise, thus:

> I wish to wrest education from the outworn order of doddering old teaching hacks as well as from the new-fangled order of cheap, artificial teaching tricks, and entrust it to the eternal powers of nature herself, to the light which God has kindled and kept alive in the hearts of fathers and mothers, to the interests of parents who desire their children grow up in favour with God and with men.
> (Kilpatrick, 1951)

The appeal to the Child's nature and to the needs that implicitly flow from this, rested on the assumption that children did indeed have a particular and specific *nature* that distinguished them from adults. Just as Coleridge, Blake and Wordsworth had, in Rousseau's wake, held up the *Child* as an icon embodying innocence, purity, and moral honesty, the Romantic idea of the Child became installed as an educational proposition in Pestalozzi's work (Kilpatrick, 1951).

Reflection:

To what extent does the school curriculum accommodate head, hands and heart? Is this a meaningful idea?

Johann Friedrich Froebel (1782–1852): German nationalism, nature and the kindergarten

Froebel was born on 21 April, 1782 at Oberweissbach, Thuringia (now central Germany) to the family of a Lutheran protestant pastor – just a year after Kant published his *Critique of Pure Reason*. Froebel was to become the educational thinker and activist most closely identified with what has become known as the progressive movement in education across Europe and certainly in England and did much to shape the child-centred philosophies that continue to influence debates around pedagogy and the nature of childhood into our own era (Liebschner, 1991).

At the age of 15, young Froebel embarked on an apprenticeship as a forester in the Thuringia Forest. Work in the forest profoundly influenced Froebel and particularly his attitude towards nature and the relationship of humankind to it; these experiences provided much of the raw material from which Froebel would distil his ideas concerning children and their education (Liebschner, 1991; Weston, 2000; Palmer, 2001). Froebel's encounter with nature as a young forester affirmed his Romanticism and inspired his belief that just as children were closer to nature, so their direct engagement with the natural world is vital to healthy growth; thereafter, this coupling of the *Child* and the natural world becomes and remains a major theme of progressivism.

After two years in the forest, Froebel enrolled as a student of Natural Sciences at the University of Jena in Germany just as Napoleon was sweeping across Europe. At this time Germany was not a unified State like Britain or France, but comprised numerous relatively small States, each ruled by separate monarchs (e.g. Prussia, Bavaria and Saxony) and the German Enlightenment became closely bound up with an aspiration to unify the German nation. Jena was a great seat of learning and played a central role in the formulation of Romantic philosophical underpinning for German nationalism as a response to Napoleon, but that went on to find calamitous, perverted expression in Nazism. Several of this nationalism's main exponents, including Fichte, Schelling and Hegel (see Russell, 1979, p. 690), taught at Jena during Froebel's time. Froebel studied literature, natural sciences and architecture, but also became attracted by these idealists' unifying, holistic vision for greater Germany. In this intellectual atmosphere, Froebel formulates his convictions concerning the contribution of children's education to building the nation as an idealized entity. It should be said that Froebel's ideas became, and continue to be, highly influential in England and the United States. However, the Anglo-Saxon reading of Froebel is frequently shorn of nationalist political convictions and it is easy to overlook the importance he attached to them. Adelman (2000, p. 112) quotes a letter written by Froebel in 1827 in which he loftily identifies a connection between his personal life and work and the good of the whole human race, but also suggests that this is expressed most tangibly through: '...blessings for my home and my native land, for Schwartzburg and Thuringia, and for the whole Fatherland itself'. This is not to say that Froebel was a proto-Nazi. Nevertheless, Nazism has tarnished the German Enlightenment (Neiman, 2009, p. 124-5) and we have to ask whether, in common with the wider critique of Romanticism, the objectified and idealized *Child* promoted by Froebel has always served the interests of real children well.

> ## Reflection:
>
> Can ideas transcend the circumstances of their formulation? How seriously should we take Froebel's nationalism in understanding his pedagogic vision and should the link between German nationalist thinkers and Nazism give us cause for concern?

In 1805, Froebel read Pestalozzi and was so impressed that he walked for three weeks to attend his school at Yverdon on the shores of Lake Geneva. Froebel was exalted by much of what he saw, but also depressed and became convinced that Pestalozzi's work lacked sufficient theorization (Adelman, 2000). However, from this time he became increasingly focused upon the education of young children and the immediate outcome was that he was appointed as tutor to the aristocratic children of Baron von Holzhausen and his wife. Despite the distractions of an illicit affair with the children's mother, Froebel used his appointment to experiment pedagogically and secured the use of a meadow in which the children prepared and tended a garden. From this practical engagement with growth and cultivation arose the idea of the *kindergarten* as a place where children could grow to organic wholeness (Weston, 2000; Michaelis and Keatley Moore, 2008).

Extrapolation from arguments *about* the nature of children to identify appropriate and formative activities *for* children lay at the heart of Froebel's emergent philosophy for the kindergarten as a new childhood institution. Alongside experiments in gardening Froebel also begins to develop his own simple toys and games through which children are facilitated to learn deep and complex truths about the world. These invented toys and games undoubtedly are precursors to Froebel's 'gifts' which we shall examine later.

In 1813 Froebel enlisted in the Prussian army, but after the fall of Napoleon at the battle of Waterloo in 1815, we see that Froebel's energies were directed back towards children and pedagogy and particularly the foundation of a number of new institutions that would do much to advance his vision for childhood. The first of these was 'The Universal German Educational Institute' in 1816 at Griesheim. Two years after founding the school, Froebel began publishing a weekly journal through which he expounded his educational ideas (see Weston, 2000, for fuller version).

Froebel is a direct heir to Rousseau and Kant through the work of Pestalozzi. His work combines the child-focused insights about human nature found in Rousseau with Kantian notions of mind, knowledge and spirituality, and all wrapped up in the practical pedagogy of Pestalozzi. Moreover, he was not content to be a prophet in the wilderness, and aspired to construct an education *method* that could be replicated as an education *system* for the great mass of children.

Based on his experience and his accumulated writings, Froebel published his most significant work in 1826 - *The Education of Man* (*Die Menschenerziehung*). The work was about education but was far from a straightforward handbook on practice (Weston, 2000). Rather, it is shot through with an intense spirituality and discusses the transcendent potentialities found in humankind using Christian cosmological and theological imagery. Yet the work's theology is a form of holistic pantheism, with the spirit of the Christ and nature conflated as the true destination for human development and for spiritual realization; in this it is far from doctrinally orthodox and even heretical to more conventional Christian convictions (Brehony, 2006, p. 170) – there are striking echoes of the mediaeval mystic theologian Meister Eckhart, (see chapter 2). At the heart of Froebel's concerns is the *Child*, whose nature, echoing Rousseau and Pestalozzi, is good and inclined towards virtue rather than original sinfulness. Froebel's engagement with nature in the forest as a young man had struck a deep chord within him that found expression in this work.

In *The Education of Man*, Froebel stresses three core principles:

1. The wholeness of the *Child*, so that there should be no arbitrary separation between school and life, with 'playing and learning and working…[forming]… a harmonious unity'.
2. That childhood is a passage through developmental stages, each of which is vital and must be completed for healthy maturation to be achieved: 'The vigorous and complete development and cultivation of each successive stage depends on the vigorous, complete, and characteristic development of each and all preceding stages of life'.

3. The centrality of play as the key to achieving harmonized, organic development and to laying secure foundations for later life for the individual and the whole species, as well as an expression of the *Child*'s active nature: 'The plays of children are the germinal leaves of all later life. Play is the purest, most spiritual activity of man at this stage, and, at the same time, typical of human life as a whole – of the hidden inner natural life in man and all things.' (Froebel, 1826 (transl. Hailman), p. 28, and discussed in Weston, 2000).

This intertwining of physical growth with stages of intellectual, moral and social development through the somewhat mystically construed medium of play, can still be found at the heart of early childhood education. Indeed it is difficult to think and talk about children without reference to the language and theoretical repertoire offered by concepts such as 'development', 'readiness', 'stages' and a very specific reading of the meaning of play, to which Froebel reputedly ascribed a moral purpose as 'the child's work' (Weston, 2000; Liebschner, 2006; although Brehony (2010, p. 5) seeks in vain for this oft-quoted slogan in Froebel's own work). The numinous character of Froebel's educational vision is an important development from what he saw and learnt at Yverdon from Pestalozzi. As Adelman suggests: '...Froebel took from Pestalozzi essential principles of pedagogy and curriculum but added another layer, another agenda about transcendence, national unity and theism, even gnosticism' (Adelman, 2000, p. 104). Hence, like Rousseau, Froebel as an Enlightenment intellectual has no hesitation in weaving the *Child*, childhood and education into big philosophical and metaphysical themes that might seem remote from the everyday social realities within which children live their lives. Arguably this sort of heavyweight vision for childhood continues to place challenging imperatives on children and young people.

In 1831, Froebel introduced the 'gifts' around which much of the children's learning was structured in the growing number schools he had established (Wiggin, 1895 and 2009). The 'gifts' have much about them that may seem commonplace to us in an early twenty-first century world. But in their time they represented an extraordinary intervention in the curriculum of early childhood education because they were designed by Froebel to embody what he saw as essential forms, processes and properties found in the world. They are a physical manifestation of the Platonic ontology, or theory of reality, that underpins his idealism (Weston, 2000). For Plato the everyday or *immanent* world is held to be an imperfect, degraded or 'fuzzy' version of the transcendent world of *ideal* or perfect forms (Magee, 1988, p. 23). By stripping away the imperfections, peculiarities and idiosyncrasies of everyday objects the gifts offer children an opportunity to encounter, experiment with and learn through a less cluttered conceptual realm of purified form and process. Therefore, through these deceptively simple gifts and the play they structure, the *Child* is enabled to engage with deep realities and truths. They were also fashioned with children in mind, being manipulable by tiny hands and formed to appeal to a child's more immediate senses. Toys and equipment akin to them can now be found on most High Streets and are fundamental to the kit and equipment found in Nursery schools wherever Western educational practices hold sway.

Froebel also championed the role of women in the education of young children over the sort of 'doddering old hacks' Pestalozzi describes (Kilpatrick, 1951, see earlier) and followed this up by making thorough training available as a passport to a hitherto inaccessible professional status. This may surprise us as inhabitants of an educational world where early childhood education is overwhelmingly staffed by women and seen as a female profession that attracts too few men.

In 1836 Froebel's lifelong endeavours achieved their apotheosis with the opening of the first 'kindergarten' (child-garden) at Bad Blankenburg in Thuringia and, such was its success that within 12 years there were over 50 of these new childhood institutions. Froebel's humanistic and philanthropic kindergarten philosophy based on freedom, autonomy and self-determination is expressed by an inscription he wrote on the fly-cover of a book owned by a friend: 'You give people their bread; let my aim be to give them themselves'. However, their success was not universally welcomed and in 1848 all kindergartens were closed by the Prussian court because there were fears that they were linked to revolutionary and anarchist activity and therefore, dangerously subversive (Weston, 2000).

It should be said that although Froebel incurred the displeasure of the political authorities, this seemed to lend him heroic status in the eyes of fellow pedagogues (Adelman, 2000); so that just before his death at the age of 70 in 1852 and while his kindergartens were still proscribed, he was acknowledged and greeted warmly by the professionally prestigious Educational Congress of Teachers (Weston, 2000). It took a further eight years before the authorities lifted the ban and kindergartens could open their doors once again. The kindergarten would, of course, go on to become a generic descriptor for institutions of early childhood education across much of Europe and the United

States and his ideas and followers went on to find a receptive home in the United Kingdom.

Conclusion

Pestalozzi and Froebel represent an important translation of Locke, Kant and Rousseau's ideas into educational practices and underline the visibility that children had achieved in the imagination of the intellectual elite by the nineteenth century. In the process they establish institutions that operate on the basis of a set of theorized Child's needs that must be met in order to learn, grow and thrive as a balanced human being. Although these institutions may appear to present children with substantial educational opportunities, for others they proceed from an idealistic objectification of the Child based on Enlightenment aspirations that may leave actual children alienated and 'abandoned in theory' (Jenks, 2005, p. 23; see Chapter 9).

Reflection:

Do intellectuals have a moral duty to others that accompanies their knowledge and expertise? Do you have any thoughts on how this might appear in highly educated teachers?

Further reading

Adelman, C. (2000), 'Over two years, what did Froebel say to Pestalozzi?', *History of Education*, 29(2), pp. 103–14.

Brehony, K. (2006), 'Early years education: some Froebelian contributions', *History of Education*, 35(2) March, pp. 166–72.

Cunningham, H. (2006), *The Invention of Childhood*, London: BBC Books.

James, A., Jenks, C. and Prout, A. (1998), *Theorizing Childhood*, Cambridge: Polity Press.

Liebschner, J. (2006), *A Child's Work: Freedom and Guidance in Froebel's Educational Theory and Practice*, Leicester: Lutterworth Press.

Palmer, J. (ed.) (2001), *Fifty Major Thinkers on Education*, London: Routledge.

Valkonova, Y. and Brehony, K. (2006), 'The Gifts and "contributions": Friedrich Froebel and Russian education (1850–1929)', *History of Education*, 35(2) March, pp. 189–207.

Weston, P. (2000), *Friedrich Froebel: His Life, Times and Significance*, London: University of Surrey Roehampton.

Website

The Froebel Institute: www.froebel.org.uk/, last accessed 17 December 2010.

3

Reclaiming Earthly Paradise: Froebelians and the Invention of Progressive Education

Introduction

Following banning and exile by the Prussians, many of Froebel's followers brought Froebelianism to England and found a willing audience for 'progressive' educational ideas and practices.

Froebelians and England

Froebel left a tangible legacy in the many schools and kindergartens found in his native Germany and the English speaking world. Moreover, there remain the Pestalozzi–Froebel Haus in Berlin and the Froebel Institute at Roehampton University, London. Each is dedicated to the education of teachers and the memorialization of his ideas. However, in the period following his death Froebel's legacy was not always so secure. To escape the Prussian ban on the kindergarten, many of Froebel's supporters came to England in 1851 and found a receptive public drawn from the middle- and upper-middle classes. History suggests that bans seldom produce their desired aims in the long run and it seems that the Prussian authorities' ban on the kindergarten lent Froebel a reputation 'as a courageous and visionary educator and social reformer' that clearly appealed to radicals in the United Kingdom and the United States (Adelman, 2000, p. 103). Among those disciples who first spread the word were Bertha Ronge and the Baroness von Marenholtz-Bulow. Ronge published a modest pamphlet in English in 1854 and established the first private kindergarten in Bloomsbury, London while writing *A Practical Account of the Kindergarten* with her husband. This was followed, in 1855, by a translation of the Baroness' exposition of kindergarten theory titled in English as *Women's Educational Mission*. This translation took Froebel's ideas beyond the coterie of exiled German nationals and to a wider audience of educationists eager to learn about progressive methods (Whitbread, 1972).

Froebel's disciples promoted his ideas vigorously, combining public lectures with open days at the kindergarten and a programme to educate kindergarten teachers in the philosophy underpinning his practical principles. By late Victorian times, Froebelianism had become embedded in the lives of many middle-class adherents and gained a certain cachet among parents who were unwilling to send their children to the new elementary schools. Further, there were many who felt that a progressive interest in education sent the right message about their family life and concern for the next generation. Wealthy families readily welcomed Froebel-trained nursery nurses and governesses into their houses, but for many who could not quite afford this, the kindergarten offered a suitable institution for the education of their children. The Froebelians went on to establish kindergartens in Kensington, Manchester and Leeds by 1860 and a training institution at Highbury Hill House in 1874 (Whitbread, 1972). The thoughts of this middle-class father, writing in 1898, underline how a proprietary interest in young children's education had, by the end of the century, become embedded in the social consciousness of the middle classes:

> …we are no longer of the same mind as our parents who sent their children straight to a public school from nursery. Rather we consider that the child's life,

from the age when he fumbles with block letters, should be a continual and graduated training for more advanced education to follow. (Parker, 1898, quoted in Whitbread, 1972, p. 38)

In England this enthusiasm was boosted by the foundation in 1894 of the Froebelian Educational Institute for the training of teachers at new college premises in West Kensington; the institution later moved to Roehampton Lane and is one of the main constituent colleges of Roehampton University. It is an indication of the appeal of the new institute that it was to be endowed by a subscription fund launched in 1892 with a target of £25,000. The scheme was an ambitious one and, besides offering training in Froebelian methods, planned to incorporate two model kindergartens and schools for children and young people aged three to fifteen. There was an explicit commitment to making Froebelian education available to the children of the poor, in that even as one of the kindergarten/schools would be for fee-paying pupils, the other was free for working-class children. However, the target sum was not reached. It seemed that the middle classes would fund their own children's education along these lines, but not that of the poor. The training college was duly built first and the fee-paying kindergarten/schools followed, but the free places were shelved (Whitbread, 1972, p. 37).

Despite these disappointments, the new Froebel Educational Institute provided a focal point for the development of the work in England and the movement gathered pace. From Froebel's encounters with Pestalozzi and his first experiments in pedagogy had sprung an international educational movement with a clearly constructed vision for the *Child* and for the transformation of society that harks back to Rousseau.

The emphasis upon a spiritual, even mystical, undertow to the practices of the kindergarten placed Froebelianism unsurprisingly at odds with the utilitarian aims and instrumentally inclined realities of the State Elementary School (see Chapter 6). However, there were those in the State sector who endorsed the child-centredness of Pestalozzi, Froebel et al., as a sort of a moral critique of the more utilitarian State system (Simon, 1965, pp. 142–7; Whitbread, 1972). However, as we shall see *a propos* the Plowden Report (CACE, 1967), attempts to turn this alternative vision into everyday practice in the State sector, especially for children in their middle years, have encountered many pitfalls and been highly controversial, dependent as the system is on taxpayers' money.

> ### Reflection:
>
> We are in an era in which we have grounds to be as concerned about the inequality between the opportunities available to the children of the rich and the poor as the Victorians who implemented Froebel's ideas in England. But can equality of opportunity be guaranteed without the active involvement of the State?

Maria Montessori (1870–1952)

Maria Montessori was born into a conservative, Catholic family in Chiaravalle in the province of Ancona, on 31 August, 1870. That year is highly significant, for it is in 1870 that Italy as a unified nation-State came into being. There was a spirit of national resurgence that accompanied the unification and, in particular, this was characterized by an anti-Church sentiment that was strongly committed to scientific rationalism and political reform. However, this radicalism did not readily translate into social transformation. Economic forces had forced rural labourers in the south of Italy into the slum–poverty of towns that were expanding all too rapidly. Thus as a young woman, Montessori found herself placed between the religious and social conservatism of her home, the intellectual radicalism of the times and the economic pressures that were transforming Italian society. This seemed to resolve itself on the one hand into the morally conservative, even authoritarian, position of the pedagogue in her educational scheme and on the other, in her convictions about the potential for radical transformation and all-round progress held out by scientific rationalism when applied to children's education (Kramer, 1988, pp. 68–71).

In the early 1890s, Montessori went to The University of Rome to study natural sciences and medicine with a view to becoming a physician. This was not an easy path for a woman at that time and she encountered initial hostility from tutors and peers, many of whom would subsequently be proud to claim to be her followers. While at the University, Montessori studied physical anthropology, a popular academic discipline that sought to classify humankind using the physical shape of the body. Among her tutors were Cesare Lombroso and Guiseppe Sergi who were pioneers in attempts to explain criminal behaviour in terms of skull shape and brain size – work that was subsequently to become widely discredited through too close an association with Italian fascism. Although this work held out little hope of reforming the criminals themselves, it did suggest to Montessori that proper attention to young children might prevent the appearance of abnormalities and the subsequent damage to the social fabric inflicted by crime (see Kramer, 1988, for fuller discussion).

Widespread economic hardship and disgust over the slum conditions in cities such as Rome during the 1890s precipitated a movement for political change that included a desire to transform elementary educational provision for all. Spurred by political zeal, Montessori took on a commission from the Association of Good Building to experiment in a slum tenement in Rome with a new form of early childhood schooling called the Casa dei Bambini – the Children's House; this was to be the cornerstone institution for the development of her method. Through her observations she proposed a theory of children's development based on consecutive stages, each of which was vital for the full, healthy development and growth of the *Child* (Kramer, 1988, pp. 110–22). We have already encountered stage theories for development in Rousseau and Froebel and Montessori's proposal adds to the vocabulary of developmentalism that continues to dominate ways of seeing children and making sense of the changes we observe in them.

Based on observation, Montessori asserted that the five senses were vital to the intellectual growth of the *Child* and that sight and touch were especially significant as means to acquiring a grasp of abstract qualities. This championing of empirical methods and of the senses as the doorway to the mind was not, of course, new and we have encountered it in Locke, Rousseau, Pestalozzi and Froebel. Thus, Montessori designed teaching materials that required children to utilize their senses in learning, for example, children would learn their letters not merely by seeing and speaking them, but the letters would be presented to them as sandpaper cut-outs so that children could trace their outline with their fingers as they read them, or that foundational objects and processes in mathematics could be acquired through the manipulation of learning materials such as graduated rods, platonic solids, colour tablets and so forth. Montessori stressed the pleasure that children take in repetition and the consistency inscribed into the graduated learning materials facilitated this repetition. For Montessori this confirmed the legitimacy of each of her developmental stages. The result was, she believed, a didactic system that properly pursued and implemented would deliver intellectual, moral and physical objectives that are the foundations upon which educated personhood is built (Whitbread, 1972, pp. 57–60). Having designed this graduated didactic pathway it was clear that the method made learning almost 'teacher-proof'; Montessori described it thus:

> Not upon the ability of the teacher does such education rest, but upon the didactic system. This presents objects which, first, attract the spontaneous attention of the child, and, second, contain a rational graduation of stimuli. (Montessori, M. (1912), The Montessori Method, New York, pp. 174-5, quoted in Whitbread, 1972)

Choice was present in the Children's House environment, but it was an important cardinal principle that children *learnt* to choose, rather than treating it as an inbuilt rational capability. Therefore, the environment was structured so as to ensure that when children did learn to choose they would select the acquisition of constructive knowledge and the merits of helping one another over less approved options. It is clear that Montessori made no bones about the need for order and direction in the classroom environment, but stressed that this was to be founded upon what she called an 'active discipline' that came from the choices made by a child and that, in turn, stemmed from an internalization of what is valued and held up to be best in the properly ordered pedagogical environment.

Montessori's child-centredness was manifested in the way in which she furnished and equipped the Children's House. As far as possible, everything was at child-scale and an emblematic feature of this was the child-sized wicker armchairs. It was vital to the project that the nature of the *Child* and the legitimacy of childhood as a period of life in its own right were acknowledged and championed within the rendering of the Method, and the furniture and spatiality were expressive of it.

Although significantly influenced by Froebel and using many of his insights and materials as her starting point, Montessori's methods set her at odds with many Froebelians of the late nineteenth and early twentieth centuries. They asserted that the Montessori method was little more than sense training and overly formal and that she neglected the *Child*'s imagination – a crushing allegation for anyone who claimed to be a child-centred progressive.

Montessori's 'Method' grappled with the paradox found in Rousseau's work – how can individual freedom based on autonomous agency be reconciled with social discipline and public responsibility? The radical libertarianism that some followers of Rousseau – e.g. Richard Lovell-Edgworth (Porter,

2001, pp. 343–6) or more recently, A. S. Neill at the radical school Summerhill (Neill, 1972) – seemed to advocate was contrary to Montessori's inclinations. For her:

> A room in which all the children move about usefully, intelligently, and voluntarily, without committing an[y] rough or rude act, would seem to me a classroom very well disciplined indeed. (Montessori, M., (1912), The Montessori Method, New York, p. 93, quoted in Kramer, 1988)

Montessori sought to resolve the paradox because desire for order and discipline stemmed from her own humanistic reading of the exponents of modern childhood and her insistence, with Rousseau et al., on the *Child* as fundamentally good and fit for the freedom that was his or her birth-right, but these rights were coupled with responsibility. Being a responsible person was the hallmark of social, political and educational progress and this came about through a disciplined approach to education. At the heart of this disciplined approach stood a learning system that although designed by pedagogues, needed to be independent and insulated from the idiosyncrasy or whim of any individual teacher. For Montessori, this means:

> .... a freedom to take action of certain kinds within certain well-defined limits....Her school is child-centered in the sense that the nature and needs of the child are the starting point for what is taught, but it is she, and not the child, who decides. (Kramer, 1988, p. 118)

Her biographer Kramer (1988) characterizes this with a certain irony as 'freedom to do the "right thing"'. At root there is the idealist's sense of hope concerning human nature, that, if given a genuine choice, people will choose virtue, honesty and interests of others over their more basic moral alternatives. As Brehony has it:

> Firmly attached to the Enlightenment project, education for Montessori was a means for the perfection of the human race, provided it were to be conducted on the scientific lines that she had outlined. (Brehony, 2000, p. 117)

But what if they do not choose 'the right thing'? It is salutary to reflect on how political systems set up to liberate, frequently turn to coercing those who are seen as not making the best use of the freedom that is afforded them.

Although the Froebel Institute and the approval of the middle classes cemented the Froebelians' position as keepers of the true faith on children's education, Montessori's methods did gain approval through the establishment of a number of private nurseries for children from wealthy families for whom the early acquisition of reading skills was regarded as vital and no hindrance to appropriately socialized development. We might reflect that the 'Montessori Nursery' is now a fixture in the landscape of private provision for early childhood care and education and that it continues to be the nursery 'brand of choice' among the fee-paying middle classes (Whitbread, 1972).

Reflection:

Do you agree with Montessori that educational systems and curricula should be independent of the interpretation or abilities of individual teachers?

Progressivism, the State and Elementary Education in the early twentieth century

The convictions of the progressives can be summarized as follows:

- ensure sound education
- promote rational intellectual, emotional, physical and moral development in line with the presumed nature of the *Child*
- secure personal and social transformation through the light of learning.

However, a sense of the need to address the goals of social justice continued to cause unease among many in their ranks and we have seen that despite Froebel and Pestalozzi's commitment to providing education for the poor, the Froebelians struggled to realize this aim. The harsh reality was that without sound finances, it was always easier to make provision for those who could pay than those who could not. Illustrative of the problems was the first free kindergarten in London that opened in 1901 for a brief period under the leadership of Adelaide Wragge until it ran out of money. At this point The

Michaelis Guild stepped in and raised funds to open more free kindergartens, and by 1908 had established them at Blackheath, Hoxton, Notting Hill and Somers Town in London. The same year Manchester Froebelians opened a free kindergarten in Salford. The first such institution in Scotland was Reid's Court Free Kindergarten, opened in 1903 (Whitbread, 1972, pp. 55–6).

Progress was slow, but while these initiatives were numerically small, Esther Lawrence, principal of the Froebelian Institute, was able to claim in 1912 that the Froebel movement was active in the majority of 'poverty stricken and deprived districts of large towns'. But dependency on private donations and subscription continued until the 1918 Education (Fisher) Act (Whitbread, 1972, p. 56). Financial difficulties were compounded by the challenges associated with class difference. Many Froebelians had been used to working with children and families from somewhat different social circumstances and at first they found themselves and their methods unprepared for the challenges presented by the children of the urban poor. Therefore, besides the usual activities centred on several types of imaginative play, singing, dancing, handicrafts and domestic training, there was a need to provide regular baths, weekly visits by a doctor and opportunities for uninterrupted sleep during the day. That said, Miss Lawrence remarked on what we might regard as a certain 'streetwise' quality and that the working-class children were far more independent and able to look after themselves than their middle-class contemporaries. Whether this was regarded as an unalloyed virtue is questionable. Many Froebelians felt that this 'knowingness' came at the price of moral rectitude and that there was an urgent need to supplement the intellectual aspects of education with direction in cleanliness, morality, order and freedom (Whitbread, 1972, p. 56). Hendrick (1997a) has identified these fears through what he sees as the discourse of the 'delinquent child' that emerges during this period, that is, the child who in the eyes of the middle classes had learned too much of the adult world and enjoyed too little of childhood.

Although attempts to introduce Montessorian progressive methods were made, their numinous view of the Child was frequently at odds with the ethos of the Elementary School (Brehony, 2000, p. 119) and received mixed reviews from Her Majesty's Inspectorate (HMI). However, State schooling was universal, passably democratic and offered some prospect of advancement for the working class, even if, in its actualization elementary education was frequently crushingly dull, authoritarian and more focused on the inculcation of narrowly utilitarian knowledge than on the children as complete people – especially under the infamous 'payment by results' regime that was not abolished until 1895. Despite the fact that progressive, rational schooling seemed to have become a naturalized home for middle-class and elitist interests (a fact that disturbed the radical conscience) it was armed with a pedagogy and child-centred vision that could offer scientific respectability both to the practices of schools and the status of the teacher. Brehony (2000) explores the way that new interest in Montessorian methods stimulated debate around the pedagogic merits of individual work over the standard fare of whole-class teaching in the Elementary school. Many of those in the new educational establishment that emerged in the wake of State intervention, found themselves drawn to the mission of the State and the vision of the progressives at one and the same time (Barnard, 1971, p. 172). H. A. L. Fisher introduced what would become the 1918 Education Act in a speech to the House of Commons in April 1917 that commended the practical impacts of universal State education in underpinning the war effort. However, he also presented a holistic vision of the child that could have come directly from a Froebelian and, arguably, laid the foundations for the child-centredness of the subsequent Hadow Report on the Primary School. It is worth reading Fisher's speech (in MacLure, 1986). Attempts by educators and educationists to reconcile this dualism run through much of the subsequent and continuing history of State education – we shall examine Hadow and Plowden and child-centred initiatives later (Chapters 7 and 8).

Rachel and Margaret McMillan: welfare, education and care

If Froebelians, such as Esther Lawrence, are responsible for the first attempts to adapt the kindergarten system to tackle the very real challenges of working with the children and families of the poor, then they laid the foundations upon which Rachel and Margaret McMillan could set out the form, practices and vision that would shape the State nursery school as an institution and arguably, offer a template for the integrated Children's Centres built on inter-professional working that are at the heart of the Every Child Matters (DfES, 2004a) strategy in the United Kingdom.

Rachel (1859–1917) and Margaret (1860–1931) McMillan were born in Westchester, New York State to Jean Cameron and her husband James

McMillan who had both emigrated from Scotland to the United States in 1858. Tragedy stalked their formative years as father and third daughter died in 1865, followed in 1877 by their mother and grandfather. This left the elder sister, Rachel to look after her infirm grandmother while Margaret travelled Europe as a suitable educational preparation to become a governess to a wealthy family. Each moved to London on their grandmother's death, where Rachel became superintendent for a young women's hostel in Bloomsbury and saw at first hand the challenges of life for the poor in the great Victorian city. The earliest ideas that would shape the philosophy and practices of the McMillans were religious and both saw their work as an extension of their values as convinced Christian Socialists (Whitbread, 1972; Moriarty, 1998; Trueman et al., 1999).

Like Montessori, the sisters' work with the poor in slum conditions was central and formative. However, their politics meant that they drew on very different sources for inspiration and mixed with noted radical political thinkers and activists of the late nineteenth century. They included William Morris, Bernard Shaw, Annie Besant, Sydney and Beatrice Webb, all left-wing Fabian Society members and prime movers in the establishment of what would eventually become the British Labour Party. At first the sisters were relatively passive attenders of socialist meetings. But, soon they were addressing meetings for workers at dock and factory gates and selling socialist newspapers on the street. Margaret had trained as an actress and clearly this stood her in good stead as an orator who could hold her audience. Their dogged personalities as well as their education, class-background and very obvious convictions meant that while the sisters repelled many of the rich and famous they attracted the devoted admiration of others. Among these they counted royalty, especially Queen Mary, and wealthy philanthropists. Margaret's capacity to reach out to social and political leaders without compromising the message was remarked on by Margaret Lamming, a student in the Training Centre the sisters established at Deptford, south-east London:

> How many lions she bearded in their dens I do not know. Prime ministers of State, MPs, Councillors, writers and important citizens – she was daunted by none of them and, when overwhelmed by fatigue, illness or depression she would continue to plead her cause to anyone with power of influence, including Royalty. (Trueman et al., 1999)

Margaret McMillan first came to know the grinding, severe poverty of Deptford from her time as manager of three elementary schools in the Borough in 1904. The slums of Deptford had become a byword for deprivation and impoverishment where population densities were high at 131 people per acre (ppa) in 1911 (by comparison, neighbouring Lewisham and Greenwich had around 25 ppa). Many families had five or more children and most lived in one room. Rachel described what she found thus:

> ...stained and tumbling walls, the dark, noisy courts, the crowded rooms, the sodden alleys all hidden behind roaring streets. Women who care no more. Girls whose youth is a kind of defiance. Children creeping on the filthy pavement, half naked, unwashed and covered with sores. (Rachel McMillan, quoted in Trueman et al., 1999, p. 12)

Levels of infant mortality and malnutrition were high and disease was rife. But then the (Conservative) Board of Education issued a policy directive that forced a transformation of the sisters' work, as Trueman et al., note:

> The plight of the youngest children became even more embedded in her developing philosophy when, in 1905, Article 53 of the Education Code stated that under-fives should be removed from the infants departments of elementary schools. This caused a dramatic drop in the number of three to four year olds in schools. The dozens of toddlers that the McMillans encountered playing in the gutters of Deptford after 1905 were a direct result of this Education Code directive. (Rachel McMillan, quoted in Trueman et al., 1999, p. 13)

In the absence of State provision for young children and spurred on both by their sense of mission and the philanthropic support of wealthy patrons, the McMillans embarked on an assault on poverty. Children's health was central to the philosophy. They had actively lobbied for the introduction of the School Medical Service that was ushered in by the 1908 Act. Furthermore, aided financially by Joseph Fels, a wealthy American philanthropist, and supported by the government's Board of Education and the newly formed London County Council, the sisters established a children and family clinic in Bromley-by-Bow in the heart of London's impoverished East End. They intended that the school clinics would be eventually spread across the whole of Britain as part of a broad assault on disease and infant mortality. In practice the clinic in Bow was hard to sustain financially, so that when they were offered premises in Deptford in 1910, they moved the clinic to the other side of the River Thames.

However, the rate at which children were cured of ailments only to reappear a few weeks later at the clinic with the same condition distressed Margaret. This underlined just how deep the roots of poverty went and the sisters realized that symptomatic treatment could never begin to tackle the problems at source. Margaret became convinced that there was a need for an assault on the environmental conditions within which the children were living and, in particular, sleeping. Thus in 1911, she set up what she called the Girl's Night Camp. Under careful supervision and after an elaborate bathing regime, girls would sleep in outdoor shelters and would all settle down under the glow of a red lantern by 8 p.m. – this was intended to assure them a sound night's sleep. Breakfast would be provided in the morning and then the girls would go off to school for the day. Although there is no evidence that McMillan intended to separate the children from their families, there is perhaps an echo here from the ideas of Robert Owen (see Chapter 4), who also suggested that if the children of the poor were to be able to make genuine progress then the influence and involvement of their families needed to be regulated. The communal aspects of the camps would seem to have a great deal in common with other contemporary movements to make fresh air and healthy pursuits available to young people from socialist-inspired experiments in community living to the Boy Scouts and Girl Guides. The girls' camp was followed in 1912 by one for the boys of Deptford (Moriarty, 1998; Trueman et al., 1999).

Margaret McMillan saw only modest success in the girls' and boys' camps and it became clear that an earlier intervention was needed. Zealous as ever and again with the help of Joseph Fels, Margaret persuaded the London County Council to permit her to develop an open air nursery on derelict land in Deptford and in 1913 the nursery admitted its first children. On admission, Margaret found that the children brought with them an array of ailments: 'tonsils, diseased glands, bad teeth, rickets, blepharitis, hernia, wasting, fits, rhinitis conjunctivitis, impetigo, cleft palate [and] bronchitis' (McMillan quoted in Trueman et al., 1999, p. 27). To aid recovery and limit the transmission of disease, especially tuberculosis, the nursery offered children a series of night shelters that were open on one side, so that the children slept under cover, but outside. The open air life was seen as essential for the health and well-being of the children. Thus a central feature of the nursery was an allotment garden that not only reclaimed the derelict land, but made nursery and garden one and the same thing.

Reflection:

What might the dual meaning of 'nursery' as a place for young children and also for raising plants suggest about the role that nature is presumed to have in effecting children's upbringing?

By combining education and healthcare, McMillan was able to illustrate the causes of a range of problems, namely, the fact that speech, hearing and intellectual development were curtailed by complaints such as ear, nose and throat infections, that physical development was stultified by forcing young children to sit still for long periods (as in infant departments of elementary schools) and fingers failed to acquire fine motor skills if there were no tasks designed to develop them. These insights clarified the aims of nursery education for Margaret, 'To educate the hand and to safeguard the speech impulse: that is perhaps the main work – of a formal kind – of the nursery school.' (McMillan, 1923, p. 23 and quoted in Whitbread, 1972, p. 61).

Margaret McMillan travelled Europe and studied intensely to learn how best to meet the intellectual, cultural and academic needs of the children. In the process she took in Froebelism and the work of Montessori in their original homes. Although she embraced their idealism, she was pragmatically eclectic in her approach to ideas and methods. Thus the nursery furnished as a childhood world was co-located with the professional provisions of the clinic and shaped by the methods of the progressive educator. This arrangement is expressive of McMillan's moral vision for a childhood world that was wrapped in adult responsibility and driven by an ethic of service.

Conclusion

Like Maria Montessori, it was in the slums that the McMillan sisters – and following Rachel's untimely death, Margaret especially – forged their template for the nursery school, and it was this environment that threw into such stark relief the difference between human potential and the grinding miseries of metropolitan reality. McMillan drew inspiration from her Christianity, her Marxist, Owenite and Fabian socialism as well as the idealism of Froebel and the practical pedagogy of Montessori. Here was a major figure who accrued huge respect through her work and who demanded that the education and care of the children of the poor be taken as seriously as that of any other. Furthermore, although her legacy has focused on the nursery and provision for very young children, she believed that her methods could be extended to reshape elementary schooling, where a more attenuated vision of human potential was the norm. The vision for the 'whole child' found in her work precedes educational opinions found in the Hadow Reports of the 1930s and particularly the Plowden philosophy that attempted a transformation of State primary education after it appeared in 1967. Finally, the McMillan philosophy is underpinned by socialist convictions concerning State intervention. Philanthropy may have facilitated her work, but she knew that realizing her goals for all children required the agency and extensive reach of the State.

Reflection:

Research the range of services provided by a Children's Centre near you. How many of the services that you identify were also provided by Rachel McMillan at her Open Air Nursery in Deptford?

Further reading

Kramer, R. (1988), *Maria Montessori: A Biography*, Chicago: Da Capo Press.

Liebschner, J. (1991), *Foundations of Progressive Education: The History of the National Froebel Society*, Cambridge: Lutterworth Press.

Moriarty, V. (1998), *Margaret McMillan: 'I learn, to succour the helpless'*, London: Educational Heretics.

Palmer, J. (ed.) (2001), *Fifty Major Thinkers on Education*, London: Routledge.

Trueman, H., Adlington, E., Marriott, F. and Steele, J.(ed.)(1999)**,** *The Children Can't Wait: The McMillan Sisters and the Birth of Nursery Education*, London: Deptford Forum.

Website

Electric Scotland: www.electricscotland.com/history/women/wh31.htm, last accessed 17 December 2010.

Part 2
Mass Schooling and Modern Childhood

4

Industry, Philanthropy and Industrial Education Systems

Introduction

Just as the Age of Enlightenment championed rational and moral progress in human affairs, it also ushered in modern capitalism and industrialization leading to a reordering of social, political and economic realities that had profound effects upon children's lives. The combined deprivations of industrialization and the visibility of children that resulted, in part, from *Emile*, inspired action which suggested that mass education was necessary and possible.

Children and industrial society

If philosophical idealism was instrumental in the construction of a modern idea of the *Child* and childhood, then there were also other modernizing forces at play that would completely transform the everyday experience of adults and children alike. These changes in economic production are generally referred to as the Industrial Revolution. Britain in 1801, with a population of around 10 million, had a largely rural, agricultural economy based on the primary production of raw materials and craft-based manufacturing (Floud and Johnson, 2004; Prince, 1976, p. 90). By 1914, Britain's domestic population had quadrupled, standing at just over 40 million and the major European powers, including Britain, were on the brink of industrial scale warfare that reflected the changes in modes and scale of production. Included among these changes were:

- transformations in communications and transport technologies
- increased flexibility in the availability of coal as the dominant energy source
- factory-based manufacturing
- a hitherto unseen harnessing of the reproductive potential of the natural world.

All this was accompanied by expansion and consolidation of the big European nations and extension of their reach into every corner of the world through their colonial empires.

Not only had Britain's population increased in sheer numbers to a historically unprecedented extent, but its geography and age-structure had changed dramatically. Industrialization was accompanied by a process known as urbanization, in which the population not only became town and city dwellers but also became acculturated to urban ways of life (Pratt-Adams et al., 2010). To give some sense of the scale and pace of the change, Manchester grew from a population of around 25,000 in the 1770s to over 250,000 by the 1820s. By 1900 Britain's population geography had changed, probably irrevocably, to become the first country in which the majority of its inhabitants were urban dwellers. However, a direct outcome of this rapid growth and of the free-market capitalism by which some entrepreneurs were amassing great fortunes was that the living and working conditions of these new urbanites were far from ideal. Observers and commentators, such as Friederick Engels (1844) who toured the slum alleys of Manchester in the 1840s, catalogued the deprivations accompanying overcrowded, insanitary and unsafe housing and the deleterious effects of long hours of toiling in factories built around noisy, dirty and lethally hazardous machinery. Children worked alongside adults, frequently undertaking especially dangerous tasks, such as servicing moving machinery because they were small and able to enter confined spaces. The worst excesses were gradually eliminated by a series of Acts of

Parliament through the nineteenth century. However it took the greater part of that century and far too many generations of children to eliminate them. Cunningham reports the experience of Joseph Hebergam, who:

> ... at the age of 17, gave evidence before a House of Commons Select Committee of 1831-2 and described this 'free labour'. He had started work, he said, at the age of seven in a worsted spinning mill near Huddersfield, working from 5 a.m. to 8 p.m. with a break of 30 minutes at noon. (Cunningham, 2006, p. 158)

Joseph noted that, as if the toil was not hard enough, violent coercion was the norm and there was an adult worker 'kept on purpose to strap'. A year after Joseph's evidence was given Parliament passed the Factory Act of 1833. The Act prevented any child under 9 from working in a factory and matched each eight hours of work for children between 9 and 14 with an equal amount of time in school – thus representing a small, but ultimately significant, legislative affirmation of the place of schooling in children's lives (Cunningham, 2006, p. 159).

The domestic growth in Britain's population was accompanied by a net out-migration towards North America and the growing colonies of Australia, New Zealand, Canada and Argentina that are described by Crosby (1993, pp. 2–3) as the Neo-Europes. Even with this net out-migration, improved sanitation and defences against disease led to a marked reduction in infant mortality rates and improved the survival rate of children into adulthood. This meant that Britain's population was not only growing, but it was young and *youthful* as never before; hence there is an obvious sense in which children were of more interest because there were simply so many more of them. This practical condition complemented the idealistic convictions of theorists, philosophers and educators, such as Locke, Rousseau, Pestalozzi and Froebel, and meant that thinking about and providing for childhood became a central concern. To quote Hendrick (1997a, p. 35):

> In 1800 the meaning of childhood was ambiguous and not universally in demand. By 1914 the uncertainty had been virtually resolved and the identity largely determined, to the satisfaction of the middle and the respectable working class. A recognizably 'modern' notion of childhood was in place: it was legally, legislatively, socially, medically, psychologically, educationally and politically institutionalized.

Thus the construction of children and theorization of childhood as the physical, moral and intellectual precondition for the future prosperity and well-being of the nation was well under way.

Robert Owen (1771–1858): children, education and the transformation of society

Robert Owen is a central figure in attempts to reverse the harsh impacts of industrialization on working people through the provision of combined education and welfare. Although his ideas were profoundly shaped by Rousseau's *Emile* he did not share the Romantics' tendency to turn their backs on industrialization; rather, his was a more direct response to the manifest material and social deprivation being imposed upon the new urban population.

Owen was born the son of a saddler and ironmonger and became a wealthy mill owner while still a young man. Indeed, by the standards of the new-monied social class to which he belonged, Owen had done very well (Palmer, 2001). Unlike so many of his fellow new capitalists, however, he became concerned about the social and physical welfare of his employees and is with justification regarded as the first modern socialist. Owen's views were far from uncontroversial. Having lost his religious faith and convictions early in life, he also lost a belief in an innate good or ill nature in human beings; rather he believed that people are a product of their environment rather than of an innate sinfulness (Owen in Claeys, 1991, p. 11). As corollary, Owen's conviction was that if society could be changed, so could humankind. As with Rousseau, society and the individual were dualistically opposed, but Owen trained his sights on the transformation of society as the means to allow the full flourishing of the individual and his or her potential. Accordingly, in 1799 Owen took over an industrial mill and village at New Lanark in Scotland, and the improvement of conditions for his workers became a passionate pursuit for him. Among the measures he took were providing housing to alleviate overcrowding, establishing a cooperative shop (the direct precursor to the United Kingdom's Cooperative Movement) that sold goods at affordable wholesale prices and the establishment of educational opportunities in the form of an Institute for the Formation of Character to be attended by children during the day and adults in the evening. Together with these new philanthropic institutions there were coercive measures in the form of fines for drunkenness that sought to steer people away from dereliction (Palmer, 2001; Sargant, 2005; Donnachie, 2005).

Owen's ideas included the development of small-scale model communities to house workers that he called 'Villages of Unity and Mutual Cooperation'. These embodied novel communistic provisions for the upbringing of children, who on reaching the age of three would be expected to sleep in shared dormitories and were compelled to:

> ...attend the school, eat in the mess-room and sleep in the dormitories; the parents being of course permitted to see and converse with them at meals and at all other proper times; every possible means should be adopted to prevent the acquirement of bad habits from their parents or otherwise...(Owen – from Mr Owen's Report, presented to the Committee of the House of Commons on the Poor Laws in the Session of 1817)

An obvious conclusion that we might draw from this is that philanthropy and dictatorial paternalism might be just two sides of the same coin.

Owen accompanied his social experiments with extensive writing and published many of the ideas that have been instrumental in the construction of his vision for children and childhood in a collection of four essays entitled *A New View of Society and Other Writings*. Essays one and two, published in 1812–13, sought to outline a rational approach to the formation of the character 'of that immense mass of population which is now allowed to be so formed as to fill the world with crimes'. In these essays, Owen proposed that human character is neither an innate feature of an individual nor predicated upon Original Sin but is a product of environment. Therefore, if the environment provided by society could be remade through the application of Reason, then, in turn, the positive moral potential found in all human beings could be realized.

Reflection:

Do you think that Owen's sense of moral duty towards the children and his attempts to offer them a better future through education, make his conviction that 'every possible means should be adopted to prevent the acquirement of bad habits from...parents' acceptable? And should this include separation?

Owen's third essay, published in 1814, is a critique of educational institutions and initiates a long tradition of scepticism from the political left about the extent to which *schooling* can be trusted as the necessary condition for sound *education*. In his third essay, Owen writes:

> Much good or evil is acquired or taught to children at an early age. Many 'durable impressions' are made even in the first year of a child's life. Therefore children uninstructed or badly instructed suffer injury in their character during their childhood and youth. (Owen in Claeys, 1991, p. 38)

Rather than seeing school as an agency for redemption of the *Child*, he suggests that it may be just another component of the malign environment that corrupts the intrinsic moral virtue found in human nature and undermines attempts at improvement. Running through the four essays is a discussion of the work of educationist Joseph Lancaster; whereas in essays one and two Owen extols the virtues of the Lancasterian 'monitorial' system for promoting 'beneficial effects' on young minds (Owen in Claeys, 1991, p. 15), by the fourth essay, he has become critical of his work and is at pains to stress that education should not seek a narrow conformity that makes all human beings alike, but recognize the differences in aptitudes and qualities found in each child. However, Owen is careful to make a distinction between imposing *narrow conformity* and securing *commonalities of purpose*, such as making everyone 'good, wise and happy'. As a socialist and agent of the Enlightenment vision, his methods are directed not only at moral transformation, but also political change and social progress (Owen in Claeys, 1991, p. 75).

Owen's championship of the rights of all, including the poor, to sound education was seen as seditious at a time when Britain was engaged in wars with Napoleon and there was agitation for political change. Besides the hostility of his own new-monied class and mill-owning associates there was also that of the Church, notably the Bishop of Exeter (Owen in Claeys, 1991, p. 20), for whom, Owen's theological unorthodoxy sounded a discordant note. Eventually the gathering forces led to the downfall of his experiment and a move from Britain to America where in 1825 he developed the community of New Harmony in Indiana.

The contribution made by Owen to the construction of a modern view of childhood and schooling included:

- his emphasis on the importance of the environment for full growth
- his assertion that education was an entitlement for all
- his conviction that the *Child* was knowable rationally and that humankind could be perfected through proper child-rearing

- his belief that the entitlements of childhood transcended class
- the continued 'normalisation' of modern Rousseauian notions of moral virtue and freedom expressed in the *Child*.

The Reverend Andrew Bell, Joseph Lancaster and the British and Foreign School society

We shall now turn to one of the main targets for Owen's discussion of sound education. Joseph Lancaster was born in 1778, the son of a shopkeeper in Southwark, London, just seven years after Robert Owen with whom he shared similar social origins. Lancaster invented a system of education that greatly influenced Owen in the first stages of the development of the communitarian ideas at New Lanark; however Owen became sceptical about the educational and social outcomes that he felt would be their result.

Lancaster converted to Quakerism as a young man and unlike Owen retained strong religious beliefs, a fact which ensured support for his ideas from many with the same convictions and who feared a general slide into atheism among the population at large. Lancaster's early zeal for his religion had led him to Bristol, where he intended to board a ship bound for Jamaica in order to be a missionary. However, at the point of commitment, he was unable to afford the fare and returned home to London. This led him to open a small school in Southwark, South London, at the age of 20 (Barnard, 1971; Taylor, 1996; Spartacusnet, 2006). The site of the school is now incorporated into London South Bank University, which has renamed this part of their estate 'The Joseph Lancaster Building'. Less than half a mile away can be found Joseph Lancaster Primary School – thus his work is memorialized at a local scale. Lancaster's school was a remarkable intervention in the lives of children in a part of London which, although traditionally poor, had seen an intensification of poverty with the advent of industrialization. Southwark was frequently depicted in the novels of Charles Dickens, (e.g. Little Dorrit) who drew on his personal experience of growing up and working as a child labourer in its mean streets.

Lancaster invited pupils to attend the school in a notice posted outside its doors: 'All who will may send their children and have them educated freely, and those who do not wish to have education for nothing may pay for it if they please' (The Lancasterian Society, 2006). Presented with such a proposition Lancaster found no difficulty in attracting interested children; however, few paid and it became difficult to attract and retain teachers in sufficient quantity and quality to teach there. Lancaster's Quaker principles, forbidding corporal punishment or violence may have compounded the problem – as a conviction it did not appeal to many less idealistic schoolmasters. Moreover, many children saw it as a liberal indulgence and made the most of the opportunity to test discipline to its limit. That said, by way of compensation for the lack of physical violence, Lancaster developed elaborate psychological means to encourage a sense of shame in miscreants – perhaps we glimpse the dilemmas that surround schemes to improve society and the problems of imposing freedom whether the recipients consent to this or not.

Reflection:

Is the psychological manipulation of children more defensible on moral grounds than physical violence?

The sizable attendance does suggest that there was considerable appetite for children to be educated in the early part of the nineteenth century. However, this and the staffing problems meant that Lancaster needed to find a way to teach large numbers of children effectively if his sense of mission was to be fulfilled. Thus, it was after reading a pamphlet by the Reverend Andrew Bell (The Lancasterian Society, 2006) about his school in Madras entitled 'A sketch of a national institution for training up the children of the poor', that Lancaster was introduced to the idea of the *monitorial system* (Spartacus Educational, 2006).

Bell proposed a hierarchical organization of the curriculum and pedagogy that was reflected in the spatial organization of the schoolroom. A master would teach a selected group of older pupils, the *monitors*, and they, in turn, taught the rest of the school in groups that were arranged in rows based on wooden 'forms'. In order to facilitate the monitorial system, a galleried classroom was designed by Lancaster and this has become one of his trademarks. The galleried classroom allowed the master to 'conduct' and survey proceedings from a raised plinth in front of the assembled group of children, who sat on their forms arranged across a raked sloping floor. Thus the idea of progression from lower to higher and from ignorance to enlightenment was reinforced. The monitors, who performed the role of pupil teachers were located at the end of each form and relayed the lesson to their charges. Despite a dispute between Bell and Lancaster over who had invented them, these arrangements became commonly identified as 'The Lancastrian System'. The system continues to be championed by the Lancasterian Society, whose motto, *Qui docet, discit* (*who teaches, learns*) expresses the particular pedagogic balance between master, monitor and pupil to which the system aspired.

The spatiality of Lancaster's classroom and the pedagogical practices and methods of the system recall Jeremy Bentham's 'Panopticon' prison designed in 1785 and which Michel Foucault saw as emblematic for modern surveillance and social control. There are also obvious similarities to the layout of a factory as another emblem of a society that had harnessed the power of nature through the steam engine. Lancaster was an educational engineer and the galleried classroom his engine for learning. Here are some of the ideas that Lancaster proposed in a paper he wrote in 1810. He is clearly mindful of the all-seeing perspective available to the master:

> THE [sic] best form for a school-room is a long square, or parallelogram. All the desks should front the head of the school, that the master may have a good view of each boy at once; the desks should all be single desks, and every boy sit with his face towards the head of the school.... These arrangements not only conduce to order, but give facility to the master in the detection of offenders.... Wherever the floor of a school-room can be placed on an inclined plane it should be so. The master being stationed at the lower end of this plane, the elevation, of the floor at the farther end of the room, would cause a corresponding elevation of the desks placed there, so that, from the platform the boys at the last desk would be as much in view as those at the first. (The Lancasterian Society, 2006)

The school in Southwark grew rapidly and within a few short years had over 1,000 pupils. Such was his fame that between 1798 and 1810 Lancaster travelled over 3,500 miles to give numerous lectures that helped to form 50 schools that, by the end of the period were educating over 14,000 pupils. Indeed, George III summoned Lancaster to attend him at Weymouth in 1805 (The Lancasterian Society, 2006).

However, Lancaster was always in debt and became increasingly dependent upon wealthy backers, who finally took over the schools and formed the

Royal Lancasterian Society to administer them. Perhaps the loss of control over the direction of his mission led Lancaster to quarrel with the trustees of the Society and in 1816 he resigned. He spent the rest of his life attempting to restart his vision, including a school in Tooting (that failed and led to bankruptcy, for which he was imprisoned) and various chequered enterprises in the United States, Canada and Venezuela. He died prematurely following an accident in New York in 1838.

Following the foundation of the British and Foreign Schools society in 1808 the Lancasterian Schools became known as British Schools and with the Church of England's National Schools laid the foundations for the State system that was ushered in by the 1870 Elementary Education Act. It should be said, that although a person of distinct religious convictions, Lancaster was not factional or dogmatic in his denominational commitments, maintaining that education should be broadly Christian and not sectarian. It seems that he followed through on his conviction, for despite educating thousands of children there is no record that any became Quakers (for a discussion of the Church's role in the development of State education, see Race, 2010).

We can gain some insight into the actual workings of Lancaster's Borough Road school through a memoir written by James Bonwick, a pupil from the age of six who went on to become its head monitor and then a British School teacher at Leicester, Ipswich and Hemel Hempstead. Bonwick published his memoir at the age of 85 in 1902 and it offers a fascinating glimpse into the life of the school in the 1820s, undoubtedly its heyday:

> The room for the boys could accommodate 500 scholars. The windows were six feet from the floor. The central part was occupied with desks and forms, fixed by iron supports. Spaces left around were for the semi-circular 'drafts' for some eight or ten lads, engaged under Monitors in reading, spelling or arithmetic . . . At the entrance end of the room was the long, raised platform for the Master's desk, etc. At the other end was placed the portrait of George III, with the motto 'The Patron of Education and Friend of the Poor'. Underneath in gold letters, were the words uttered by our late Queen's grandfather to Lancaster in an interview of 1805 – 'It is my wish that every poor child in my dominions be taught to read the Holy Scriptures.' (Bonwick, in Burnett, 1994, pp. 169–75)

This was a time just after the end of the Napoleonic Wars, so perhaps the rather sycophantic royalist tone is understandable; however, it also alerts us to the fact that this was an era before the State funded, directed or underwrote mass education in any really significant extent and so sponsorship by the great and good was essential to survival.

Despite the emphasis placed on reading the scriptures (selections from which constituted the only reading material on offer) Bonwick recalls a diversity in the curriculum that might surprise us, especially given the narrowness advocated by Lancaster's near-contemporary and founder of the Sunday School Movement, Hannah More (see Chapter 5). After the youngest children had learnt their alphabet by tracing letters in sand, they ascended 'up' the successive forms and were offered a diet of arithmetic, spelling, reading, geography, singing and science. Rudimentary and uncritical as the content was, it at least offered an introduction to the possibilities education afforded, and enabled James Bonwick to build a career in teaching, inspecting schools and seek his fortune in Australia (Bonwick in Burnett, 1994, pp. 169–75).

Lancaster's work represents a milestone in the construction of schooling as the dominant institution in most modern children's lives because of its capacity to operate on a mass scale. Indeed scale was the issue, and the 500 pupils Bonwick refers to would probably have been overseen by a single adult, with the burden of teaching placed on young monitors. Furthermore, such was his faith in youth, that Lancaster would select monitors aged 14 or 15 to set out and establish schools of their own at some remove from the original location – reduced salary bills may also have been a factor!

Conclusion

Lancaster's is a formulaic approach embodying an industrial, pragmatic and non-Romantic vision of education that allies moral purpose to the industrial and engineering spirit of the times. It is a modernizing project with roots in technical-rationalist Enlightenment values, and is at odds with the spiritualized, numinous vision found in Pestalozzi and Froebel et al. Lancaster's vision of the *Child* has more of Locke's Anglo-Saxon empiricism and commitment to futurity than the progressives' idealistic appeal to the integrity of childhood as a stage of human life that stands in and of itself. The differences emphasized here, including those with Owen, would not become less pronounced with time. Indeed they continue to animate debate about the form, content and purposes of an education that seeks to be effective as well as morally appropriate.

Reflection:

Imagine a debate between Froebel and Joseph Lancaster for which each prepares by outlining the strong points in their respective educational systems and institutions. Would there be any virtues they both identify and could agree on?

Further reading

Barnard, H. C. (1971), *A History of English Education from 1760*, London: Unibooks.

Owen, R. (1991), in Claeys, G. (ed.), *A New View of Society and Other Writings*, London: Penguin.

Palmer, J. (ed.) (2001), *Fifty Major Thinkers on Education*, London: Routledge.

Taylor, J. (1996), *Joseph Lancaster: The Poor Child's Friend*, West Wickham: Campanile.

Website

The British Schools Museum: www.iguidez.com/Hitchin/british-schools-museum/, last accessed 17 December 2010.

The Robert Owen Museum: www.robert-owen-museum.org.uk/, last accessed 17 December 2010.

5

'Christian Children All Must Be...': Moralists, Moral Panics and Empire

Introduction

The Industrial Revolution not only had a devastating material impact on children's lives, but it also inspired a series of moral panics about the condition of their souls. This inspired the Church of England and other Christian moralists to take a defining stake in education and schooling.

Church of England National Schools and the Clapton sect

Until the Industrial Revolution, the position of the Church of England at the heart of most communities in England was assured. Apart from the sizeable minority of non-conformists who counted themselves as Methodists, Baptists, Congregationalists and independents of various sorts, Anglican Communion held sway and the vicar or rector was a powerful figure in village or market town life. However, industrialization changed all that as the towns and cities were heaving with the new urban labouring classes and ties to established religion were increasingly tenuous. Many in the Church of England looked on with horror at the prospect of a godless generation of children and so a body of Church worthies decided to take action that was:

> designed to illuminate the surrounding darkness and to rescue the children of the poor, particularly in the new industrial and manufacturing towns, from heathen-ism and barbarity. (Canon Charles Smyth on the occasion of the 150th Anniversary of the Foundation of the Society, on 12 October 1961) (The National Society for Promoting Religious Education, 2003)

Thus it was, in 1811 at the home of Joshua Watson in Lower Clapton, Hackney that the National Society was founded with the ambition to place a school, founded upon and promulgating the tenets of the Church of England in every parish of the land, including the new urban areas. The founding group became known both as 'The Clapton Sect', or alternatively 'The Hackney Phalanx', and were closely associated with a broader attempt to revive the Church of England through a return to what they saw as traditional 'High Church' values and practices that had much in common with Roman Catholic forms of worship. The *Clapton* sect (from Hackney in North East London) should not be confused with 'The Clapham Sect' (from South West London) – we shall look at their contribution to the construction of schooling and childhood later.

Joshua Watson was a wealthy wine merchant born in 1771, who had made his money early, but decided to leave the city in order to devote his energies to defending and promoting the Church of England in times of tumultuous change that included the rise of Napoleon Bonaparte in the wake of the 1789 revolution in France. A widespread fear of revolution in England meant that the National Society came into being at a time of perceived crisis and was, in many ways, shaped by it. Thus armed with the belief that: 'In the whole field of education, there is nothing more vitally important than the inculcation and the apprehension of Religious Truths' (The National Society for Promoting Religious Education, 2003), Watson and his friends set about establishing a national education system based on Church values, beliefs and convictions.

At the inaugural meeting, with no less a figure than the Archbishop of Canterbury in the chair, the purpose of the Society was identified as being:

> That the National Religion should be made the foundation of National Education, and should be the first and chief thing taught to the Poor, according to the excellent Liturgy and Catechism provided by our Church.

Furthermore, there were two main objectives for the children of the poor. First:

> to teach them the doctrine of Religion according to the principles of the Established Church, and to train them to the performance of their religious duties by an early discipline;

And second:

> to communicate such knowledge and habits as are sufficient to guide them through life in their proper station. (The National Society for Promoting Religious Education, 2003)

Thus the aims and objectives for Christian education and the schools' task in reproducing the *Christian Child* were formulated under the shadow of perceived crisis. A typical expression of this moralizing sentiment about the iconic Christian child is to be found in the Christmas carol 'Once in Royal David's City', published as a poem in 1848 by Miss Cecil Humphries in her *Hymns for Little Children*: 'Christian children all must be mild, obedient, good as He'.

The schools of the National Society had much in common with Joseph Lancaster's because both had been inspired by the experience and writings of the Reverend Andrew Bell, who after a stint as a colonial clergyman in Madras and rector of Swanage in Dorset, UK, had published in 1808 his educational manifesto entitled: *A Sketch of a National Institution for Training Up the Children of the Poor* (see Chapter 4).

Hannah More and the Clapham sect

The High Church party of 'The Clapton Sect' had their counterpart in the evangelicals of 'The Clapham Sect' and both were responses to the apparent weakness of the established Church of England (Project Canterbury, 1999). However, whereas the High Church exponents believed that the key was for the Church to return to traditional forms of worship through a version of Christianity that was a blend of Englishness and Catholicism and that placed sacraments at the heart of religious observance, the evangelicals sought to counter what they saw as a dangerous secularism and tendency to godlessness through preaching and conversion. A leading member of the Clapham sect was Hannah More, a writer, moralist and friend to many in the literary and political elite of the time.

Hannah More was born near Bristol in 1745 and died in 1833 at the age of 88. She was the daughter of a politically conservative schoolmaster and education clearly ran in the family bloodline, for in 1758 her eldest sister established a school for girls in Bristol. Hannah More was educated at her sister's school and she went on to become a teacher there. In 1774, as a young playwright – a less than usual occupation for a young woman at the time – she and her sister travelled to London where she fell in with the contemporary literary and political elite, naming the celebrated theatre manager David Garrick among her friends and sharing acquaintance with Samuel Johnson, Edmund Burke, the Elizabeths Montague and Carter and Prime Minister Horace Walpole (Project Canterbury, 1999; Porter, 2001, pp. 467–9; Stott, 2002).

However, it was around 1785 that More's life and aspirations changed as she underwent an evangelical religious conversion. Following this, her loyalist politics, concern for the poor, abolitionism and matronal brand of feminism became focused on education as the vital outlet for her newly acquired evangelizing sense of purpose. She became a leading member of the Clapham sect which identified her with many of the radical and evangelically attuned voices of the time, including the leading opponent of slavery, William Wilberforce. Her most celebrated educational work was *Strictures on the Modern System of Female Education*, published in 1799 and it achieved the distinction of being compared to her near-contemporary Elizabeth Wollstonecraft's seminal *Vindication of the Rights of Women* of 1792. In her *Strictures*, More forcefully argued that education had failed women, by offering little more than a trivial diversion in place of preparation for their important roles as 'companionable wives, rational mothers, or moral examples to the wider society' (Stott, 2002) – another version of the apprenticeship discourse for childhood (Mills, 2000 and Chapter 1).

However, while these sentiments concerning the education of women and ending the abomination of slavery may strike us as passably progressive, her views on the purpose of education took on a considerably more socially conservative hue:

> Beautiful is the order of society when each according to his place, pays willing honour to his superiors – when servants are prompt to obey their masters, and masters deal kindly with their servants; – when high, low, rich and poor – when landlord and tenant, master workmen, minister and people…sit down satisfied with his own place. (More, 1799, in Stott, 2002)

Armed by this morally founded world view she set up a Sunday school in 1789 as the first step in the establishment of the Sunday School movement. It should be noted that the supposed moral peril of the child had a galvanic effect upon the imagination of her fellow evangelicals, whose convictions owed much to an underlying pessimism concerning human nature. In consequence, the terms for the education being offered are distinctly conservative; for example, eschewing radical social transformation, More makes a moral distinction between what happens during the working week and the possibilities for spiritual redemption offered by Sunday School education:

> they learn of week-days such coarse works as may fit them for servants. I allow of no writing for the poor. My object is not to teach dogmas and opinions, but to form the lower classes to habits of industry and virtue (More, 1799, in Stott, 2002)

If such naked exhortations for education to reinforce rather than revolutionize the social order strike us as merely indicative of their times, then the vigorous commitment to halting social change found in her views on children and by implication, on human nature still have a capacity to shock:

> Is it not a fundamental error to consider children as innocent beings, whose little weaknesses may, perhaps, want some correction, rather than as beings who bring into the world a corrupt nature and evil dispositions, which it should be the great end of education to rectify? (quoted in Hendrick, 1997a; Hendrick, 1997b)

More clearly has Rousseau and what she saw as the heresies of the Romantics in her sights. In place of Rousseau's Apollonian vision of the *Child* as morally virtuous, More proposes its Dionysian polar opposite as chaotic, disordered and in urgent need of redemption (Jenks, 2005, p. 65). Once again, and not for the last time, the *Child* becomes embroiled in metaphysical disputes over human nature and a site on which the struggle between revolution and conservatism can be played out. However, More was no child hater, and she perhaps epitomizes the oft quoted evangelical aphorism that 'God hates the sin, but loves the sinner'. Accordingly, she was opposed to corporal punishment and there was nothing of 'spare the rod and spoil the child' about her work, preferring bribes and inducements over physical coercion.

If religious zeal was the driving force for so much of this educational philanthropy, there were those who advocated a more secular approach to the problems of both the quality and the quantity of provision. Therefore, in 1836 a Central Society of Education was formed in order to advocate and lobby for a centrally controlled State system of education. The Society launched its campaign through a number of education Bills put before the Houses of Parliament through the 1830s; however, none of them came to anything. Although never a realistic proposition on economic grounds, the secularism at the heart of its proposed State-centred system posed moral and religious problems. This is not to say that the Central Society's scheme was irreligious, but its distinction between 'general' and 'special' education struck a discordant note with many (Barnard, 1971, p. 98). General education was the core of the curriculum and would be given by the teaching staff; but 'special' education was to be turned over to ministers of various Christian denominations who would have a right of entry to schools. For many in the National Schools and Church of England camp, this decentring of religion, religious institutions and its ministers was unacceptable. The Church of England was still confidently embedded as the established religion of the state and it was not about to relinquish either its primacy or moral influence over the Nation's children. That said, it was estimated in 1833 that only one in ten children were in schooling that was deemed acceptable (Barnard, 1971, p. 98) and spurred by this we see Dr. Hook, the Vicar of Leeds, publish a pamphlet in 1846 with the title *On the Means of Rendering More Efficient the Education of the People* that advocates a schooling system similar to that proposed by the Central Society.

Reflection:

Debates continue around the respective influence of religious and secular visions for children's education. Do you think faith schools are easier or harder to justify in a multicultural society?

Ragged Schools and the social gospel

Alongside the work of the British and Foreign Schools (Chapter 4) and the attempts at moral and spiritual reclamation of the National School Society, there appeared what began to be known popularly as 'Ragged Schools' with the foundation of the London City Mission in 1835. The informal name was confirmed in 1844 when the Ragged School Union (later the Shaftesbury Society) was formed under the aegis of illustrious patrons, including Lord Shaftesbury and Charles Dickens, and committed itself to a broad vision of the poor child and its needs. A staple diet of instruction in reading, writing, arithmetical calculation and religious instruction was supplemented by concern for children's general physical, moral and spiritual welfare that was frequently extended to the well-being of adult factory workers. In a contemporary source, the Ragged School movement was likened to a tree, with the connotation of reaching out into hitherto untouched areas of deprived urban life. Therefore, in addition to its work in the education of poor children (including evening and Sunday schools), we find branches with coffee and reading rooms, Bands of Hope (an influential contemporary temperance society that aimed to rid the nation of what they saw as the curse of alcohol), 'Penny' banks offering opportunities for thrift and saving, as well as refuges from violence and, respectively, women's and men's clubs (Smith, 2009). The remedy reveals much about the diagnosis of the problem – not merely that there were limited educational opportunities for the children of the poor, but also an absence of appropriate social institutions and purposeful associational activity for them. Although the 'schooling societies' established a format for children's education that has endured, there is much about the Ragged School movement that continues to shape youth and community work with its emphasis on the construction of sustainable social capital institutions as a foundation for community regeneration and renewal.

The origins of the Ragged Schools are the subject of keen debate, for unlike the British Schools of Lancaster and the National Schools of Watson, there was no single guru-like progenitor and they came into being in a rather more organic fashion. Smith (2009) identifies the first 'ragged schools' as, variously the brainchild of John Pounds (1766–1839) a Portsmouth cobbler, Sheriff Watson from Aberdeen who set up an 'industrial school' in 1840 to educate poor and vagrant children and Thomas Cranfield who set up a 'Sunday School' in Kingsland Road, Hackney as well as a 'day school' near the London Bridge as early as 1798. The fact that there were 'ragged', 'industrial', 'day and

Sunday' schools existing simultaneously underlines their growth from disparate non-conformist churches as well as the relatively lowly status of their originators. This undoubtedly accounts for the prejudice they faced from the more established echelons of educational opinion and the tensions that occasionally arose with illustrious patrons of the movement.

Whatever may be said of the more demotic, spontaneous and popular character of the Ragged Schools, by the middle of the nineteenth century they had attracted a number of august patrons who saw in them a worthy commitment to self-help that was deserving of charity. Among the supporters was the great novelist and social commentator Charles Dickens, who in a correspondence with a contemporary newspaper and referring to Ragged Schools, wrote:

> I offer no apology for entreating the attention of the readers of The Daily News to an effort which has been making for some three years and a half, and which is making now, to introduce among the most miserable and neglected outcasts in London, some knowledge of the commonest principles of morality and religion; to commence their recognition as immortal human creatures, before the Gaol Chaplain becomes their only schoolmaster; ... (The Literature Network, 2006)

Dickens had first-hand experience of the deprivations of an impoverished childhood and of gaol when his own father was imprisoned as a bankrupt. Furthermore, he was unequivocal in his views on what he saw as the national disgrace of education during his time. In the preface to Nicholas Nickleby he refers to:

> the Monstrous neglect of education in England and the disregard of it by the state.

He continues the theme in Great Expectations, and we infer that his bitter personal experience meant that he did not give his approval lightly.

We can sense the effort required to comprehend the unprecedented growth of these new urban manufacturing populations. A sense of compassion for the urban poor is at least matched by fear of where the propagation of an irreligious, insanitary and seditious populace might lead. The fear, bordering on moral panic surrounding the condition of what were regarded as near-heathen urban masses is palpable, that is, there were souls to be saved, but the stability of society also had to be secured and key among a range of measures was the education and redemption of the young. In consequence rescuing the fallen child becomes emblematic for ensuring the future moral and spiritual health of the nation. Burdening children with the weight of the future can be no less prevalent in current discourses on how social degeneration might be reversed and remedied.

Reflection:

Can you think of any contemporary social ills for which the education of the young is seen as the best route to ensuring long-term change or improvement? Scan the news; how often is education invoked as a necessary response to intractable problems?

Chief among the supporters and advocates of Ragged Schooling was Anthony Ashley-Cooper, the seventh Earl of Shaftesbury. Lord Shaftesbury was one of the most celebrated evangelical Tory aristocrats of his age and through the Shaftesbury Society that campaigned to abolish child labour, has become a towering figure in child welfare reform of the Victorian era. Shaftesbury became involved in the efforts to effect changes to working conditions for women and children in mines and factories in the 1830s but met with determined opposition from many of the mill owners and those who benefitted from the system. In 1841, he was sent a manuscript written by a former child labourer named William Dodd detailing the privations and physical disabilities caused by child labour at first-hand. Shaftesbury determined to use the manuscript and Dodd's experience as the basis for publishing *A Narrative of the Experience and Sufferings of William Dodd, A Factory Cripple* and *the Factory System: Illustrated* in 1842. Shaftesbury caused a huge stir and widespread outrage within Victorian England and change, albeit gradual, was set in motion (Ashley-Cooper, 1841 and 1842). Schooling played its part in this, as the Factory Act of 1891 subordinated factory working to schooling (made possible by the 1870 'Forster' and 1880 'Mundella' Elementary Education Acts) by raising the minimum age for the employment of children from 10 to 11.

As a high-Tory aristocrat, Shaftesbury's huge patronal presence and popular identification as leader of the Ragged School movement was not universally welcomed, especially by the non-conformists, whose outsider instincts had infused the schools with their particular ethos. However, the growth of the schools and the movement was prodigious. Thomas Cranfield from Hackney, East London, by dint of his energy, enthusiasm and organizational abilities had 'built up an organisation of nineteen Sunday, night and infants schools' across the poorest parts of London by the time of his death in 1838. In1840, the London City Mission reported that in the previous year five new Ragged Schools had been established and that 570 children were attending them. However, by 1867 this number had swollen to 226 Sunday Ragged Schools, 204 Day Schools and 207 Evening Schools with an average, over-all attendance of more than 26,000 children. The rapid growth in numbers gave rise not only to one specific problem of success, namely the provision of adequate number of teachers, but also teachers possessing sufficient quali-ties to undertake the work. The 200 or so identified Ragged School teach-ers in 1844 had swollen to over 1600 by 1851 – an eightfold increase in just seven years. This sowed the seeds of what was to be an abiding criticism from those interested in more mainstream educational institutions and that sur-faced with the advent of the 1870 Elementary Education Act; namely, that the educational standards in many Ragged Schools were inadequate and that weak or poorly equipped teachers were undermining the lofty, stated ambi-tions of the movement. Indeed, when it came to confrontations between the two systems following the passage of the 1870 Act, these shortcomings came to be deployed as a rationale for the benefits of a regulated State system of education with which the Ragged Schools could not compete, and their fate was largely sealed (Smith, 2009).

Barnardo – Ragged School teacher and child 'rescuer'

There is one Ragged School teacher whose name became emblematic for child welfare; he is Thomas Barnardo, born in Dublin in 1845 and better known as 'Dr' Barnardo. In 1862 at the age of 17, Barnardo underwent an evangelical religious conversion and from that point developed and maintained a zeal-ous commitment to spreading the Christian gospel. His mission to save the fallen children led him to the overcrowded, unsanitary slums of Stepney in East London, where in 1867 he was instrumental in opening a Ragged School at Hope Place. His work brought him into daily contact with many children, each with stories to tell about their plight; however, it was in the coldest part of the winter of 1869–70 that he met a child who, according to the legend, would redirect the course of his life and be the spur to the establishment of the charitable foundation now known simply as *Barnardo's*, which continues to be a major contributor to contemporary debates on childcare and welfare.

One night Barnardo was taken by a boy named Jim Jarvis to a semi-derelict building in which numerous homeless and orphaned children lived. From that day, it is said, Barnardo resolved to provide for Jim Jarvis and his like by the provision of orphanages for parent-less children. A. E. Williams (Barnardo's secretary for some seven years) writing a seminal history of the movement in 1953 asserted that:

> In the short space of forty years, starting without patronage or influence of any kind, this man had raised the sum of three and a quarter million pounds sterling, established a network of Homes of various kinds such as never existed before for the reception, care and training of homeless, needy and afflicted children, and had rescued no fewer than sixty thousand destitute boys and girls. (Williams, 1953, p. 75)

Williams was clearly no impartial observer of Barnardo's work; however, others have been less enthusiastic. He encountered long-running resistance from the Catholic Church, who objected to what they saw as an attempt at re-education by converting children and young people away from Catholicism. Further, for many children 'rescue' became irrevocably entangled with the purposes of Empire as they were sent abroad to the colonies for what Barnardo believed was a new start and an alleviation of what he saw as the evils both of overcrowding and the shortcomings of parents and families (not all were orphans). The Empire had provided a 'safety-valve' for the disenfranchised, disillusioned and convicted, including children, certainly since the early seventeenth century when ships took huge numbers of children from England to Virginia (Cunningham, 2006, p. 98). This forced migration was all part of a desperate battle against the demons of crime, delinquency and godlessness that stalked the high Victorian imagination whenever the luridly perceived urban morass came to mind. We see it in the writing of Dickens and the gritty work of the contemporary engraver Gustave Dore.

The conflation of a colonial fresh start and evangelical zeal not only sought to convert these children to the righteous and deserving ways of the Christian Child but also constructed them as children of the Empire. They were thus allowed to make the transition from lost to found, from lives of dissipation to active agents for the generative extension of sound Christian value, wealth and civilization overseas. All too often their actual experience fell short of this as many died on the voyage and those who survived were prone to disease, abuses and other ills (Cunningham, 2006, p. 98).

Public schools, Muscular Christianity and Imperial childhood

While we see growth of provision for a newly invented 'public child' under the evangelizing outreach of the churches and the strengthening convictions about the role of the State through the nineteenth century, the elite, longer-established and male-dominated educational institutions also underwent significant transformation. These included the 'Public Schools' – an unhelpful English misnomer for institutions offering schooling to children from social and financial elites and not to be confused with the more demotic *public* elementary schools that did nothing of the sort. Public Schools included elite institutions, such as Eton College, Harrow and Winchester as well as former grammar schools including Tonbridge, Manchester, Shrewsbury and the King's Schools at Canterbury, Worcester and Rochester and former guild schools, such as Merchant Taylors. Despite offering education almost exclusively to the wealthy, these schools continued to enjoy status as charities and thus were exempted from the full rigours of other businesses similarly founded on commercial principles.

Rapid social change, the growth of new-monied classes, new educational ideas and a rejuvenated redemptive and evangelizing mission in the Church of England expressed through education, generated impatience with the practices and frequent barbarities of the old schools. A central figure in the transformation of the Public School system was Dr Thomas Arnold (1795–1842), headmaster of Rugby, and in the eyes of A. P. Stanley – Arnold's biographer of 1844 – the saviour of the English Public School system (Rouse, 1898).

W. H. D. Rouse, writing a history of Rugby School in 1898 before the advent of Thomas Arnold as headmaster, tells us that:

> The system as Arnold found it at Rugby was not unlike to the administration of a conquered state. The Headmaster was an autocrat, dispensing punishments with no unsparing hand. He and his colleagues alike were looked on as the natural enemies of boyhood, set over them by a mysterious dispensation of Providence to interfere with personal liberty and enjoyment. To these rulers the boys rendered a

grudging obedience, which ceased when it ceased to be enforced. They had their own organisation, by which the weaker were slaves of the stronger; and their own code of honour, mercilessly strict among themselves, but lax towards their masters....Differences between them were settled by an appeal to brute force, not only amongst the younger, where it was natural, but amongst older boys already on the verge of manhood. (Rouse, 1898)

Thomas Arnold was a product of the system thus described, having been educated at Winchester College and Oxford, where he had become a fellow of Oriel College when aged only 21. Arnold's educational philosophy was rooted in a commitment to the values of liberal culture that was fired by his own education in the Classics and in the centrality of religion and religious values. When appointed headmaster of Rugby he also ensured that he was made school chaplain, so that he could guide the religious development of his pupils as well as their intellectual, moral and physical development (Stanley, 2009).

Arnold's work is most famously celebrated in *Tom Brown's Schooldays*, a work of fiction, published in 1857 by Thomas Hughes. Hughes portrays Arnold's transformative regime as headmaster of Rugby School through the eyes of Tom as he moves from 'new boy' to manhood. The book is written as a paean to Dr Arnold (who had died prematurely at the age of just 47) and the educational methods and philosophy he brought to bear in addressing the violent, bullying culture that Rouse describes above. These topics aroused considerable debate on the publication of the book and in the preface to the sixth edition, Hughes reproduces correspondence from the readers. In the following excerpt we should note how the argument is predicated on futurity as much as on morality and an analogy is made with the treatment of animals; however, what should not escape our attention is the way in which 'boy', the Public school catch-all for its pupils, is modified to 'child' (with its more nurturing connotations) and how the argument draws implicitly upon the connotations surrounding this construct and that makes the distinction a telling one:

A boy may have moral courage, and a finely organised brain and nervous system. Such a boy is calculated, if judiciously educated, to be a great, wise, and useful man; but he may not possess **animal courage**; and one night's **tossing** [rough treatment while helplessly wrapped in a blanket], or bullying, may produce such an injury to his brain and nerves that his usefulness is spoiled for life...A groom who tried to cure a shying horse by roughness and violence would be discharged as a brute and a fool...the person who thinks a child of delicate and nervous

> organisation can be made bold by bullying is no better. (Hughes, 1857 and 2007, sixth edition, preface)

We are witnessing Arnold's transformation of the Public School into a more complete and enlightened *educational* institution imbued with a new sense of responsibility to children and young people *as people*.

Changes to the Public School tradition were not significant with regard to the numbers of children who directly experienced these institutions; however, on account of their elite social status, they have exerted ideological influence over mass State provision by establishing a value setting that continues to shape the ethos of schooling and the discussion of its purposes (see Mangan, 2000, for a discussion of the particular place occupied by sport in this ethos). This ideological dominance is obvious in the huge popular acceptance given to elite schooling and its mores in *Harry Potter and the Philospher's Stone* and subsequent stories (Rowling, 1999). Just as Quidditch is central to the curriculum at Hogwarts, so it was on the playing fields where Arnold's Public School ethos found expression through sport as a moral calculus for the modern era. According to C. L. R. James (1963), the triumvirate of Thomas Arnold, Thomas Hughes (author of *Tom Brown's Schooldays*) and Arnold's son Matthew (poet, intellectual and first Chief HMI) re-conceptualized sport as the embodiment of honour, fair play and healthy physical, mental and spiritual recreation and as a means to virtue that came to be known as *Muscular Christianity*. For Arnold, the classical, Corinthian and Spartan codes of Ancient Greece resonated with Christian virtue and values, and could be translated not only into scholarship, but also into the practice of play and then through them into the exercise of responsibility in national and imperial affairs. As Huggins puts it:

> Athleticism became a civilising offensive, aiding Christianity and education in the character-conditioning and health of sometimes badly behaved, brutal or brutalised pupils, and promoting school identity. (Huggins, 2004, p. 31)

Thomas Hughes expresses these themes in the penultimate chapter of *Tom Brown's Schooldays* through an exchange between Tom, his fellow pupil Arthur and a master during their last cricket match:

> '...But it's more than a game. It's an institution,' said Tom.
> 'Yes,' said Arthur, 'the birthright of British boys old and young, as **habeas corpus** and trial by jury are of British men.'

'The discipline and reliance upon one another which it teaches is so valuable, I think,' went on the master, 'it ought to be such an unselfish game. It merges the individual in the eleven; he doesn't play that he may win, but that his side may.' 'That's very true,' said Tom, 'and that's why football and cricket, now one comes to think of it, are much better games than fives, or hare and hounds, or any others where the object is to come in first or to win for oneself and not that one's side may win.' (Hughes, 1857 and 2007, pp. 225–6)

We note that the chief criterion for the superiority of a game is a moral one. It is through the Public School ethos that we see the transformation of sport and games into strictly directed, codified forms whose laws represent a logical calculus underpinning moral action as much as practical regulations governing play. It was the Public Schools who led in setting the tone for this new moral muscularity and who secured the place of sport in the curriculum. In Huggins' view:

The school house system, playing fields and team game competitions, cups and colours gave a major boost to the systematisation, reorganisation and regulation of modern sports, as former public school boys carried their sports into the wider world…Complex concepts such as those of 'manliness' or 'athleticism' were developed to aid the process, with notions of 'fair play' added later, and linked to imperialism and militarism. Huggins (2004, pp. 31–2).

Cricket was held to have a particular place in the moral scheme and when articulated as a practical discourse on manliness, was explicitly opposed to the perceived degeneracy of the lower classes and their cruder, more violent sports and pastimes. Clem Seecharan has written of the importance of this particular muscular vision of masculinity and education and its export to colonial societies through the newly founded elite schools; here it exerted a quite specific influence on Caribbean intellectuals and their self-conscious development within a profoundly racialized society. Cricket's particular capacity to invoke an essential English pastoral memory offered reinforcement to the cultural power of the colonizers and, thus, their grip on the colonial imagination. Echoing Williams (2001, pp. 15–6), Seecharan argues that:

…cricket in Victorian and Edwardian England was impregnated with notions of the cultivated essence of a pastoral Englishness, the sustainer of a moral superiority that validated their imperial mission. (Seecharan, 2006, p. 14)

The mystical and imagined 'pastoral Englishness' that cricket embodied was vital in the planters' attempts to justify the brutal actuality of their status as increasingly reviled slave owners by presenting themselves as *civilizers* and *tamers* of savage, tropical disorder. The attempt to maintain moral superiority locally and secure acceptance back in Britain was underwritten by the establishment of schools for the plantocracy's sons that were inspired by the mystique that had grown up around elite public schools of Eton, Harrow and Rugby (Simon, 1965, p. 109). In practice the scion Harrison College, Combermere and Lodge Schools that were founded in Barbados were more like the grammar schools for the new-monied, upper middle class that were springing up all over Britain, but like them they made up for their *parvenu* status, by being fiercely aspirational (Sandiford and Newton, 1995). Seecharan (2006, p. 20) asserts that at the heart of their curriculum were the 'three Cs' – cricket, Christianity and the classics – and grasp of each provided a series of shibboleths that regulated access to professional, social, political, economic and intellectual mobility for the children of a growing non-white middle class. Thus, in the aspirant Victorian imagination the pursuit of an appropriately conceived manliness through school sport (Huggins, 2004, pp. 74–9) combined with the 'three Cs' becomes a recipe for a childhood well spent.

Reflection:

What part – if any – should discourses of 'moral rescue' play in the education of the poor and disadvantaged? Examine any recent policy; does a concept of moral rescue continue to inform aspects of thinking about the opportunities education can offer to poor but able pupils?

Further reading

Barnard, H. C. (1971), *A History of English Education from 1760*, London: University of London Press.

Chandos, J. (1985), *Boys Together: English Public Schools, 1800-64*, Oxford: Oxford Paperbacks.

Mahmood, S. (2009), *A History of English Education in India*, New York: BiblioBazaar.

Mangan, J. A. (2005), 'Eton in India: the imperial diffusion of a Victorian educational ethic', in McCulloch, G. (ed.), *The RoutledgeFalmer Reader in History of Education*, London: RoutledgeFalmer.

Miller, P. and Davey, I. (2005), 'Family formation, schooling and the patriarchal state', in McCulloch, G. (ed.), *The RoutledgeFalmer Reader in History of Education*, London: RoutledgeFalmer, pp. 83–99.

Sandiford, K. P. and Newton, E. H. (1995), *Combermere School and the Barbadian Society*, Mona: University of West Indies Press.

Seecharan, C. (2006), *Muscular Learning: Cricket and Education and the Making of the British West Indies at the End of the 19th century*, Kingston, Jamaica: Ian Randle.

Website

The Ragged School Museum: www.raggedschoolmuseum.org.uk/nextgen/, last accessed 17 December 2010.

6

State Schooling and the Construction of 'Public Childhoods'

Introduction

Through the combined ministrations of the British Schools, the Church of England and the Ragged School Movement, education had become a central organizing feature of many children's lives, but not all. It would take landmark legislation in 1870 to begin the process of establishing a universal State education system in England and Wales thereby contributing to the construction of schooling as a general condition for childhood in Western industrialized societies.

The educational landscape in England and Wales before the 1870 Elementary Education Act

Before moving on to examine Forster's 1870 Elementary Education Act and the impact it had in setting the conditions for the creation of schooling as an institutional norm for twentieth century *public* childhoods, it is helpful to consider the condition of schooling in England on the eve of the Royal Assent being given. Education for the wealthy and well-to-do remained in the hands of the Public, post-monastic 'King's' and long-established grammar schools (Barnard, 1971). For the vast mass of the population there were institutions established by the Voluntary societies largely based either on the Lancastrian non-conformist British and Foreign Schools or the Church of England National Schools. It should also be said that, although smaller in scale and influence at this time, there were following Catholic emancipation in 1827 a growing number of Catholic schools under the auspices of the Catholic Poor School Committee. In addition, as we have seen, there was the looser and more diverse non-conformist provision of the Ragged School Union with its social vision and well-heeled patrons. Clearly religion played a vital role in the justification for education and the formulation of these institutions and their curricula. However, despite the aspirations to ubiquity of both the Voluntary societies and the Ragged Schools, provision was too patchy and dependent upon an uncoordinated investment of limited time, energy and resources (Smith, 2009).

To understand the breadth and quality of the provision of the pre-1870 education institutional landscape it is instructive to look at Dame Schools. These 'institutions' offered a benchmark for popular education systems at this time, because as the least systematic, worst organized and poorly regulated schools, they are frequently regarded as the weakest link in the chain of provision. Dame Schools offered little more than the most rudimentary instruction in literacy, numeracy and other practical skills, such as sewing, for a basic fee. Those who ran and taught in these schools were usually unqualified, used their own homes and had a level of education that marked them out from the bulk of the rest of the population – but usually not by much.

Charles Dickens refers to a Dame School in *Great Expectations,* and the great Victorian childhood moralist paints a desultory picture through young Pip's eyes of the limited opportunities afforded those scholars who, we conclude, had the great misfortune to attend. In the following passage Pip soon realizes that curriculum, pedagogy, resources and conduct at the Dame School overseen by Mr Wopsle's great-aunt all fall well short of what is required to meet his aspiration to make himself 'uncommon' and 'to get on in life':

> The Educational scheme or Course established by Mr Wopsle's great-aunt may be resolved into the following synopsis. The pupils ate apples and put straws down one another's backs, until Mr Wopsle's great-aunt collected her energies, made an indiscriminate totter at them with the birch-rod. After receiving the charge with every mark of derision, the pupils formed in line and buzzingly passed a ragged book from hand to hand. The book had an alphabet in it, some figures and tables, and a little spelling – that is to say, it had had once. As soon as this volume began to circulate, Mr Wopsle's great-aunt fell into a state of coma; arising either from sleep or rheumatic paroxysm. The pupils then entered among themselves upon a competitive examination on the subject of Boots, with the view to ascertaining who could tread the hardest upon whose toes. (Dickens, 1861 and 1994, p. 69)

If this is drawn from life, we might wonder what became of the author's less talented or fortunate contemporaries and any aspirations they shared to become 'uncommon'! These weaknesses, combined with rapid urban growth and patchy provision sealed the argument in favour of substantive State intervention to ensure the possibility of uniform coverage and this was the premise of the legislation of 1870.

The 1870 Elementary Education Act, schooling and childhood

The 1870 Elementary Education Act ranks as a landmark piece of educational legislation and by creating the conditions for a sea change in children's core experience of childhood its impact cannot be overstated. The Act confirmed school as the dominant institution of childhood beyond the family, and established being a 'scholar' and latterly a 'pupil' as the normal condition for children from the age of five. Thus, *being schooled* becomes the central, universal condition around which the social patterns, temporal rhythms and spatial locus of children's lives would come to be wound.

The Act was put through Parliament by William Edward Forster (1819–86), a leading member of the Liberal government led by Gladstone. Forster was born into a Quaker family in Bradpole, Dorset. He began his career as a lawyer and then moved on to become a wool trader; however, alongside his commercial interests, Forster was always interested in politics and was an active member of the campaign against slavery, counting Robert Owen among his friends. In 1850 he married Jane Arnold, the eldest daughter of Thomas Arnold, the reforming headmaster of Rugby Public School, portrayed in *Tom Brown's Schooldays* by Thomas Hughes. Jane's family had illustrious credentials in mid-Victorian educational and literary circles. Besides being a celebrated poet, her brother Matthew Arnold was also Her Majesty's first Chief Inspector of Schools. Political interests led Forster to become MP for Bradford in 1861 and following the 1868 election that brought Gladstone to power he was given an important role in government as 'Vice-President of the Committee of Council on Education'.

Despite its landmark status, Forster introduced the Bill that would become the 1870 Elementary Education Act, as a relatively modest measure (MacLure, 1986). He was at pains to stress that the new legislation would not abolish any existing schools (a nod towards the Ragged Schools and the general fears about the secularizing effects of State intervention) but would allow for 'infilling' where provision was patchy or non-existent; moreover, that this would be 'at least cost of public money'. The approach was to be organic rather than revolutionary.

If the Act of 1870 established the conditions that made it possible for all children to be schooled under the aegis of the State, it was not until the 'Mundella' Elementary Education Act of 1880 that this became compulsory and universally free (Barnard, 1971, pp. 168–71; Aldrich, 1982). Clearly it is possible to explain the push for universal education from a number of interests and perspectives; however, it is perhaps worth distinguishing the reasons and explanations for universal education from the social institutions it was instrumental in creating.

There were the interests of employers in the new industries. It was increasingly important that workers had a sufficient grasp of literacy, numeracy and other basic knowledge and skills to be productive and useful. Then there were the ever present moral concerns that united so many observers despite their denominational differences – the fear of an emergent heathen, urban mass proletariat that stalked the Victorian middle- and upper-class imagination. For these moralists, schooling became identified, along with the microcosmic social order based on values of modesty, sobriety, respect and adherence to biblically ascribed morality found in the Christian family, as the antidote to disorder and rampant godlessness.

However, the totalizing intervention of Forster's Act was not welcomed by all. Besides conflicts with economic interests, there were concerns about a creeping secularism in schooling that State involvement seemed to facilitate. As we have seen earlier, these concerns dogged attempts to universalize education under the umbrella of the State through the nineteenth century and came to a head in a very public show of anger from Lord Shaftesbury and the Ragged School Union. If the Church Societies felt that their pre-eminence and authority were threatened, the threat to the Ragged Schools was their very survival. As predicted, many Ragged Schools dwindled away during the 1870s and the new School Boards took over several existing buildings and reconstituted them as Board Schools. Shaftesbury explicitly described this as no less than a 'national calamity' because in the process the Board Schools, and by implication the State, were riding roughshod over philanthropic, self-help instincts of patrician Tories (such as Shaftesbury) and seemed to be propagating State secularism rather than the gospel. Following a number of heated controversies and in response to what appeared to be an inevitable tumble into the abyss, the Ragged School Union reinvented itself as sponsor for the boys (and now young people's) club movement (Smith, 2009). Other doyens of the movement followed Dr Barnardo's lead and translated the Ragged School ethos into a set of educational institutions with a philanthropic sense of mission, *inter alia* George Williams, founded the YMCA and Quintin Hogg established Regent Street Polytechnic in central London (Simon, 1965, p. 62).

Inasmuch as the 1870 Act was seen as a progressive measure on the domestic front it was also motivated by fears of external developments. The unification of Germany under the Prussian leader von Bismarck in 1871 underlined rumbling anxieties within Britain about its rise as an industrial, military and imperial power, and there was a widespread acknowledgement that an effective system of education underlay this nascent superiority. It is ironic that after Froebel's kindergartens had been banned by the Prussian authorities and many Froebelians who had sought refuge in Britain were gaining an intellectual hold on sections of the educational establishment, that the State authorities adopted key characteristics of the Prussian system when turning the legislation into practice (Chapters 2 and 3; Barnard, 1971, p. 172). Among these were the spatial and organizational form of many of the Board

Schools that sprang up after the passage of the Act. This was especially true in London, where E. R. Robson, the chief architect to the School Board of London set about designing a template for the many 'triple-decker' schools that were the hallmark of the Act's infilling vision and still represent a defining icon in the landscape of urban education (Bannerjee, 2008). Although most of Robson's schools were designed in what was seen as the appropriately secular, English vernacular architectural style known as Queen Anne Revival, the layout of classrooms based on the separation of children by age around a central common hall space, follows a pattern established in Prussian schooling and is clearly embodied in an alternative educational philosophy from the galleried classrooms of Lancastrian and National schools. It is intriguing to reflect on just how many children's childhoods have been regulated by the age-based social order built into the bricks and mortar of school buildings – where physical and intellectual growth is underwritten and mediated by the ritual of staged annual transitions from room to room, standard to standard, floor to floor and teacher to teacher.

The advent of the Elementary School certainly changed patterns of children's engagement with school, particularly after 1880 when attendance became compulsory. In 1870 there were 1.7million pupils in Elementary schools in England and Wales; by 1891 this number had risen to 4.8 million (Copeland, 1999). The numbers are indicative of the scale of the transformation in the rhythm and geography of children's lives and of what Hendrick (1997b) has called the growing 'compulsory relationship' between children, their families and the State during this period. Just as the nineteenth century transformed so many other aspects of life, it also transformed childhood through its identification of schooling as the quotidian condition for children's habitus. Besides the separation of childhood and adulthood that it achieved, Hendrick (1997b) captures the depth and breadth of this transformation by suggesting the following as social, and even political, effects of this new compulsory universalism:

- standardization of knowledge in favour of that learnt at school, rather than other informal contexts that include the family
- reinforcement of a common class identity
- the moral censure of child labour
- the right of strangers to assault children
- the promotion of the idea that the nation's future lay in the hands of children as a quite specific group.

> **Reflection:**
>
> You have been reading a great deal of material from educational history; why might this be important for social constructionists?

Compulsory schooling and the working child

Besides the religious objections, there were other sites of opposition. The gradual move towards universal schooling and moral censure of child labour led to tensions with the actuality of children as workers in the United Kingdom as well as the United States. Beyond the school gate, there was a widespread view that putting children to work was not just important for the home economy, but also the natural condition for *working* class children to inhabit. Furthermore, there were fears that schooling might make people less than comfortable with their divinely ordained lot in life. This was not a view confined to those with an obvious interest in maintaining a compliant labouring class, but is found in contemporary accounts where families complain bitterly that their children have been, in a memorable phrase, turned from 'useful to useless' through compulsory preoccupation with schoolwork rather than engagement with financially remunerated labour that added to a family's economic security (Tomes, 1985). It is a sentiment that continued to be echoed a century later, when a traveller parent was clear about what he saw as the damage done by education:

> My children never had education. I reckon education destroys a lot, I do…The young people today, the moment they sit down they got to have a book in their hands. It's all wrong. I don't reckon that a lot of education is any good. If you've always got a book in your hands you aren't got any time to do anything else. (Zuma, 2009)

These tensions meant that although the school-leaving age was made compulsory through the 1880 Elementary Education Act there continued to be special provisions for children aged 10 and 11, whereby they could attend school half-time and work the rest. Furthermore, the hierarchical

'Standards' through which school classes were organized did not adhere strictly to age bands. Depending on the school board that held jurisdiction, pupils could leave school before the age of 13, but only after demonstrating that they had reached a particular standard and passed the required examinations.

Compulsory schooling and the discovery of the 'ineducable child'

Making school compulsory also meant that schools found themselves confronted by children who had hitherto not attended. Often this was because these children were described as 'dull' or 'backward', even 'ineducable', and thus would not benefit from education (Copeland, 1999). The sudden visibility of pupils with what we would now describe as special educational needs was an unexpected consequence of the legislation and shocked the educational establishment. Further, this was the era of 'payment by results' and the annual tests ruled the curriculum; children who could not contribute to the standing of the school in academic tests were regarded as a liability. But more fundamentally, the universal education Acts had gone some way in making the extent and depth of poverty in the home country all too visible.

As a consequence, two Royal Commissions of enquiry were set up almost simultaneously during the 1880s to address the challenges. The first in 1886 was the Cross Commission under the chairmanship of Sir Richard Cross and was entitled the Royal Commission on the Elementary Education Acts (RCEEA). However, early in deliberations, the Cross Commission (1886) decided that the education of children who were at that time usually referred to as 'feeble-minded', 'educable idiots' and/or 'imbeciles', fell into a category it described as *such other cases as from special circumstances would seem to require exceptional methods of education*. Therefore the second, the Egerton Commission, was set up within six months of the Cross Commission and was entitled The Royal Commission to Examine the Education of the Blind, Deaf and Dumb, etc. (RCBDD&).The 'such other cases' came to be represented by the 'etc.' in the Egerton Commission's title and thus, as a distinct afterthought, the idea of 'special' education was introduced into the landscape of schooling. Although provision for this group was seen as an attempt to limit and even diminish the extent of 'pauperism', the terms of the argument are not especially philanthropic:

> The blind, deaf and dumb, and the educable class of imbeciles form a distinct group, which, if left uneducated, become not only a burden to themselves but a weighty burden to the State. It is in the interest of the State to educate them so as to dry up as far as possible the minor streams which ultimately swell the great torrent of pauperism. (RCBDD&, p. 3, and quoted in Copeland, 1999)

The Elementary Education Acts of 1870 and 1880 and the Egerton and Cross Royal Commissions they precipitated, were, therefore, in large part responsible for the construction of categories of children distinguished from the 'normal' child and the consolidation of a vocabulary comprising 'feeble-minded', 'idiot' and 'imbecile' to identify these categories.

Reflection:

Why might these socially constructed terms have gone on to become popular terms of general abuse (and continue to be so)? How do you feel about hearing them being used?

Children's experience of the new Board Schools

It should be noted that State schooling was not always received negatively by children and their families. Alongside being a substantial intervention in the lives of children and precipitating a thorough re-invention of childhood, the 1870 Elementary Education Act also produced a school building boom with few urban neighbourhoods and townscapes unaffected by the new Board Schools. The social and personal impact of this building boom comes through in autobiographies of many who attended these schools. Often the 'before and after' contrast is stark; engraver Frank Galton (b.1867) first attended a parish school in St Pancras, London where all the boys' classes were in one large room (Rose, 2001). According to his own account, the teachers were incompetent and miserably paid and one of them could only maintain discipline 'by sheer brute strength'. However, at age ten he transferred to a mint condition Board School, where he enjoyed professionally trained teachers, orderly classrooms, and French lessons.

Likewise, his contemporaries offered equally enthusiastic, even loving testimonials:

> .... a wonder building, sumptuous and indeed palatial beyond belief, with its large classrooms, brand-new equipment so different from the mouldy patchwork of the [old] school, the desks with lids. (John Eldred, 1955, in Rose, 2001)

> We all thought it marvellous, judging by the standards of those days. It was a fine building...: it had flushed toilets, heated water pipes in the class-rooms, and a playground, asphalt of course, but, alas, no playing-field with soft green grass. (Lord Taylor of Mansfield, 1977, in Rose, 2001)

> ...the smell of copal oak varnish as the big windows, desks, partitions and fittings were of pitch-pine well and truly varnished, even today if I get a whiff of oak varnish I remember the new school. Two other features of the school of which we were justifiably proud was that it was the first school in Bolton to be lit by this new electricity, the other feature is that it was the first in central heating with radiators and constant supply of hot water for domestic purpose. (Ellis, 1978, in Rose, 2001)

Their sense of wonder is palpable and points to a social revolution whose impacts have largely become invisible to our gaze.

Economy, health and schooling in the early twentieth century

By 1900 there had been 30 years of explicit commitment to the principle of universal access to an elementary school education and the signature institutions that would shape children's experience of education (and with it so much of their childhood for the first half of the new century) were in place. The landscape of Britain's towns and cities had been augmented by a rash of new school buildings, and the Board School rising above a sea of low-rise Victorian terraces had cemented the place of schooling in the life of the nation and the lives of what were now imagined as 'the Nation's Children'. Further, in a spirit of optimism, Ellen Key pronounced in her best-seller, that the twentieth century would be 'The Century of the Child' (Key, 1909; Lengborn, 1993).

Despite the changes brought about through schooling, the early years of the twentieth century were years of economic hardship for the poor. Between 1899 and 1913 the average wage declined in real terms by almost 10 per cent and despite short-term fluctuations and improvements, growth within the economy was sluggish enough over the succeeding decades to ensure that they only just recouped the lost value on the eve of the Second World War in 1939. The pernicious effects of this decline in real incomes were matched by the reality of unemployment which reached hitherto unknown rates and levels during the 1920s and 1930s, peaking at nearly 21 per cent of the workforce and totalling around three million in the early years of the 1930s (Whitbread, 1972).

The statistics point to a nation where malnutrition and disease were still all too common. Thus in 1901 the philanthropic sociologist and social investigator Seebohm Rowntree carried out a survey of poverty in Britain; he gathered a wealth of data concerned with incomes, expenditure, employment, nutrition, housing and health. Based on the evidence gathered in the survey, Rowntree identified what he called Primary and Secondary Poverty. Primary Poverty was identified as insufficient family income to meet costs; Secondary Poverty existed where there was sufficient income, but expenditure included items that were regarded as unnecessary, such as alcohol. Rowntree concluded that around 13 per cent of the population of Britain lived in Primary Poverty and 14 per cent in Secondary. The conclusion that 27 per cent of Britain's people lived their lives in debilitating poverty was shocking and Rowntree was able to persuade David Lloyd George, the Liberal politician who was to become Prime Minister between 1916 and 1922, to introduce social welfare reforms, including the introduction of Old Age Pensions and National Insurance during the period of the Liberal government (Hattersley, 2010). It is obvious that family poverty means childhood poverty and there is no doubt that many children in Britain grew up in conditions of grinding impoverishment during the first third of the twentieth century. Add to this the fact that whereas life expectancy had increased during the late Victorian period and continued to do so during the early years of the twentieth century – owing to improvements in the survival of young people and adults after they had grown out of childhood – infant mortality rates remained stubbornly high during the years before the First World War (Foley, 2001, p. 10).

Rowntree's findings and the conclusions to be drawn about the health and well-being of the nation's children had been preceded by a very obvious and shocking insight into the effects of poverty and its implications for the nation. A series of embarrassingly disastrous defeats and reversals in the South African or Boer Wars of the late nineteenth and early twentieth centuries had shown that too many of Britain's young male population were simply not fit enough to fight. On the brink of war in 1898, the British Army numbered 225,000 men, its largest complement for 40 years. However, as Judd and Surridge observe:

> ...the poor quality of the recruits rendered its efficiency somewhat suspect....the health of recruits was often so poor that despite the healthier environment and regular meals, many new soldiers never fully developed physically. Most were in their late teens when they joined and many were already stunted by poverty; one glaring feature of the war would be the height difference between the officers and their men. (Judd and Surridge, 2002, p. 60)

The Boer Wars of 1899–1902 are well documented as providing a catalyst for the emergence of child welfare initiatives as it became clearer that the Victorian Poor Law system was inadequate to meeting the widespread impoverishment and deprivation that they so disturbingly exposed (Cox and Dyson, 1972). It was at this point that the State began to offer services for the children of the poor that went beyond measures to induce moral redirection; moreover, the new-found universal reach of Elementary schooling presented the means to embrace the nation's children and address their health (Foley, 2001, p. 10). Thus, the emerging analysis of the wars as less than triumphant, together with the emergence of the rival Labour Party as a political force representing working-class people, encouraged the Liberal government that swept to power in 1906 to catch the national mood and introduce a range of social welfare measures. These measures consolidated the principle that the State had an interest in direct intervention in public health and laid the foundation of the Welfare State that would emerge, fully fledged, some 40 years later after the Second World War. Despite being caught between the political interests of the left in securing welfare reform on behalf of the working class, and fierce opposition to any radical legislation from the Conservative and Unionist majority in the House of Lords (the upper legislative body in the United Kingdom) (Cox and Dyson, 1972), it should be said that there was also a gradual and pragmatic realization that healthy workers were more productive, and thus these measures went beyond notions of philanthropy to gain acceptance owing to a degree of self-interest among employers (Hennessy, 1993, p. 125). As a result, mitigating the deprivation of tomorrow's workers and soldiers became a priority, so that children's health and welfare services precede the wider assault on poverty made by the National Health Service by some decades.

Thus the Interdepartmental Committee on Physical Deterioration was set up in 1904 and included a focus on children's health; this was followed by five further reports between 1910 and 1916 (Foley, 2001, p. 10). Although these reports were clearly overdue, their assumptions about why poverty and deprivation exist, may strike us as disturbingly un-progressive. Rowntree had pointed to the social and environmental factors that shaped poverty, but perhaps by identifying secondary poverty as in part 'self-inflicted', the door was left ajar for a more moralistic analysis of the problem by those who were only too ready to make the poor themselves responsible for their poverty, rather than indict the slum conditions in which they lived. In particular, child poverty was 'naturalized' by making mothers responsible for the poor health of the nation's children:

> Highly influential reports by George Newman, the Chief Medical Officer to the Board of Education...blamed women for the bad management of their households, their ignorance concerning care of children and their lack of a proper sense of maternal obligation...Newman was repeatedly to recommend the education of working class women to raise the standard of domestic competence and to install the proper ideals of motherhood and home life in British girls and women...he, and others, ignored statistical evidence available at the time showing infant mortality to be primarily a feature of inner city slums. (Foley, 2001, p. 10)

A direct result of these reports and policy developments was the development of a regulated and professionalized force of health visitors and midwives; much of this work had hitherto been loosely regulated and rooted in middle-class notions of voluntary charity work, especially in the case of health visiting and infant welfare work. However, more directly relevant to education and schooling was the passing of a raft of legislation that variously reinvented and consolidated schools as not only educational, but also social welfare institutions. Universal schooling had created the conditions whereby the nation's children and youth could be reached and influenced pretty well in their entirety by the State. Not for the last time would schools be commissioned as the vanguard for social reform – a sort of 'policy horse' saddled with the State's hopes of redirecting and transforming the aberrant, anti-social or wayward behaviour of the populace through its children.

Reflection:

Schooling is frequently invoked as an agent of social change, but how powerful is it and what can realistically be achieved through education?

Legislation arising from this 'social welfare turn' in policy included the Education (Provision of School Meals) Act 1906. This measure permitted the Local Education Authorities (LEAs) that had replaced the School Boards (Local Education Authorities were created by the 1902 Education 'Balfour' Act and placed under the direction of a central government School Board) to provide school meals for schoolchildren as they saw fit; this provision for the poorest children was made a compulsory duty in 1914 (Foley, 2001, pp. 12–14). Clearly, that schools should offer meals to those most impoverished pupils was a response to the perceived malnutrition and deprivation of the era. As the service grew, it became obvious that providing a nutritious hot meal was fundamental to any hope of educational progress. School meals, 'dinner-ladies', cake, pink custard and cabbage now became inseparable from the daily social life and routines of the school and a much mythologized part of the culture of the State-regulated childhood experienced by the *public child* as children spun their own culture around the daily reality of school dinners. Here are children's playground rhymes from the 1950s:

> Say what you will,
> School dinners make you ill,
> And shepherd's pie
> Makes Davy Crockett cry;
> All school din-dins
> Come from pigs' bins
> -That's no lie.

> If you stay to school dinners
> Better throw them aside,
> A lot of kids didn't,
> A lot of kids died.
> The meat is of iron,

The spuds are steel,

If that don't get you

Then the afters will.

(Traditional from Opie and Opie, 1959, p. 162–4)

As a social welfare measure school meals certainly made a significant contribution to the health of the nation and seemed to have become a fixture of school life. More recently concerns over nutritional standards, largely led by the high-profile campaign of celebrity chef Jamie Oliver (JamieOliver.com, 2010), have re-ignited debate over school meals and their place in assuring the health of the nation's children.

In 1907 the School Medical Service was set up following the passage of the Education (Administrative Provisions) Act. This allowed for School Medical Officers to be appointed whose role was to ensure that all children were inspected on entry to school and at regular intervals thereafter. They were also responsible for inspections of school premises, were charged to follow up outbreaks of infectious diseases and could make home visits to those who claimed to be ill, but were deemed suspect. The School Medical Service was placed under the aegis of the medical branch of the central Board of Education along with services responsible for 'handicapped' children and maternity and infant welfare (Foley, 2001, p. 12). These measures emphasized a medicalized approach to tackling poverty, malnutrition and disability rather than one based on environmental or social explanations.

The establishment of the School Medical Service meant that for the first time, all the nation's children were weighed, measured and assessed. These statistics facilitated research and research led to theorization that would shape the construction of the Child as a medicalized and physical entity. This scientifically based theorization of the Child shaped professional practice; furthermore, it established the terms for identifying a 'normal' childhood guaranteed through the institutions of the State (Foley, 2001, p. 14). However radical the intentions, these measures contributed to the transformation of Rousseau's active and agentic *Emile*, into the passively conceived Child of expert theoretical discourse and theory, around which standardized schooling for normative children could be constructed.

If the role of the school was being augmented by these provisions and associated new professional practices, its curriculum was also subject to a re-think in response to the panic about the welfare of the nation. The demise of Payment by Results in 1897 had potentially freed the curriculum of the elementary school from the restrictive shackles of teaching to the test. However, despite its unpopularity, the impact of abolition was not as immediate as might be imagined and it was nearly a decade before a substantial body of teachers who had never worked under the Payment by Results regime emerged (Burnett, 1994). Daisy Cowper, born in Liverpool in 1890, tells how with the appointment of a new, progressively minded headteacher, the tone, if not the actual content, of her elementary school curriculum changed after the abolition of the Revised Code and Payment By Results:

> School now began to be a daily delight, with a kind teacher ready to praise, and interesting lessons: life began to be more or less what the poet called a 'grand, sweet song…We had no painting, or drawing, or physical exercises, but what you've never had, you never miss, and there was certainly never a dull moment…(Burnett, 1994, p. 204)

These changes provided an opportunity for educational progressives to become increasingly influential in State education. Despite the challenges of cuts to the education budgets, the National Froebel Institute had become a vocal, respected and influential contributor to educational debate during the early years of the twentieth century (Liebschner, 1991, pp. 88–104).

Reflection:

When we are assessing learners we frequently speak of 'right' and 'wrong' answers or being 'correct' or 'false' without much thought. Do these terms suggest a moral as well as an intellectual judgement on children?

Elementary schooling, nation and empire

We have looked at the role of sport and the colonial curriculum in constructing imperial identities; however, there were also curricular tendencies nearer home that sought to entrench an authentic Englishness within the curriculum as the birthright of the nation's children while also addressing the concerns for their health and welfare. Among the activities deemed fit to inculcate these values and qualities were folk dance and song. Thus responding to the urging of Cecil Sharp (a musician, folk-song collector, school inspector and founder member of the English Folk Dance Society) folk dance was included in 1909 as a component of the elementary school curriculum. Sharp was clear about the 'easy' and 'efficient' physical benefits that English children would experience by including folk dance within the curriculum, for:

> Dancing promotes physical culture in an easy and efficient manner; easy, because, being presented as an amusement, it is pleasurable; efficient, because physical actions performed under the stimulus of emotion, naturally and unself-consciously, are less calculated to produce a stiff, wooden and mechanical bearing than those that are executed, in response to the word of command, for the sole purpose of developing the body. (Sharp, 1912, in Gammon, 2008)

However, the place of education in sustaining a national identity, inflected by notions of race, is also present in Sharp's advocacy of this particular form of dance:

> In the folk dances of their own nation children have a form of artistic expression which must, from their very nature, be especially suited to them. (Sharp, 1912, in Gammon, 2008)

Sharp's point, Gammon asserts:

> ... is clear enough, the products of the race are the best material for educating the race. Here Sharp is articulating ideas of essential, elemental Englishness. (Gammon, 2008)

Sharp asserts a moral imperative to educate children in and through Englishness; his ideas may seem strange to us living in an era when multiculturalism has been installed as a core ethic for the curriculum and subsequent events, including two world wars in which antagonists drew motivation and justification from nationalism and race, have tended to upstage a more naive reading of Sharp's sentiments. In short, they now appear inappropriate, even sinister, for a globalizing age; imagine the popular reaction to the following complaint against cosmopolitanism in the curriculum found in his *English Folk-Song: Some Conclusions* published in 1907:

> Our system of education is ... too cosmopolitan, it is calculated to produce citizens of the world rather than Englishmen. (Sharp, 1907, in Young, 2010, p. 67)

Ironically, in his advocacy of pre-industrial folk dance and song, Sharp champions a naturalized English childhood that is only made possible through the actuality of mass schooling and social changes that attended industrialization, including the growth of a national rail system and newspapers (Faith, 1994).

The rest of the curriculum was also not immune from the project to affirm national identity, and there was the important business of preparing a metropolitan population to assume their position at the heart of the world's largest ever empire. Therefore, whereas Sharp's nation-building focus was on the direct affirmation of Englishness, other areas sought to achieve the same effect by emphasizing the study of peoples who were *other* to the domestic population. Subjects such as geography were obvious candidates for the task of imperial education. Walford (2001) describes a set of readers in geography called *Alternative Geography Readers* produced in the 1890s, of which Book three for children in Standards six and seven (i.e. children aged 11–13) was entitled *The British Empire* in which Australia is described through the eyes of a British explorer:

> In 1873, Colonel Warburton, with thirty camels, succeeded in reaching the western coast from the centre of Australia. The journey occupied eight months.

Warburton goes on to offer a judgement on Aboriginal people and their culture:

> They are the very lowest in the scale of humanity, and I cannot conceive how anything could fall much lower. They do not even take the trouble to put a few bushes up to shelter themselves from the sun or the rain – when it does rain, though I don't know when, for I didn't see it; the sun is hot enough. (Walford, 2001, p. 55)

It should be added that not all indigenous and subject peoples were regarded as pejoratively as those in Western Australia; however, this neither ruled out the implicitly hierarchical racist thinking that structures the narrative nor a presumed right to patronize:

> The Maoris, or natives of New Zealand, are a much superior race to the natives of Australia. They are intelligent, brave and daring, and capable of civilisation. (Walford, 2001, p. 55)

These were the curriculum materials intended to inspire the foot soldiers, sailors, mechanics and clerks of the empire for their particular role in sustaining the British imperial mission at home and overseas. However, besides propagandizing half-truths and distortions on curricular material, there was a more complete and ideological sense in which childhood was recruited in the service of the empire. This was in the deployment of the child and childlike qualities as metaphors for all subjugated peoples.

In a distortion of the Rousseauian vision for the *Child*, the idea of childhood innocence could be put to use to other, less savoury ends in the curriculum of the elementary school. An essential idea instilled in the minds of Britain's poor was their intrinsic superiority to the millions of subjects of Queen Victoria found in the colonial lands overseas. An ideology of superiority to others, of course, served both to motivate the future servants of the empire and to achieve acquiescence by suggesting that British children should be grateful for their lot. The assertion of superiority frequently took the form of comparing colonial subjects to children who had an ingenuous, childlike nature which called out for decisive and strong leadership:

> Africans and people of African descent were often deemed childlike and so, it was argued, required the wisdom and guidance of whites. (Diptee, 2006, p. 190)

The deployment of the *Child* as a metaphor was not confined to the disparagement of sub-Saharan African peoples and became pervasive throughout the British Empire; here it is found in the following quotation from an old 'China hand' cited in a paper by De Groot:

> Treat them as children; make them do what we know is for their benefit. (De Groot, 2000, p. 44)

Nor were Church authorities beyond *othering* subjugated populations through this process of infantilization; pictures of children were frequently used to teach young people in Britain about the challenges and achievements of missionary work. In the following passage, children are invited to sympathize with those described as less fortunate overseas and, no doubt, be grateful for their own lot:

This picture is a photograph of a little boy born in a heathen land – the Solomon Islands. Until ten years ago, no missionary had been to the part where this boy's home is, and the people there were dark and cruel and wicked. But to-day, hundreds of them know all about Jesus, and many of them love Him. This little boy is now in our Mission Schools, and he, with scores of other children, is being taught the way of truth and purity. But there are thousands upon thousands of children in the islands of the Pacific still in the heathen darkness. Their homes are full of evil, their lot is very sad, for they are surrounded by wicked people. We want you to help to make known to them the joys of the Christian faith. (Thomas, 2000, pp. 305–6)

There are not only messages about social and racial order here, but also the civilizing mission of the empire; further, the child is presented as an innocent among 'wicked people' who, in consequence, needs to be rescued and redeemed – the recruitment of the nation's children to achieve this goal follows from the final sentence.

The First World War and the 1918 Education (Fisher) Act

Times of national emergency change the social and political landscape. At these times existing institutions and provisions are tested to their limits and those that are not up to the test will be seen as needing reform. The First World War represented one such emergency and thus at its end we see a major piece of educational legislation in the 1918 Education Act, also known as 'The Fisher Act'. It was named after H. A. L. Fisher, the President of the Board of Education in Lloyd George's wartime coalition government, as also Vice-Chancellor of Oxford University and member of an aesthetic and intellectual elite that included his brother-in-law, the composer Ralph Vaughan Williams (Judge, 2006). The 1918 Act is an attempt to do for secondary education what the 'Forster' Act of 1870 had done for elementary education nearly 50 years earlier (Barnard, 1971; Vaughan Williams, 1988; Academic, 2004; Spartacusnet, 2005). The shortcomings of a State system where many children left school at 12 with only patchy provision for them to progress further in full-time education were becoming obvious. Besides a need to bring administrative arrangements for the whole system up to scratch for the post-war era, the main thrust of the 1918 Act was to do the following:

- Extend schooling provision to age 14 and free young people from what was described as 'the injurious effects of industrial pressure'.
- Introduce 'part-time day continuation schools' beyond 14 for all young people unless they are clearly engaged in another programme of instruction.
- Improve elementary education and through it the physical health of the population.

(See Fisher's introductory speech in MacLure, 1986.)

Despite being passed as the 1918 Education Act, it was proposed by Fisher in a White Paper presented to Parliament in August 1917. Placed in its context, this was 15 months before the war was won; the second of three disastrously bloody battles at Ypres on the western front was coming to a tragic close; soldiers from the United States were just beginning to appear on the western front; and, the October Russian Revolution had yet to occur. In short, the Bill was introduced while the war was very much *on* and the outcome unclear. However, Fisher proposed that:

> We have reached a point in our history when we must take long views. We are a comparatively small country, we have incurred the hostility of a nation with a larger population and with a greater extent of concentrated territory and with a more powerful organization of its resources. We cannot flatter ourselves with the comfortable notion, I wish we could, that after this War the fierce rivalry of Germany will disappear and hostile feeling altogether die down. That in itself constitutes a reason for giving the youth of our country the best preparation that ingenuity can suggest. (from MacLure, 1986)

The sense of the nation's youth as its future prosperity and defence was palpable. Tragically, of course, the prophecy implicit in the fears about Germany's fierce rivalry were to come to pass, and for many of the nation's youth the 'best preparation' meant preparation for the Second World War, just as the welfare measures implemented through elementary schooling before the First World War prepared young men to be fit for the trenches.

Fisher continues, suggesting that the new Bill is important for the democratic health of the nation at a time when the extension of the right to vote to women was very much under debate:

> ...we are making a greater demand than ever before upon the civic spirit of the ordinary man and woman...and how can we expect an intelligent response to the demands which the community propose to make upon the instructed judgement of its men and women unless we are prepared to make some further sacrifices in order to form and fashion the minds of the young...(from MacLure, 1986)

Fisher was, along with his illustrious relatives, a member of the intellectual elite, and in certain passages there is a suggestion that the ideas of Pestalozzi and Froebel with their holistic view of the Child have taken hold:

> ...education is one of the good things of life which should be more widely shared than has hitherto been the case, amongst the children and young persons of this country...We assume that education should be the education of the whole man, spiritually, intellectually, and physically, and it is not beyond the resources of civilization to devise a scheme of education, possessing certain common qualities, but admitting at the same time large variation from which the whole youth of the country, male and female, may derive benefit. (from MacLure, 1986)

Fisher acknowledged that these qualities of genuine education were available to the children of the 'well-to-do' as he has it, but believed that they should also be available to the poor. In outline we see many of the arguments that would shape educational policy over the twentieth century, namely how can a mass system: provide for individual difference; promote opportunities fit to the individual needs of children and young people; and, transcend narrow vocational instrumentalism?

In actuality, the 1918 Act was mixed in its achievements. The leaving age was extended to 14 with a provision for further extension to 15 (as, ironically, it already was in Germany) at a later date and following revision to the grants system for local authorities, all elementary school fees were finally abolished. As for the proposed part-time day extension schooling for those aged 14 and above, this was undermined by the economic travails of the 1920s and the 1930s. However, where the Act failed to create new institutions, it endorsed them in principle and expressed what a growing consensus of opinion was seeing as necessary to the further development of the educational system and to securing the economic prosperity that should flow from it. As Fisher acknowledged in the Parliamentary debate on the Bill, the war had proved the worth of elementary school education because British army volunteers could largely read, write and perform the calculations necessary to utilize the weapons of modern warfare (MacLure, 1986).

However, developments did not have wholly positive effects. The limited achievements in extending the age range for State education 'upwards' relieved the pressure for more education sufficiently to undermine the efforts of those seeking to extend universal provision for the under fives, thus holding back a national State system of nursery education. Thus, although the Act did acknowledge the merits of education for children aged two to five and made grants available for this purpose few LEAs took up the opportunity (Whitbread, 1972, p. 67).

In general, apart from the modest advance in extending schooling to 14, the economic difficulties of the inter-war years meant that much of the momentum for change built up by the late Victorian Acts of Parliament was dissipated. In addition to the issues surrounding extension of the school-leaving age, education and child welfare reformers separately and together struggled to make progress in implementing curricula and pedagogies in line with what were seen as the progressive insights of the relatively new professional groups of psychologists, educationists and educators (see next chapter). It is striking that in most educational reports during this period there is an obvious grasp of what should be done, but implementation of change and reform seem continually to be deferred in a nation pre-occupied by a mixture of war, economic slump conditions and the challenges of keeping an empire together (see discussion of Hadow in Chapter 7).

Reflection:

Education is frequently depicted as a driver of economic development; but here we see educational development stymied by weak economic conditions – can education really drive or, in reality, does it follow economic development?

Despite the enlightened and somewhat refreshing rhetoric found in Fisher's Bill, the actuality of elementary school education for working class and other disadvantaged children was anything but ideal. Much of the curriculum, whether explicit or hidden, seemed directed at disciplining the children of the poor in preparation for a life of grinding industrial labour. The instrumentalism that characterized the education of the poor and sought to reproduce their social subordination was implicitly underpinned by moralizing notions that had not changed since the days of Hannah More and the evangelicals. Indeed, in contrast to the virtuous, agentic Child imagined by the Romantics and progressives, the elementary school child was conceived as disordered, morally weak and in need of strict regulation and redemption (Walkerdine, 2009). The following recollection, from a woman who had endured elementary schooling during the late 1920s, illustrates in a single, everyday incident the impoverished educational goals, the moral pessimism concerning working-class children and the day-to-day violence that underpinned the Elementary School ethos:

> Every morning we marched in to the strains of 'March Militaire'. It was very regimental and very harsh and, erm, we used to have to sit up very stiff and straight with our arms folded behind our back.
>
> 'Good morning girls' and we'd have to say 'Good morning Miss Morgan' or whatever her name was.
>
> The curriculum I think, was very basic – reading, writing and arithmetic, just a general idea of things. Erm, more, I think, to slot you into the role in which working class children were going to, to go into in those times and that was mostly into the factories with monotonous, ordinary jobs. Erm, if there was any potential in the children then they didn't bring it out.
>
> On this particular morning, I remember, the teacher had called the register and she was now surveying us and this was going to be the first lesson of the day, which was Copywriting. And she wrote a word on, on the board called 'abundance'. Er, suddenly, the word abundance conjured up a picture of three little buns dancing. So I scribbled on a piece of paper three little buns dancing and even a little caption coming out of their mouths, you know, 'tra la la la la ... tra la la la la'. So the teacher advanced to the middle of the room and, er, she gave me one cursory look and said, 'come out, fetch the cane'. So you had to come out of the classroom and collect the cane from the corner of her desk and take it in and she would follow you in. Well she followed me in and I had three strokes on that hand and three strokes on that hand. And she told the class that I was a disruptive influence and it was something that would not and certainly could not continue, a state of affairs that couldn't or wouldn't ... she wouldn't allow to go on. And after

you'd had the cane you had to return the cane to its rightful place, then stand in the hall for the rest of the morning. And that was all because I happened to make a little drawing of three funny little buns dancing!

(Joyce Storey, born 1918 in Gloucestershire, on life at Two Mile Hill Elementary School in the late 1920s, speaking in 1991 for Channel 4's 'A Century of Childhood – School', transcribed by the author).

Reflection:

What motivates the teacher to describe Joyce Storey as a 'disruptive influence', are there implicit assumptions concerning human nature and the status of the poor that underpin such an assessment?

Further reading

Burnett, J. (ed.) (1994), *Destiny Obscure: Autobiographies of Childhood, Education and Family from the 1820s to the 1920s*, London: Routledge.

Castle, K. (1996), *Britannia's Children: Reading Colonialism through Children's Books and Magazines*, Manchester: Manchester University Press.

Grosvenor, I. (2005), '"There's no place like home": education and the making of national identity', in McCulloch, G. (ed.), *The RoutledgeFalmer Reader in History of Education*, London: RoutledgeFalmer, pp. 273–85.

Maguire, M., Wooldridge, T. and Pratt-Adams, S. (2006), *The Urban Primary School*, Maidenhead, UK: Open University Press.

Pratt-Adams, S., Maguire, M. and Burn, E. (2010), *Changing Urban Education*, London: Continuum.

Simon, B. (1965), *Education and the Labour Movement, 1870–1920*, London: Lawrence & Wishart.

Part 3
Schooling in the Century of the Child and Beyond

7

Brave New Worlds and Rhapsody Renewed: New Rationalities, New Institutions and Old Ideas

Introduction

Despite the relative stagnation of the Elementary school as the central institution of State education during the first half of the twentieth century, in other spheres these were times of change. As a generality, wars change things and the First World War was no exception in exerting a profound effect upon the social and political restrictions of the deeply deferential society of the Victorian and Edwardian eras that preceded it. Furthermore, if the war changed things in the social and political realm, then in the intellectual sphere change was already well underway, in 1905 and 1915 Albert Einstein transformed physics with the publication of his theories of Relativity, the cubist painting movement of Pablo Picasso and Georges Braque became increasingly prominent in the run up to the declaration of war in 1914 and Igor Stravinsky had scandalized the musical sensibilities of Paris at the first performance of his ballet, the Rite of Spring in 1913 (Ross, 2009). But importantly, Ludwig Wittgenstein had begun work on his *Tractatus Logico-Philosophicus* (Wittgenstein, 2001), a work that he completed in the Austrian trenches of the Italian front and carried with him into captivity as a prisoner of war in 1918 (Monk, 1991). The *Tractatus* is especially significant, in that it tests the technical rationalism at the heart of Enlightenment philosophy, with its crystalline logic and rarefied debates over mind and matter, to destruction point, and clears the way for social constructionism and associated theories of knowledge that characterize so much of subsequent intellectual life (Wittgenstein, 1952; Heaton and Groves, 2005; Monk, 2005). As far as childhood and education are concerned, new ways of theorizing the *Child* and associated ideas about curricula and pedagogy were emerging. These drew on the emerging disciplines of the mind, including psychology and psychoanalysis, as well as philosophers who trained their sights on the education of the young.

Freud and psychoanalysis

Sigmund Freud comes out of the late nineteenth century culture of Vienna and his work has imprinted itself indelibly upon the intellectual world of the twentieth century and beyond. Freud spent most of his life in Vienna until the advanced age of 79 when he left for England to avoid the anti-Semitism of the Nazis; he died a year later in 1939. Freud was a doctor who developed an interest in hysterical or nervous diseases in his patients (Thurschwell, 2000). However, as much as his work was the foundation stone for a vast array of psychotherapeutic methods and is still in use today, he is just as important for offering a model of mind with profound philosophical implications for an emerging understanding of childhood and its contribution to the formation of the mature adult.

Freud challenges the model of the mind as an entity suffused by a unitary consciousness and solely devoted to the exercise of rational faculties that we find in Descartes. Instead, Freud proposes that the conscious mind, what he calls the *Ego*, is complemented by an unconscious mind, the *id*, which is the site of our deepest desires, drives and imaginings, including those that shape our sexual appetites. Furthermore, the moral strictures of wider society are manifest in another structural layer Freud called the *super-Ego*, that imposes further pressure on us to keep our unconscious desires in check (Thurschwell, 2000).

Moreover, Freud's assertion that children are not asexual beings provoked a controversial reconsideration of children's development. He contended that they experience a developing sexuality that passes through successive stages identified by the three foci or erotogenic zones for desire, namely, the oral, the anal and the genital (see Thurschwell, 2000, pp. 54–6). Disruption or repression of sexual desire can lead to arrested development, an unhealthy fixation of the libido on the erotogenic zone at which the arrested development occurs and subsequent appearance as neurosis in adulthood (for a discussion of children's sexuality that includes historical evidence for changing values and beliefs, see Kehily and Montgomery, 2009).

Freud's work was not educational and is not directly concerned with pedagogy, but it emphasizes the importance of children's early upbringing and, in particular, the practices of the early years (Maynard and Thomas, 2004, pp. 42–3). Taking Freud seriously clearly places imperatives on early childhood education since those who deal with young children appear to be in greatest jeopardy of getting things wrong or of inducing lifelong neuroses or psychic disorders (Graham, 2009 p. 20). Freud and his followers' work also found resonance with progressive educators because he seems to justify their more intuitively formed concern with 'the whole child' as well as the implied advocacy of childhood as a period of life in its own right. Followers who were influenced by psychoanalysis include the clinicians Donald Winnicott and John Bowlby, whose promulgation of successful attachment as the foundation stone for healthy growth and psycho-social development continues to shape institutional practices and clinical diagnosis in early childhood (David, 2004, p. 33; Walkup et al., 2007, pp. 81–5).

Freud's disciple, Wilhelm Reich developed work on avoiding sexual repression and was for a time a great friend of the radical educationist A. S. Neill. Neill was committed to the doctrines of radical or *scientific* education and sought to take the doctrines of the progressives to their logical conclusion through the foundation of Summerhill School in 1921. The school's ethos was shot through with notions of freedom and the achievement of well-being for the psyche alongside the attainment of more conventional intellectual goals. Neill (1972) states in his autobiography that Reich would often say, 'Bend the tree when it is a twig and it will be bent when it is fully grown'; read as repression (bending) and resultant neurosis (being bent) this is emblematic for the importance of childhood for subsequent health and well-being, and offers a Freudian justification for the intuitions of child-centred, progressive education. For the progressives, Freud and his followers offered a vindication of their fear of the repressive, normalizing, stifling tendencies of society and its harmful effect upon the 'natural' child that goes back to Rousseau – Reich's 'twig and tree' organic metaphor could have come out of *Emile*.

Susan Isaacs: child observation, psychoanalysis and play

Susan Isaacs was a follower of Freud, but along with Melanie Klein challenged the male-centeredness that they saw in his work; both preferred to stress the mother-child relationship and the importance of a nurturing, maternal role in infant psychological development. Besides her contributions as a proponent of psychoanalytic theory, Isaacs was also an educationist who interpreted the pedagogical and curricular implications of what Freud had to say about children, their childhoods and the sorts of institutions that might foster learning and the development of the child to maturity.

Susan Fairhurst (later Isaacs) studied philosophy at the University of Manchester and the newly emerging science of psychology at Cambridge University – despite not being able to take a full degree because she was female. In 1924 she applied to undertake scientific work with young children at what was to be an experimental school in Cambridge called 'The Malting House School'. Her role was to 'conduct education' at the school but also carry out close observations on the children (Jackson, 2004, pp. 99–100; Graham, 2009).

Isaacs used the opportunity presented by the school to elaborate her theories on child development. Developmental theories of the child and the idea that the nature of the child can be described and theorized have become so completely assimilated into the practices of teachers and the structure of children's institutions that it is easy to overlook her importance in establishing new insights into children's education and development. Isaacs' work is placed in a tradition about children that certainly goes back to John Locke and *inter alia* embraces elements of Rousseau, Pestalozzi, Montessori, Freud and Dewey. These theorists shared a common belief that children impose a moral imperative for action in modernizing progressive societies, and that education should be one of the principal arenas for that action.

Between 1933 and 1943 Isaacs held a professorship at the University of London's Institute of Education and was able to influence educational practice and early years' policy, both through the books she wrote under her own name and the regular parental advice column she wrote for *The Nursery World* as 'Ursula Wise' (*ursa* is Latin for *bear*, hence her moniker translates as 'Wise Bear') (Graham, 2009, p. 208). Susan Isaacs' educational creed was summed up well when 'Ursula' wrote:

> The aim of education is to create people who are not only self-disciplined and free in spirit, gifted in work and enjoyment, worthy and desirable as persons, but also responsible and generous in social life, able to give and take freely from others, willing to serve social ends and to lose themselves in social purposes greater than themselves. (Isaacs in Gardener, 1969, p. 171)

Isaacs combined child observation and psychoanalytic theory to underpin many of the core, and frequently more intuitive insights found in earlier child development theorists and, like so many others, she places play at the centre of the child's development. Just as Freud had asserted the existence of a complex sexuality in children, Isaacs compounded this by arguing that children also possessed a complex inner life of emotions. As Drummond, (2000, p. 229) suggests, through play and its capacity to rehearse and express fantasy, children are able to construct a bridge between inner and outer worlds and set out on the path to becoming fully rational, expressive human beings with a capacity to exercise and receive compassion. As an educationist, the implications for schooling were that play, not formal instruction in English, mathematics or other subjects, should be squarely at the heart of both curriculum and pedagogy for young children. Furthermore, that what she called 'the child's joy of discovery' should serve along with play as the primal force that drives children to embrace the practical business of living and thereby, contingently, to discover a purpose for the more formal requirements of reading and writing (Llewellyn-Jones, 2004, pp. 195–6; Graham, 2009, pp. 203–4). It was not for the pedagogue to deny the place of mathematics, English or chemistry in the intellectual life of the child, but to structure and control an environment within which this instinctual propensity to discover would catalyse the child's learning – as an attempt to reconcile the nature of the child with its cultural environment this could have come from Rousseau's *Emile*. Isaacs was clearly at odds with the Elementary School tradition with its formal instrumentalism and passive view of the learner. However her work found approval in the mid-1960s' progressivism of the Plowden Report (CACE, 1967); moreover, the idea of play continues to animate resistance to what are seen as encroachments on the natural development of the Child by centralized curricula and institutional reform.

Reflection:

Do you think educators have responsibilities beyond just catalysing or facilitating learning? What if a child's 'joy of discovery' is not roused by the stimuli we offer?

Piaget and developmentalism

The separation of childhood as a distinct condition from the rest of humankind that finds expression in idealist constructions of the Child, gained impetus during the 1920s and 1930s through the work of a Swiss biologist named Jean Piaget (1896–1980). If scientific proof were required to show that childhood represents a qualitatively different domain to that of adulthood, Piaget appears to provide it through a theoretical schema that has become so engrained and naturalized that it passes as the indisputable truth about children and childhood. His ideas are given extra credibility through their derivation from empirical experiments, showing that children's thinking does not simply operate at a lower bandwidth than that of adults, but is qualitatively *different* (Prout and James, 1997, p. 11).

Piaget had studied Freud and worked in psychoanalytic clinics and was familiar with Freud's theory of infant sexuality and development. Although Piaget is frequently pigeonholed as a psychologist, this underplays his roots as a biologist (he published his first scientific paper at the age of ten – a single page description of an albino sparrow). He described himself as a 'genetic epistemologist'. By this he meant that his work sought to understand the biological roots of children's cognition and how they were expressed in a staged process of development leading to adulthood. Crucially his work is concerned with *how* young children think, rather than more conventional questions about *what* they think (Morgan, 2007, p. 65). Through a series of experiments involving jars of water, beads and models of mountains, Piaget suggested that children's thinking follows a progressive developmental path comprising four successive stages from birth to young adulthood. Furthermore, although the trajectory of the pathway leads to the acquisition of mature adult reason that looks very like Cartesian rationalism, at each stage children think and operate intellectually in ways that are qualitatively different from reasoning adults. Crucially, each stage must be entered into and completed if an adult rational capacity, identified as the stage of 'formal operations' is to be achieved. The necessity to be faithful to the sequential steps of each developmental stage is reinforced by the suggestion that these steps represent a natural order. Piaget's interests in natural history come through, especially the early influence of Levy-Bruhl who proposed the intriguing idea that the development of each human individual follows a sequence that retraces the evolution of the whole species, albeit over a much shorter period – an idea frequently formulated as *ontogenesis recapitulates phylogenesis* (Prout and James, 1997, p. 11; Mooney, 2000, pp. 59–81). In educational terms, Piaget's work suggests that it is not merely unhelpful to offer children tasks and material that they struggle with, but futile if they are at a 'developmental stage' that differs from the demands of the task.

The distinctive nature of childhood as a separate state from the rest of human life suggested by earlier theorists, for example, Pestalozzi, Froebel and Montessori (see Chapters 2 and 3), is affirmed by Piaget through the methods of experimental science. Thus he lends credence to the more intuitive insights of the progressives and those who sought to reconstruct childhood and childhood's institutions along these lines. Indeed, Piaget's work would be central to the construction of 'developmentalism' as the dominant ideology shaping the language and practices not only of the children's professions of care, paediatrics, education, law, child guidance and psychology, but also that of toy and clothing manufacturers as part of a global industry of childhood. Indeed, Hall (2000) has argued that in combination with Susan Isaacs, Piaget's work has exerted a profound and seminal influence on the emergence of new curricula for young children and cites their particular influence upon science education.

A further aspect of Piaget's work that appealed to the progressives was his emphasis on *activity* as the foundation for thought and that therefore underlines the merits of a pedagogy founded on discovery learning and activity methods rather than formal instruction (Bruce, 2006, pp. 98–99; Mooney,

2000 p. 61). Piaget therefore proposed that even those thoughts that seem most abstract and removed from the concrete world of empirical experience – justice, freedom and the divine – have their roots in the concrete world and in physical activity associated with it. Thus, if children's learning is to be effective, it must be rooted in concrete experience. This seemed to echo Rousseau's conviction that learning by doing was to be preferred over learning by being told and suggests an order of priority for the relationship between language and thought – a question that had been at the heart of Western philosophical enquiry since Descartes. By proposing that thought derives from action, the social medium of language is deemed less significant than the child's individual engagement with the world and his or her attempts to make conceptual sense of it. Piaget's child represents the apogee of the individualistic, interiorized view of human nature based on the cogito, and that has its roots in the Enlightenment project and Descartes' dualistic distinction between mind and matter.

Critics of Piaget, deploying feminist and post-colonial theory (Walkerdine, 1984; Burman, 1994), have pointed to an excessive Eurocentric and masculine emphasis found in his work, with individualism and rationality as the hallmarks of maturity and the presumed end point for the development of the Child (Walkerdine, 1984 and 2009; Burman, 1994; Prout and James, 1997; Jenks, 2005). Further, they doubt whether the unitary view of the Child at the heart of Piaget's work informs us about the diversely differing lives of real children (see Chapter 9).

Piaget's assertions about the relationship between thought and language and his emphasis on the individualized, rather than social, character of learning and concept formation, brought him into contention during his lifetime with a developmental psychologist working in the newly formed Soviet Union named Lev Vygotsky (Mooney, 2000, pp. 81–95; Daniels, 2001; Daniels et al., 2007; Walkup et al., 2007, pp. 52–8). Deriving inspiration from a reading of Marx, Vygotsky stressed the importance of language and social context in the construction of thought and the development of the child to maturity. Vygotsky died relatively young and was largely unknown in the West until Jerome Bruner introduced his works in the 1970s; therefore while Piaget is cited in the Plowden Report, the works of Vygotsky are absent. The emphasis upon the social nature of learning found a receptive audience among educators, especially as a post-Modern cast of mind came to prominence in Western intellectual life, so that as

Piaget's star has waned, so Vygotsky's has shone brighter. Arguably, the radical implications of Vygotsky's work frequently seem to go unrecognized, being presented as merely offering an alternative gloss on Piaget or as *Piaget plus*. However, his work represents a shift away from the stubborn dualisms, for example, mind–matter, individual–society, that have plagued Western thinking since the early Enlightenment, with profound implications for our view of human nature in general and how children construct their knowledge and understanding within networks of social relations, in particular. His work has more in common with the post-Enlightenment social constructionism of Wittgenstein and Heidegger than the rationalism that is at the heart of Piaget's work, and has exerted significant influence on social cognition theorists such as Lave and Wenger (1991).

Reflection:

Why do ideas rooted in science seem to exert so much purchase on our thinking?

John Dewey and the child-centred philosophy of education

John Dewey (1859–1952), a member of a largely American school of philosophy known as *philosophical pragmatism*, was a major contributor to the development of the social constructionist standpoint and an influential contributor to educational theories emerging during the 1920s and 1930s. For Dewey, like other social constructionists (see Introduction), knowledge is always referenced to the meanings shared in a social context, rather than to absolute, unchanging or essential truths; therefore they find it more helpful to speak of the world that is constructed around this knowledge as constituting a *social reality* rather than as *reality* without qualification. Therefore, philosophical pragmatists argue that whereas intellectual traditions, for example the scientific tradition, may suggest that we commit to theories and beliefs on the basis of whether or not they represent reality accurately, in practice, we commit to theories and beliefs that prove their *usefulness* to us (Rorty, 1999, p. 33). Rorty, a philosophical follower of Dewey, goes on to suggest that this is consistent with a recognition of the implications of Darwin's Theory of Evolution, namely, that we are evolved, clever and socially situated primates who are adept at finding and sharing smart ways to solve problems, whether these concern providing food and shelter on a day-to-day basis or explaining the big questions – birth, death and the meaning of the world. Moreover, that while it may be the solution to a problem that grabs our attention, the achievement of social cohesion and the cooperation necessary to solving it, is actually just as important. In educational terms, this means that the *processes* of inquiry by which social realities are constructed should demand our attention at least as much as the *products* that are their outcome (Russell, 1979, p. 777).

Dewey translates this process-based understanding into his educational philosophy; the child's impulse to inquire is bound up with growth and is entirely consistent with a philosophy that stresses the importance of the child being allowed to be a child. The education system, he argued, should embrace these impulses to growth as the core of a genuine child-centred approach rather than concentrate on the obsessive pursuit of what the child is to become, that is, with *futurity*. Dewey saw schooling as too preoccupied with learning knowledge that was external to the child rather than with a pedagogy that facilitates each child to mobilize its curiosity and learn through active discovery; for example, it is the difference between, on the one hand, being told to memorize the times table because it needs to be learnt, and on the other being offered experiences that lead to the discovery that the operation of multiplication can substitute for laborious repeated additions. But, for Dewey, an effective and pragmatic pedagogy should not ignore the important and powerful cultural heritage found in subject-knowledge; he does not see this in opposition to child-centredness. To make his point, Dewey contrasts strictly child-centred approach, wherein:

> The child is the starting point, the center, and the end. His development, his growth, is the ideal...To the growth of the child all studies are subservient; they are instruments valued as they serve the needs of growth...subject matter can never be got into the child from without. Learning is active. It involves reaching out of the mind....It is he and not the subject-matter which determines both quality and quantity of learning. (Dewey, 1902, p. 9)

with a more traditional subject-centred approach to the curriculum, in which:

> Subject-matter furnishes the end, and it determines the method. The child is simply the immature being who is to be matured; he is the superficial being who is to be deepened; his narrow experience which is to be widened. It is his to receive, to accept. His part is fulfilled when he is ductile and docile. (Dewey, 1902, p. 8)

Dewey seeks to identify a pedagogy that will bring these two into a state of resolution by challenging the assumption that child and curriculum are inevitably and unbridgeably opposed to one another (Lawton and Gordon, 2002, pp. 172–3; for full discussion of Dewey's philosophy, see Pring, 2007). Rather, he suggests that we view them as more fluid and open to active, reconstructive negotiation:

> Abandon the notion of subject-matter as something fixed and ready-made in itself, . . . cease thinking of the child's experience as something hard and fast; see it as something fluent, embryonic, vital and we realize that the child and the curriculum are simply two limits which define a single process. Just as two points define a straight line, so the present standpoint of the child and the facts and truths of studies define instruction. (Dewey, 1902, p. 11)

The challenge is familiar to any conscientious teacher who has tried to match subject matter (the thing to be learned) with the needs and capabilities of the learners (what they know and where they are 'at'). Even as excessive emphasis on subject matter risks overlooking the child's capacity to make sense of what is to be learnt, so being rigorously child-centred may curtail access to new ideas with the consequence that nothing substantially new is learnt.

Reflection:

. Look back at the passages from Rousseau's *Emile* in Chapter 1. Are there similarities between Dewey and what Rousseau proposes about how the teacher should unobtrusively facilitate the child's learning?

It should be noted that Dewey works from the assumption that the child has agency and an active disposition towards learning that enables him or her to negotiate over the meaning of subject matter in this way. Dewey derived inspiration from the American Froebelian kindergarten movement that had sought to articulate an appropriate interpretation of their guru's work, and in particular, from Froebel's stress on the importance of play. In return, the Froebelians and progressives welcomed the philosophical endorsement and fresh impetus that Dewey gave them; although it should be said that whereas Froebel's *Child* is conceived individualistically, Dewey's conception is rooted in a social view of human nature (Pring, 2007). He published his ideas in *The School and Society* (1899) and *The Child and Curriculum* (1902). However, it was Professor J. J. Findlay who introduced these works to UK readers in 1908 and Dewey would become one of the influences on the work of the Hadow committees that shaped new thinking about primary education in the United Kingdom (see Chapter 8 and Dearden, 1968, pp. 11–12).

Sir William Hadow and primary schooling with progressive accents

A glance at Dewey's dates puts him in the same generation as the McMillans and like them his work and influence comes to fruition during the first half of the twentieth century. Dewey is probably the major philosopher most directly identified with pedagogy and education (Russell, 1979, p. 774) and his ideas were certainly well received by the existing audience of progressive educators (Dearden, 1968, pp. 1–12). They also took root in a series of influential government reports that prepared the ground for the 1944 Education Act. These were the Hadow reports, the first of which appeared in 1926 and set out a blueprint for secondary education; the second, published in 1931, addressed elementary schooling and proposed its metamorphosis into the primary school of the post-war years; and the third, from 1933 examined the condition of nursery education.

Sir William Hadow (1859–1937) was an eminent academic musician and composer who had been Vice-Chancellor of both Durham and Sheffield Universities and chair of the Consultative Committee of the Board of Education.

Reflection:

Examine the brief biographies of William Forster (1870 Elementary Education Act – Chapter 6), Herbert Fisher (1918 Education Act – Chapter 6) and Sir William Hadow; Can you identify any similarities in their family, intellectual and social connections? Does this suggest that ideas concerning the *Child* and childhood had become the property of a particular cultural elite and also explain how they gain a hold on the imagination of the educational establishment? (see Chapter 2) Will elites always shape education?

The first report was commissioned by Ramsay McDonald's first Labour government, but its recommendations were shelved by the Conservative government that succeeded it. This report distinguished between the child of primary schooling and the state of adolescence and used this to propose a developmental rationale for distinctive educational and institutional provision. In a memorable passage, Hadow colourfully paraphrases Brutus in Shakespeare's Julius Caesar:

> There is a tide which begins to rise in the veins of youth at the age of eleven or twelve. It is called by the name of adolescence. If that tide can be taken at the flood, and a new voyage begun in the strength and along the flow of its current, we think that it will 'move on to fortune'. We therefore propose that all children should be transferred, at the age of eleven or twelve, from the junior or primary school either to schools of the type now called secondary...(The Hadow Report, 1931, in MacLure, 1986)

The Report appears to use 'primary', 'junior' and 'elementary' interchangeably. However, it is worth remarking that by standing these concepts alongside each other, some distinguishing differences begin to emerge. This process of distinguishing primary education from the elementary school tradition that became so important in framing the arguments of the post-war progressives, is taken a step further in this second Hadow Report (Board of Education, 1931). This report is subtitled 'The Primary School' and was commissioned by the Labour government that took over office in 1929. It is less celebrated than the earlier report but offers a broad sweep across educational provision for children under the age of 11 and 12. As such it represents the first coherent attempt to delineate the aims, character and curriculum of primary education to be found in a government document; subsequent echoes of Hadow are to be found in the Education Act of 1944 as well as the Plowden Report (CACE, 1967) and, more recently, the *Cambridge Education Review* (2009). Moreover, the influence of Dewey is plain:

> ...the curriculum of the primary school is to be thought of in terms of activity and experience rather than knowledge to be acquired and facts to be stored. (The Board of Education, 1931)

Further, the phrases constructed around active verbs in the following passage underline the commitment of Hadow to *activity methods* and to a view of the teacher as facilitator of the child as an active agent in the construction of their own learning:

> ...the primary school can do nothing more useful than **to help children gain** a thorough command of their mother tongue, **to use books freely** as a source of information and pleasure, and **to express their ideas readily** in writing. (Board of Education, 1931, 'The Hadow Report') (MacLure, 1986)

Besides Dewey, other contemporary thinkers on education and children that we have come across are cited in Hadow. Expert opinion and evidence was supplied by Sir Cyril Burt, the eminent educational psychologist, on intelligence and social deprivation and, as corollary, the appropriateness of distinctive schools and streaming to meet these needs. We also hear echoes of the Froebelians' insistence on play, practical activity and experiential discovery as justification for Hadow's view of the child as an active, agentic learner with a humanistic capacity for 'sympathy, social spirit and imagination'. Furthermore, a view of the school 'not as the antithesis of life, but as its complement and commentary' is promoted (Selleck, 1972, p. 123). The idea of the distinctive rather than diminished character of the pre-adolescent child is evident as Hadow is at pains to stress that the development of secondary schooling should not provide:

> an excuse for offering inferior accommodation to children under the age of eleven, nor...the view that classes in primary schools may properly be of a larger size than those in schools for children over the age of eleven...(Hadow, in MacLure, 1986)

Any assumption that 'younger equates to lesser' as justification for the continued subordination of childhood to adulthood, is thereby challenged – a view that the theoretical work of Piaget served to underline.

In an echo of Susan Isaacs' insistence upon useful and meaningful knowledge in the curriculum, the report warns against:

> ...inert ideas – that is, ideas which at the time when they are imparted have no bearing on a child's natural activities of body or mind and do nothing to illuminate or guide his experience. (Hadow, in MacLure, 1986)

By contrast the report advocates the 'good primary practice' that was the epistemological cornerstone of the progressives, and goes beyond the acquisition of basic skills to endorse education's role in facilitating children's entitlements as members of civil society, so that the primary school's:

> ...aim should be to develop in a child the fundamental human powers and to awaken him to the fundamental interests of civilized life so far as these powers and interests lie within the compass of childhood.... (Hadow, in MacLure, 1986)

The last phrase is significant and condenses much about the report's construction of the Child and childhood. The emphasis is on being a child, rather than becoming an adult – futurity can wait. This commitment to the validity of childhood in and of itself was compounded by the more detailed structural recommendations made for primary education by the report. Drawing on the arguments of developmental theorists (including Jean Piaget and Susan Isaacs), Hadow's report on the primary school (1931) advocated separate infant (5–7) and junior (7–11) primary schools with curricular provision to match these developmentally defined stages. At the junior stage the emphasis on activity and experience was discussed in relation to recognizable subjects. However, for the infants, Hadow recommended a curriculum organized under three broad, more experientially focused headings:

1. natural activities' – including play
2. expression training' – including handwork
3. formal instruction in the three Rs' (reading, writing and arithmetic).

However, the report was at pains to stress that formal instruction had no place for the under sixes (Whitbread, 1972). The latter proposal locates Hadow's imagined child well within the tradition of childhood discourse that stresses the natural and ordered unfolding of capabilities found in Rousseau and running through the work of Pestalozzi, Froebel, Piaget and Isaacs. We should note that whereas the recent *Cambridge Primary Review* (2009) echoes similar sentiments, the Early Years Foundation Stage has generated controversy precisely around this question of when formal learning should start (see the arguments of the Steinerians in Chapter 9).

Following the publication of the second Hadow Report on primary education, the committee went on to examine nursery schooling and published its third report in 1933. The emphasis was again progressive and it is clear that the welfare orientation of the McMillans is imprinted on its proposals. Miss Freda Hawtrey, a Hadow committee member, wrote in the report that although not wholly conceived on welfare grounds, the nursery school was:

> a desirable adjunct to the national system of education. In districts where the housing and general economic conditions are seriously below the average, a nursery school should, if possible, be provided....Apart from purely social and economic considerations model nursery schools for children from the age of two onwards are educationally desirable. (MacLure, 1986)

As we have seen, the impact of Hadow's three reports was limited at the time of publication. However, in this last report they maintained a consistent prescience. It would take until after the Second World War for the proposals to be realized, but realized they were, and the post-war history of education owes much to the foresight of Hadow's committees and their infusion of these new theories into the discourse of primary education – even if, in certain cases they generated controversy and subsequent conflict over educational aims and practices.

Reflection:

Many of these ideas rest on the presumption that it is important to identify and establish the right conditions for a good childhood so as to ensure growth to healthy adult maturity. Is this an argument for childhood as a state of 'being' in its own right or the futurity of 'becoming'? Can we have *being* without *becoming* or vice versa?

Further reading

Daniels, H. (2001), *Vygotsky and Pedagogy*, London: Routledge.

Daniels, H., Cole, M. and Wertsch, J. V. (2007), *The Cambridge Companion to Vygotsky*, Cambridge: Cambridge University Press.

Drummond, M. J. (2000), 'Susan Isaacs: pioneering work in understanding children's lives', in Hilton, M. and Hirsch, P. (eds), *Practical Visionaries: Women, Education and Social Progress, 1790–1930*, Harlow: Longman.

Mooney, C. G. (2000), *Theories of Childhood: An Introduction to Dewey, Montessori, Erikson, Piaget and Vygotsky*, St Paul, MN: Redleaf Press.

Palmer, J. (ed.) (2001), *Fifty Major Thinkers on Education*, London: Routledge.

Pring, R. (2007), *John Dewey: A Philosopher of Education for Our Time*, London: Continuum.

Ross, A. (2000), *Curriculum Construction and Critique*, London: Routledge.

Russell, B. (1979), *A History of Western Philosophy*, London: Counterpoint.

Slavin, R. E. (2009), *Educational Psychology: Theory and Practice*, New Jersey: Pearson.

Thurschwell, P. (2000), *Sigmund Freud*, London: Routledge.

Website

John Dewey: Progressive Education in the 1940s:www.youtube.com/watch?v=opXKmwg8VQM&feature=related, last accessed 17 December 2010.

8

The Shape of Jazz to Come: Plowden, Progressivism and Discourses of Difference

Introduction

Despite endorsement by establishment figures such as Fisher and Hadow, the ideas of the progressives concerning curricula and pedagogy made little impact on State schooling until the late 1950s and the 1960s when the agnosticism of the 1944 Education Act concerning the curriculum facilitated manifold possibilities for improvisation, experiment and development. This era saw the most sustained attempt to bring the progressive vision for the child together with mass schooling and despite being widely regarded as an apparent failure, the experiments in pedagogy, curriculum development, school-building and teacher education that it saw, continue to shape educational debates, policy and the professional consciousness of teachers.

Changing times and child-centredness

When Ornette Coleman produced his iconoclastic album entitled 'The Shape of Jazz to Come' in 1959 and Bob Dylan sang 'The Times They are a-Changing' in 1964,they each offered anthems for times of social, political and techno-logical change, as anti-establishment movements demanding civil rights and nuclear disarmament were on the march, fuelled, in part, by an expansion in higher education for the baby-boom generation. Guidance manuals on child rearing had become best-sellers through the work of Dr Benjamin Spock; and, popular culture flooded print, radio and television media with sport, music and fashion, creating its own celebrities along the way.

The cultural world of children was not immune to these changes, and con-flicts over the proper place of culture in children's lives had been ongoing cer-tainly since the Walt Disney film factory first brought Mickey Mouse (1928) and Snow White (1937) to cinemas and drew in huge youthful audiences. The creation of a popular cinematic culture for mass consumption by children seemed to challenge the cosier, middle-class storybook world of E. Nesbit (*The Railway Children* – 1905), Frances Hodgson Burnett (*The Secret Garden* – 1910), Arthur Ransome (*Swallows and Amazons* – 1930), and their like. Although frequently given by aunts and uncles at Christmas and on birthdays, books by these icons of children's literature were probably actually read by very few children; their worthiness was beyond question, but compared with watching the movie, they represented hard work. Anxiety about the growing influence of popular culture in children's lives, and even schooling, is a theme that, as we shall see later in this chapter, Plowden (CACE, 1967) touched upon.

However, the cultural politics of childhood were not confined to those identified strictly as children. When Joni Mitchell sang 'I came upon a child of God, he was walking along the road…' as the opening lines of her anthem for the Woodstock pop festival of 1968, she was speaking for a hippy genera-tion who identified re-admission to the Garden of Eden as a duty to be pur-sued and a return to the innocent verities of childhood as their desired state (Mitchell, 1969; Young, 2010).

Along with these changing convictions about the culture of childhood and its popular currency, there were also significant changes in the educational orthodoxy and convictions of many educators. The introduction of longer training courses and wider access to universities and degrees were changing the status of State-school teachers, advisers and educationists. Many of these felt empowered beyond mere day-to-day classroom matters and welcomed the professional legitimacy afforded by progressives' theorization and doctrinal certainties (see George Baines' obituary later in this chapter and Burke, 2009). It was also the case that the widespread, although not total, abolition of the 11+ and the move towards comprehensive schooling had removed the pressure both to teach for the test and to stream by 'ability' in the primary school. Furthermore, despite other changes that were underway, the 1944 Education (Butler) Act still held sway and ensured that substantial control over questions of curriculum and pedagogy was retained by headteachers and their staff.

The cultural pressures for change both in children's lives and on conventional educational institutions were, with great prescience, identified by Marshall McLuhan as the product of an incipient electronic revolution, he wrote:

> Today's television child is attuned to up-to-the-minute 'adult' news – inflation, rioting, war, taxes, crime, bathing beauties - and is bewildered when he enters the nineteenth century environment that still characterizes the educational establishment where information is scarce but ordered and structured by fragmented, classified patterns, subjects, and schedules. (McLuhan and Fiore, 1967, p.1 8)

Thus it is that a new educational radicalism focused on the Child and highly critical of traditional schooling emerged, but one whose pedigree extended like the links of a chain back, deep into the Enlightenment and the work of Locke, Rousseau, Froebel, Dewey and Isaacs. It should be said that, despite the romanticism of many adherents of the coming child-centred educational revolution, others point more pragmatically to the galvanic effect on the North American imagination of the launch of Sputnik by the Soviets in 1957 – it seemed that the United States risked slipping behind technologically, and the work of theorists, including progressives such as Piaget and Dewey, was recruited to restore the intellectual edge of American schooling in mathematics and science (Griffiths and Howson, 1974).

By contrast, there was another strand to the construction of the cultural world of childhood that excited huge interest by those wishing to champion a less commercial or technological conception of the Child and that challenged the institutionalization of childhood by schooling. Children's folklore seemed rooted in their everyday world and studying it appeared to tap into an old, deeply rooted and naturalized childhood culture. The ethnographic work of Iona and Peter Opie was central to this as between 1951 and 1959 they assembled *The Lore and Language of Schoolchildren* as their seminal work. The authors are at pains to stress that the copious material found in the book comes outside the world of the school; the précis on the dust-jacket of the first edition is eloquent in expressing not only what the book is about, but also the meaning and importance the authors attach to the material and to their work:

> Based on information collected during the past eight years from five thousand children in England, Scotland, and Wales, this volume is a disclosure of the lore and language natural to the modern schoolchild when out of school. It is a record of his strange and primitive culture, including seasonal customs, initiation rites, superstitious practices and beliefs, innumerable rhymes and chants (800 are given here in full), catcalls and retorts, stock jokes, ruderies, riddles, slang-epithets, nicknames, and the traditional juvenile argot which continues to flourish in street and playground, largely unknown and certainly unheeded by the adult world. Indeed this study, which describes, for instance, the omens children observe on the way to school, and the traditional pranks they play on householders after dark, is the first full survey of the subject to have been made. Further, the historical annotation throughout the work reveals that many of the formulas children use today, for example when begging, fighting, pulling hair, and denouncing a sneak, are the same as they have been for generations; and the comparative lore which has been assembled from other countries, particularly the United States, establishes that much of the schoolchild's chant and custom is international. (Opie and Opie, 1959, dust jacket)

We might note several things here: the apparent opposition of this folk-world of childhood to the institution of school; its opposition to the adult world; the claims to authenticity deriving from the antiquity of the content and themes; and, the claims to universality – all of which conspired to support the revival of romantic conceptions of the Child as the authentic foundation for a good childhood.

Reflection:

Why do you think traditional folk forms with no traceable authorship and apparently transmitted from generation to generation aurally, such as those collected by the Opies, offered a construction of childhood that appealed to and confirmed the convictions of the educational progressives?

Plowden: the child and social justice

It is at this juncture that in 1967 we see the publication of a highly influential, yet also controversial report from the Central Advisory Council for Education (CACE), under the aegis of the DES, entitled 'Children and their primary schools', but more popularly known as the Plowden Report (CACE, 1967) after Lady Bridget Plowden, the CACE's Chair. The report represents the high-water mark for official sanction of progressivism in the State educational system and the best attempt to date to marry the universal provision of the State primary system with the pedagogic and curricular traditions of the progressives that had hitherto largely either been confined to the private sector or curtailed by being seen as only suitable for very young children.

The Plowden Report (CACE, 1967) has come to be identified with its advocacy of child-centred education and, therefore, primarily as a lengthy essay on curriculum and pedagogy in part because this is where its many opponents, such as the authors of the Black Papers (e.g. Cox and Dyson, 1970), concentrated their fire. However, the full terms of reference for the report stressed that it was to be an enquiry into the social circumstances of schooling and, in particular, the mitigation of poverty and what it called 'cultural deprivation'. Therefore, it is important to stress that curricular and pedagogic advances are presented as means to this end and not an end in themselves. As Jones puts it, from the Plowden Committee's point of view the access that educational changes were opening up:

> ... was not enough. To open nursery schools, or to abolish selection at 11 or to raise the school-leaving age were from this point of view necessary measures, but not sufficient. (Jones, K., 2003, p.83)

The emphasis placed on the social geography of State schooling is reinforced by the aerial photographs of schools in their urban and suburban contexts bound into the report – a very 'sixties' collectivist message that progressive social and educational development goes hand in hand with progressive, rationally executed Town and Country Planning. Furthermore, it suggested that the pursuit of equality of opportunity may be insufficient because of its built-in tendency to produce unequal outcomes – no doubt mindful of the shortcomings of the 1944 Education Act and its tripartite system – so that releasing the potential within children may also need to be accompanied by what was then a new administrative principle of 'positive discrimination' and therefore it advocated the identification of Educational Priority Areas (EPAs) to achieve this (CACE, 1967, paragraph 151).

> ## Reflection:
>
> Have we witnessed this attempted concatenation of progressive educational themes and social justice objectives before?

However, although there is a social message in Plowden, the report enshrines the *Child* as the wellspring for its priorities through the oft-quoted credo:

> At the heart of the educational process lies the child. No advances in policy, no acquisitions of new equipment have their desired effect unless they are in harmony with the nature of the child, unless they are fundamentally acceptable to him. (The Plowden Report - CACE, 1967, paragraph 9)

The report is at pains to establish the Child and the idea that *he* has an inviolable nature as the still centre around which everything else should revolve. It is a truism that the male pronoun was routinely used as catch-all during this era; however, its use also points to the assumption that the concept of the Child represents a unitary, universal and naturalized reality– thus, to switch from 'he' to 'he or she' is not merely a matter of gender 'hygiene', but challenges the validity of universalist assumptions and implicitly proposes a more complex relationship between childhood and other sociological variables such as gender – and, as we shall see, by extension ethnicity.

It should also be stressed that the attempt to combine child-centred, progressive pedagogy with the provision of equality of opportunity and its concomitant, social mobility, had a long pedigree. Despite the fact that their methods had been most enthusiastically received and patronized by the middle classes, Pestalozzi, Froebel, Montessori and, of course, the McMillan sisters had all sought to make progressive methods available to the children of the poor and thereby, pursue greater social justice.

Plowden acknowledges the influence of the Hadow Reports of 1926, 1931 and 1933 on State education (Board of Education, 1926, 1931 and 1933), asserting that Sir Henry Hadow 'has the right to be regarded as the architect of the English educational system as we know it'. Indeed, the report suggests that as the first major review of primary education since the 1930s, Plowden's task was to assess how far the intentions of Hadow had been realized. Thus, Plowden represents a direct extension from Hadow's emphasis upon activity and learning through experience and his desire to see a genuine primary education emerge from the straitening regime found in most elementary schools. However, Plowden was able to illustrate its discussion of child-centredness through examples of what progressive primary schooling actually looked like. This is because a significant body of practitioners were implementing, or attempting to implement, the vision and the numerous photographs bound into the report underline the point.

Before examining one such practitioner, it is worth reflecting on the irony that just as Plowden articulates a universalist construction of the child, the report's interest in the amelioration of poverty and the pursuit of social justice through positive discrimination, tends towards a more sociological understanding and a construction of the child that is enmeshed with social class. As Britain's State-school classrooms became more obviously multiracial (Troyna and Williams, 1986) and as feminist critiques (e.g. Walkerdine, 1984) began to take hold, tensions emerged around whether child-centred pedagogy was neutral with respect to ethnicity and gender and therefore had the capacity to promote social justice; indeed, was it meaningful to speak of the *Child* as a unitary, naturalized presence at the 'heart of the educational process...'? (CACE, 1967, paragraph 9). We shall examine some of these critics later.

Plowden: a 'progressive' at work

Typical of the progressives, was George Baines, one of a generation of headteachers who through the 1950s and 1960s were instrumental in introducing broadly 'child-centred' methods into primary school practice and who is cited as having contributed evidence in person to the Plowden committee (CACE, 1967). The fact that headteachers would or could count themselves as educationists and innovators in matters curricular and pedagogic, is in itself indicative of the prevailing professional, intellectual and even political climate surrounding education under the aegis of the 1944 Act. In other words, although the Act established a national system, it was at pains to ensure that decisions concerning teaching and teachers were made as close as possible to the point of their impact and by the very people who were responsible for their intervention. Matheson (2004) has described this as a 'national system, locally administered'. Therefore, curriculum and pedagogy were the concern of the school and even LEAs and their advisers (later to take on a more authoritarian mantle as 'inspectors' in a signal change following the 1988 Education Reform Act and the advent of the inspection regime that accompanied the establishment of the Office for Standards in Education, more recognizable via its acronym, OFSTED) had to tread diplomatically when seeking to influence school practice at this micro level.

Baines became headteacher of Brize Norton Primary School and then Eynsham County Primary School in Oxfordshire during the 1960s just before Plowden's publication. At the heart of his and other progressives' philosophy was the belief that education should be dictated by the needs of the child and not the convenience of the teachers. Clearly there are echoes of Rousseau, Froebel and Dewey's respective constructions of the Child in his philosophy (CACE, 1967, paragraph 9; Burke, 2009).

Baines believed that if the children's needs were paramount, then the teacher's vocational task was to offer themselves to the children in pursuit of the fulfilment of those needs:

> I am sure that teaching is an art and that teachers are artists. The teacher teaches what he is, more than what he knows, and as an artist, involved and giving of himself with love. (Burke, 2009)

The implicit anti-instrumentalism here and the suggestion that teachers' vocation is to give themselves with 'love', connects us again to the rather numinous and holistic spirituality of Pestalozzi and Froebel. Aspects of Baines' philosophy were expressed in a sloganizing, almost formulaic fashion. He proposed that there were six 'selves' to be acquired in order by the children – *self-awareness, self-confidence, self-direction, self-discipline, self-criticism and self-esteem* and that these would attained through the exercise of three 'I's – *industry, integrity and imagination* (Burke, 2009). However, his work was not narrowly conceived and he was at pains to stress the importance of constructing physical and social environments that could foster learning. He was concerned with school layouts, furnishings and the regulation of time and learning space through timetabling. His innovations in the spatial arrangement of his school brought him to the attention of educational architects and gave him direct influence over the design and building of a new school at Eynsham, Oxfordshire, England that would embody his ideas about children and effective learning. Catherine Burke continues in his obituary (*The Guardian*, 28 October 2009):

> George wanted the building itself to be a kind of teacher, with a 'geography' that the children could understand, and with as wide a variety of spaces as possible supporting different kinds of activity. Under the guidance of Edith Moorhouse, a senior adviser for primary schools in Oxfordshire, the design of the school became a model for others to follow with its vertical groupings of children – groups of mixed ages within the whole primary range of 5-11 – domesticated 'home bays' with cooking areas, 'book corners' for quiet study, and separate bays for art, craft and nature study.

Architects took up the ideas and Eynsham offered a blueprint for the open-plan primary school with its flexible closures and child-friendly facilities. Indeed, open plan became the standard solution to the challenges of bringing curriculum, pedagogy and environment into an integrated facilitative whole for subsequent generations of primary school children and teachers. Whether all teachers felt comfortable with the new arrangements is a moot point and many retained enough scepticism about the new pedagogy and its claim to be the beginning and end of 'good primary practice' to ensure that sliding screens were largely left closed and child-friendly spaces were only used if they could be surveyed by the teacher's eye. The romantic faith in the virtuous nature of the child was not shared by all.

Reflection:

Do teachers still construct themselves as educationists in the way that George Baines did?

Post-Plowden: the critics and opponents begin to circle

Despite being welcomed by many educationists, Plowden was not received sympathetically in all quarters. The subordination of children's futurity (or what it was to become) to childhood conceived as a state in its own right, seemed to a gathering band of critics to underplay the importance of real concerns including employability and the importance of being able to read, write and perform calculations effectively. The idea that the prioritization of creativity and choice would lend learning such purpose and meaning that skill acquisition would follow naturally (rather than the other way around) was challenged by critics and opponents, who were dubbed as knowledge-centred traditionalists by the progressives (who were, of course, by contrast child-centred). These critics found a voice through the publication of a series of 'Black Papers' by the right-wing *Critical Quarterly Society* (e.g. Black Paper Two, Cox and Dyson, 1970) in the late 1960s and early 1970s. Many of the arguments and contributors found in the Papers would become central to education policy during the Thatcher years. Contributors included the novelist Kingsley Amis and poet Philip Larkin, each of whom had perfected a particular brand of irritability, as well as educationists, the psychologists Sir Cyril Burt and Hans Eysenck and the Conservative politician Angus Maude who made the most of his party's period of opposition by opposing progressivism (Race, 2001).Often the tone was splenetic and combative, seemingly as concerned to prop up existing establishment practices and institutions as critique the arguments of the progressives. What surfaced as a conflict of educational ideology may have been as much about generational differences between those who had fought the Second World War and youthful progressives riding the economic buoyancy of the sixties (Young, 2010, p. 326).

It should be added that proponents of a progressive transformation in the nation's schooling frequently justified their convictions by identifying with the social justice mission that Plowden had articulated and were keen to emphasize the conservative instincts and Conservative political affiliations of their opponents. However, Labour politicians, including Cabinet minister Anthony Crosland, were also critics of progressivism. Those with working-class roots felt that they owed their social mobility to the opportunities for a formal, classical-humanist and didactic education found in the institutions invented by the 1944 Act. For them social change required working-class children to be given the levers of power through access to the professions and they suspected that progressivism offered merely access to a romantic backwater of hazy self-realization.

In actuality the heyday of Plowden-esque practice based on discovery methods and child-centred practice was short-lived. Research by Bennett (1976) showed that there seemed to be few tangible educational benefits for pupils taught under progressive regimes. Certainly (and crucially) on an emotional level children may be more anxious and hence worse off than their more formally educated peers. Ross (2000) notes that Bennett's (1976) findings made headline news – such was the appetite of newspaper editors and proprietors for these sort of findings. However, when a few years later Bennett felt compelled to re-examine his data, he found the picture it painted less clear-cut – needless to say, the papers paid little or no interest to a more nuanced or uncertain conclusion.

Despite equivocation over Bennett's findings, the tide was turning on progressivism at a policy level in State education. With the advent of the National Curriculum in England and Wales in 1988 (HM Government, 1988), the *Child* that is essential to Plowden's world view has been supplanted by the *pupil*. To be a pupil is to possess a status that is fully assimilated to the world of school, that is, in turn, the dominant institution other than home and family in defining the meaning of childhood. To be a good pupil is to be punctual, obedient, willing and industrious while climbing the ladder of knowledge, skills and understanding set out by the curriculum.

As a further response to this changing environment, progressive educational practice in its purest form became largely restricted to early childhood, the area that had been its heartland since the failure of the Froebelians (see Chapters 2 and 3) to make headway against the utilitarian tendencies of State education from the 1870s.

Reflection:

Why do you think the case for child-centred and progressive educational methods becomes harder to make as children grow older? Are there any discourses of childhood operating to shape thinking here?

The politics of the whole child: discrimination and difference

If Plowden attempted to usher an era when the central working assumption of primary education was the necessity of *starting with the child* or being *child-centred*, then by the early 1970s it was becoming increasingly obvious to some observers that some children were never placed at the centre of curricular or pedagogic decisions. This crystallized in the publication in 1971 of a seminal indictment of the treatment of black pupils in British schools by the community activist, politician and academic Bernard Coard, with the challenging title: *How the West Indian Child is Made Educationally Subnormal in the British School System: the Scandal of the Black Child in Schools in Britain.*

As a community activist, teacher, politician and academic, Coard had worked with many children and young people who had been categorized in contemporary parlance as Educationally Subnormal commonly abbreviated to ESN – a term that lost currency following the Warnock Report (DES, 1978). His work had led to the growing conviction that special education, and ESN schools in particular, was being used 'as a convenient dumping ground for black children who were anything but "educationally subnormal"' (Coard, 2005). However, Coard had no hard data and struggled to see how he could bring the matter to wider attention. Then in 1970 an *internal* report from the Inner London Education Authority (ILEA) about all of its Special schools and their pupils was leaked to him.

This report gave him the data he sought, and he set about compiling his book over the summer months of 1970, 'By the time the summer was over I had written 210 typewritten pages, outlining the many problems black children were facing, why, and what I felt should be done about them' (Coard, 2005). It is at this point that Coard decided that his book's title should directly address black parents as a 'call to action'. Initially, publication was not easy; however, he was at length helped by media experts and community activists to place the pamphlet in influential hands. The result was extraordinary as every newspaper covered it 'positively and accurately in its news and in many of its columns'; radio and TV talk shows invited Coard to discuss his work and the BBC made a series of documentaries prompted by its findings. Further, *The Guardian* published a complete and crucial chapter of the book on its editorial page. Coard tells of how the educational 'establishment' response evolved:

> The first was to rush out their spoke[s]persons to deny everything. At first, they said on radio and TV that the book was 'a pack of lies'. Within days, based on the feedback they were getting, and the fact that I would read directly from their 'internal' report on the electronic media, they amended their position to: 'There is some truth in it, but most of it consists of lies'. By the third week of sustained publicity following the book's publication, they had moved to say 'most of it contains some truth, but there are many untruths too'. By the end of six months following

> publication, they had surrendered. It was now acknowledged to be 'accurate', and was now 'recommended reading' at Teachers Colleges and Schools of Education in many parts of the country! (Coard, 2005)

The findings of Coard's book set an agenda for future debate over the subject of 'race' and opportunity in British schools and, as he had hoped, had a galvanic effect upon the community of black parents:

> The black community's response to the book was incredible. Thousands of black parents in small groups throughout the country began meeting, and several parents' groups were formed. Black supplementary schools were formed up and down the country. Some estimates put the number of these schools at as many as 150. Black youth groups were formed, and existing ones held regular discussions on the scandal and what their members could do to help. (Coard, 2005)

Moreover, it challenged the legitimacy of a unitary view of the *Child* with quite specific ramifications. First, it opened up a different perspective on the experience children had of their childhood, and suggested that the relationship between childhood and other sociological variables, such as ethnicity, could not be overlooked. Second the proposition that there was a universally effective pedagogy designed around the characteristics of a romantically conceived child looked distinctly ethnocentric; but more importantly, and as a stinging challenge to the educational establishment, racist practices were deeply inscribed in schooling and made education distinctly unequal and discriminatory. The book's assertion that there is a 'West Indian child' takes hold of the language of identity and with it the agenda of debates around difference as a sociologically and politically informed notion. The effect is to begin to destabilize the *Child* as a unitary construct.

Coard's book certainly painted a signally different picture of education and schooling from that found in the Plowden Report (CACE, 1967), published just four years earlier. In chapter 6 of Plowden, the committee sought to address the 'Children of Immigrants' (it should be noted that statistics used in the report classified a child born in the United Kingdom to parents who had entered the country after 1955 as actually an 'immigrant child'!). Plowden's treatment is couched heavily in terms of the *problems* schools and teachers are presented with by parents and children as a consequence of immigration, there is no acknowledgement that schools themselves may be the problem. Further, racism is conceived as something that is located in the 'prejudices' of the adult world beyond the school gate, but not inside and certainly runs

counter to its romantically optimistic construction of the Child and its natural virtue:

> Most experienced primary school teachers do not think that colour prejudice
> causes much difficulty. Children readily accept each other and set store by other
> qualities in their classmates than the colour of their skin. Some echoes of adult
> values and prejudices inevitably invade the classroom but seldom survive for long
> among the children. It is among the neighbours at home and when he begins
> to enquire about jobs that the coloured child faces the realities of the society
> into which his parents have brought him. (The Plowden Report - CACE, 1967,
> paragraph 179)

It is assumed that the *Child* with its presumed natural innocence is the
key actor around which children's cultural worlds revolve. Thus imbued
by Rousseau's notion of innate moral virtue the children are on the one
hand irreproachable, but also are prey to the pernicious effects of faulty
socialization. Despite the 'colour-blindness' of children and schooling that
the report claims, it broadly endorses one of the most controversial policies conceived as a way to engineer racial *integration* (see Mullard, 1985
for a discussion of the evolution of Home Office policy on race from the
late 1950s up to the 1980s; Sarup, 1986; Race, 2010). This is the policy of
'dispersal' which meant bussing pupils from their home communities and
schools because:

> When the concentration of non-English speaking children in a particular school
> reaches a level which seems to interfere with the opportunity for other children
> to learn, or with the teacher's ability to do justice to the immigrant children, there
> may be a demand for dispersal of the immigrants. The Secretary of State for
> Education and Science in Circular 7/65, advised local authorities to avoid heavy
> concentrations of immigrants in particular schools. (The Plowden Report – CACE,
> 1967, paragraph 193)

This policy was unsurprisingly controversial and mindful of this, the report
was keen to stress that 'Children should be given special consideration on
account of their language and other difficulties and not on account of their
colour' (The Plowden Report – CACE, 1967, paragraph 194). In practice, skin
colour rather than whether a child was an 'immigrant' per se, was the reason
for the policy and therefore for deciding whether a particular child should be
'dispersed'. The report also, however, cites a somewhat equivocal objection

to the practice by a teacher described as having: 'long experience in a notoriously deprived district', who wrote:

> We have to accept that there are going to be schools in many of our cities with an intake largely coloured....Dispersal at the primary stage, except on a limited geographical basis, is administratively difficult and psychologically unsound. (The Plowden Report – CACE, 1967, paragraph 194)

In this, Plowden reinforces a construction of the child that is rooted in the universalism of the progressive tradition and is re-articulated through the psychological individualism of theorists such as Piaget (see earlier chapters). In consequence, the policy is primarily interpreted with an eye to the harm it might do to the well-being and self-concept of the child, not because of broader social injustices that it propagates and entrenches or the damage done to community relations. The language is of problems and it is the responsibility of the parents and pupils from black and minority ethnic backgrounds to resolve it by accepting dispersal as a policy and practice.

Typical of the effect of the policy was the experience of one young man from Bradford growing up in the 1960s. He describes the way in which his 'dispersal' was justified by the authority's assessment of him as a non-English speaker 'when in fact, English was the only language I could speak!' (Channel 4, 1989) Clearly, in this case Plowden's assertion that the main criterion for 'bussing' should be linguistic, served as a fig leaf for discrimination on the basis of skin colour.

Plowden is far from alone in the emphasis it places on the psychological and individualistic notions of self-concept and self-esteem in explaining the educational performance of children and young people from black and minority ethnic backgrounds. These ideas were also reinforced by Milner (1975) who had undertaken research into children's racial attitudes and sought to explain how children's identities were formed. The broad proposition of the work was that black children internalize the overwhelmingly negative cultural environment of a predominantly white society and that this is expressed as a negative, self-deprecating view of themselves and of black culture. It would then follow that, if true, the curriculum and schooling should seek to compensate for this by concentrating on emotional or affective goals in order to redress the problem. From the late 1960s we therefore see the emergence of special curricular areas, notably Black Studies in order to build the pride and self-esteem that is supposedly so lacking. We should note that 'the problem' is constructed almost entirely in terms of the individual children. It is seen as an expression of their pathology rather than as a question of inequality and racial prejudice from other individuals or the institutions within which the children live and grow. It should be noted that whereas black young people were having their problems with self-esteem addressed in Black Studies, their peers were studying more traditional curriculum subjects, such as mathematics, science or history. (Sarup, 1986). The actual reinforcement of inequity through the supposed compensatory practices of the institution is glaring and obvious!

Milner's (1975) findings were refuted in an influential study undertaken by Maureen Stone. Stone (1981) assembled evidence to show that the need for 'multi-racial education' that included curricular interventions such as Black Studies, was wrongly conceived and based upon psychologistic arguments about self-esteem that were empirically unsupported. By contrast, evidence from a close examination of other institutions such as supplementary and community schools demonstrated that there was no problem with self-esteem among young black people, but that it was the schools and their unquestioned practices that required attention. She revealed Black Studies as more about a solution to the challenges presented by young black males than an attempt to compensate their low self-image. Stone concludes her study with an indictment of much that is sacred to liberal, child-centred educational orthodoxy:

> ...self-concept research and theory and teaching styles based on these ideas have little to contribute towards an understanding of how West Indian children in Britain should be educated, and may have contributed towards the low attainment of such children – because they stress affective goals of self-expression, self-fulfilment, happiness and so on as the basis of their teaching methods. It has been suggested that teaching methods associated with mastery of skills and knowledge and the development of abilities should be substituted for affective-type goals which are vague, and give teachers access to aspects of pupil personality which should be private, extending teacher control of areas of pupil personality which are unnecessary for instructional purposes. Whilst not decrying all attempts at curriculum innovation and creativity, the need for schools to retain a commitment to the mastery of basic intellectual skills and competencies by all children has been expressed. (Stone, 1981, pp. 253–4)

The progressives' notion that the school should concern itself with the *whole child* is openly questioned. Further, Stone (1981) implies that limits should be placed on the State's involvement in the lives and education of children and young people, so that schools should discharge their educational responsibilities towards the child but not transgress territory that really is not their concern. This mounts a challenge both to the universalist theoretical assumptions underlying progressivism that had acquired widespread consent within public education, and to the right of the State to impose an increasingly compulsory and intrusive relationship upon children and their families. Coard and Stone were thus significant contributors to emerging discourses that stressed difference and thus, in turn, to the work of Prout and James (1997) who with others sought to liberate real children from being 'abandoned in theory' (Jenks, 2005, p. 23). We shall look at their work in the next chapter.

Reflection:

Plowden sought social justice armed with a universal concept of the *Child*; but Stone suggests that the acknowledgement of difference is crucial. Do you think the cause of social justice is better served by a concept of universal rights founded on the Enlightenment idea of the *Child* or by the recognition of particular differences in children's childhood experiences based on class, ethnicity and gender? Can you have both?

Further reading

Claire, H. (2004), *Not Aliens: Primary School Children and the Citizenship/PSHE Curriculum*, Stoke: Trentham.

Griffiths, M. and Troyna, B. (eds) (1995), *Antiracism, Culture and Social Justice in Education*, Stoke: Trentham.

Jones, K. (2003), *Education in Britain: 1944 to the Present*, London: Polity Press.

Race, R. (2010), *Multiculturalism and Education*, London: Continuum.

Robinson, K. and Jones Diaz, C. (2006), *Diversity and Difference in Early Childhood Education: Issues for Theory and Practice*, Maidenhead, UK: Open University Press.

Ross, A. (2000), *Curriculum Construction and Critique*, London: Routledge.

Sarup, M. (1986), *The Politics of Multiracial Education*, London: Routledge & Kegan Paul.

9

Can Things Only Get Better? New Labour, Quality of Life and Beyond

Introduction

When Marshall McLuhan prophesied that growing up was the new work, he must have had early twenty-first century childhood in mind. With the optimism that accompanied the election of the first UK Labour Government for 18 years in 1997 came an invigorated commitment to do something about the state of childhood in Britain, and particularly child poverty.

The United Nations Convention on the Rights of the Child (UNCRC): universal rights and difference

Although introduced some eight years earlier in 1989, the United Nations Convention on the Rights of the Child (UNCRC) is vital to understanding the intellectual and legal landscape within which the New Labour government elected in 1997 was operating. By definition, the child and its rights are core constructs for the UNCRC and when the United Nations General Assembly endorsed these constructs in November 1989 it placed them on an equal legal footing with those for generic human rights. The terms for these rights are proclaimed as:

> ... children's right to enjoy leisure, recreation and cultural activities; their right to enjoy and practice their own culture, religion and language without fear of persecution or discrimination; and their right to privacy, protection and autonomy. (MacNaughten and Smith, 2009, p. 162)

Furthermore, the Convention confirms the participatory rights of children to freedom of expression, especially over matters affecting them. Crucially for education, in Article 29 the UNCRC asserts that 'the education of the child shall be directed to...

> The development of the child's personality, talents and mental and physical abilities to their fullest potential; ... respect for the child's parents, his or her own cultural identity, language and values... The preparation of the child for responsible life in a free society ....(UNCRC, 1989, Article 29)

There are three points we can tease out from these clauses. First we see a commitment to the idea of development that understands children's intellectual, moral and, some would say, spiritual growth as happening in parallel to physical growth. Second, however, this apparent naturalization of emotional and intellectual change is counterbalanced by reference to the social worlds within which children live and the importance of the cultural stock they derive from them. Third, the statement embodies a hefty chunk of futurity in expressing the need to prepare children to take their place in society.

If there are core values for educational constructions of the *Child* in the early twenty-first century then the ideas of *development, cultural context* and *futurity* found in the UNCRC statement could make a strong claim to primacy; moreover they seem pretty incontestable. Nevertheless, these values may not be entirely congruent and the Article can be seen as an attempt to reconcile difficult and contradictory elements, namely, can the idea of childhood that is underpinned by development as a naturalized and, therefore, universal process through which children reach maturity, be reconciled with culturally different understandings of the child and meanings for childhood? Or to what extent does the futuristic idea that children need to be prepared eventually to take a responsible place in society only make sense because the Article presumes a rather Western notion that children exist in some unique childhood space outside of the rest of society?

Writing on behalf of children and young people in post-colonial Africa, De Boeck and Honwara (2005) challenge the provenance of the idea of the *Child* that is the Convention's core construct; suggesting that the UNCRC's universal child rests upon highly Eurocentric assumptions and is rooted in Western Enlightenment values that curtail its capacity to embrace difference; indeed, they suggest that far from being liberatory, the Convention can work against the interests of children whose lives and circumstances are not congruent with those values:

> ... children and youth are often perceived through opposition to adulthood and as 'people in the process of becoming rather than being'. This view predominates in international law on children's rights (Ennew, 2002). The need to establish global standards of child protection led to the universalization of a specific definition of childhood. Several international agreements define a child as anyone below the age of eighteen (UN Geneva Conventions; UN Convention on the Rights of the Child; The African Charter of Rights of the Child). Here, children and youth appear as pre-social and passive recipients of experience. They are portrayed as dependent, immature, and incapable of assuming responsibility, properly confined to the protection of home and school (Thomas, 2000). This concept developed amongst the middle class in Europe and North America and has been universalized in such a way that youngsters who do not follow this path are considered either to be at risk or to pose a risk to society. Children who are 'out of place' (Connolly and Ennew, 1996), who do not readily fit within Western cultural fantasies of children as innocent and vulnerable, are quickly perceived as demonic, discontented and disorderly and are often feared and punished as a consequence. Parents who do not follow normative Western child-rearing practices are immediately seen as irresponsible (Levine et al., 1994). (De Boeck and Honwara, 2005, p. 12)

Indeed, many sub-Saharan African nations felt sufficiently moved to write the African Charter on Human and People's Rights (ACHPR) as an alternative that conflates children and young people's rights with those of mature adults. The ACHPR entrenches what Chinouya and O'Keefe (2003) describe as the notion of *Ubuntu-Hunhu* expressing a principle of 'duty, respect for one another and social solidarity' that locates the child within social networks held together by responsibilities as well as rights, rather than as an independent, individualized and autonomous actor. Perhaps this better reflects cultural contexts where it is not considered unusual for a child to be responsible for younger siblings and their care or to take a reasonable share of family-based work. A recent popular television programme addresses these issues under the banner of 'The World's Strictest Parents' (BBC, 2010b), in which somewhat wayward young people from the United Kingdom (raised, we infer, under a more liberal construction of childhood) encounter very different parenting practices in other parts of the world with fascinating consequences; the socially constructed status of childhood and youth is manifest.

Clearly there are challenges that attend the speed and manner in which different values and perspectives are brought together in a globalizing world, moreover, that this coming together is not a meeting of equals. Differences in wealth, military power and cultural dominance mean that dialogue is seldom on equal terms. There are perils and potential moral difficulties associated both with the rejection of universalism in favour of a particularistic emphasis on cultural difference, just as there are in enthroning a universal view of the child that rides roughshod over difference and may undermine a child's identity. Perhaps the strength of the UNCRC lies not in an intellectual or academically acceptable resolution of this dualism, but in the strategic and political possibilities it opens up; notably in insisting that children's opinions and voices are listened to and contribute to decisions concerning them as a matter of social justice.

Reflection:

Do you think social justice stems from supporting cultural differences or assuring universal rights? Are these mutually exclusive?

A New Paradigm for the Sociology of Childhood

An important academic intervention that rode this difficult dualism between asserting rights and proclaiming difference was found in Alan Prout and Alison James' *A New Paradigm for the Sociology of Childhood*. This had been published originally in 1990, but it was following publication of the second edition in 1997, just as New Labour came to power, that it generated academic interest across a wide spectrum of child-related disciplines.

Prout and James' (1997) work was prompted and supported by a growing body of criticism aimed at Piagetian developmentalism and its role as a 'scientific' justification for more intuitive insights concerning the conflation of biological growth and cognitive development as braided strands in the *Child*'s journey towards adulthood (Walkerdine, 1984 and 2009; Richards and Light, 1987; Burman, 1994). Rousseau and subsequent progressives had placed emphasis on childhood as a state of *being* rather than *becoming*. However, these critics argued that developmentalism merely entrenches the 'being–becoming' dualism rather than settles it. First, this is because it is underpinned by an equally stubborn dualism that presumes a rigid distinction between adults and children – almost as if they are separate species; and second, because it is implicit that 'normal' adults are the product of socialization within 'normatively' arranged childhoods – *being* is a way of *becoming*! Moreover, they criticized the way in which developmentalism had become embedded in the practices of child professionals and their associated institutions across a broad front of education, care, social work, health and play – and consequently, beyond criticism or dispute.

Prout and James' (1997) 'New Paradigm' represented an attempt to set out articles of faith concerning childhood and catalyse a process of review and change in how children and their childhoods are imagined. The New Paradigm is social constructionist in its accommodation of diversity and challenges the idea of a universal, natural childhood, thus:

> The immaturity of children is a biological fact of life but the ways in which this immaturity is understood and made meaningful is a fact of culture. It is these 'facts of culture' which may vary and which may be said to make of childhood a social institution. It is in this sense, therefore, that one can talk of the social

> construction of childhood and also…of its re- and deconstruction. In this double
> sense, then, childhood is both constructed and reconstructed both for children
> and by children. (Prout and James, 1997, p. 7)

The social constructionist position means that it is possible to speak of many
childhoods rather than a single naturally founded and universal childhood.
They go on to suggest that we should think of children's experience of their
childhoods as always in relation to other sociological variables of ethnicity, class
and gender. Indeed, the New Paradigm takes us further, because this relativist
position challenges the existence of childhood as an absolute, real or given state,
so that whereas in some circumstances it may be useful to see little people as
children, in others, class or ethnic affiliation or gender identity or the experience
of disability may offer more meaningful bases for understanding and expressing their experience as people, whether we stress the child–age dimension of a
person's identity over, say, their social class is down to what is considered meaningful in the prevailing social circumstances (see Chapter 8). This is not to deny
the biological immaturity of the people we categorize as children – that would
be patently absurd; rather it is to assert the historical provenance of the idea of
childhood, and specifically, in Holloway and Valentine's words:

> Only in 'modern' times has physical immaturity been socially dealt with through
> the historical process we call childhood (Holloway and Valentine, 2000, p. 4; see
> also Connell, 1987, p. 79).

Thus childhood is a way of understanding, knowing and providing for the
group of people so defined; the question is, does it seem that real children are
benefiting from the processes and institutions that coalesce to construct their
childhoods?

The New Paradigm served as a rallying point for a new inter-disciplinary
area known as Childhood Studies and a research agenda that sought to offer
solutions to the challenges of growing up in societies where rapid change
in economy, in social structure and relations, in patterns of consumption,
and in media and communications had become the norm. Furthermore,
Prout and James' (1997) social constructionist standpoint provoked debate
in academic circles about the meanings held at large about childhood at a
time when actual children's lives seem to have come under substantial pressure from poverty, materialism, anxieties about schooling and the economic
health of the nation as well as fears about any number of abuses and dangers

lurking within strangers, road traffic and the internet. Prout and James (1997) and contributors, including Kitzinger (1997, pp. 165–89), indicted romantic ideologies of the *Child* for failing to make children and childhood safer because of their overriding imperative to protect children's innocence and shield them from the challenges that everyday life presents. Indeed, innocence, as the preferred state within which children should live their lives, is to be seen as part of an adult rhapsody on childhood that is rooted in, and legitimized by, the Enlightenment construct of the Child – maintaining innocence is rarely high on the agenda when children are consulted about their lives. The Enlightenment objectified children and is responsible for the construction of institutions and practices which express adult priorities, yearnings and mores.

Reflection:

Why do you think adults are frequently more concerned to protect children's innocence than children are? Can children take greater control of this debate?

The range, complexity and, at times contradictory qualities of these adult ways of seeing children and making sense of childhood is manifest through the work of Mills (2000, pp. 7–38). Following a trawl through various cultural and literary sources concerning children, he comes up with six ways of seeing, namely:

1. children as innocent
2. children as apprentices
3. children as persons in their own right
4. children as members of a distinct group
5. children as vulnerable
6. children as animals.

Mills suggests that each implies that being a child is a socially constructed role and quotes Waksler:

> To recognise that 'child' is a role is to suspend the assumption that childhood has some absolute, real, transcendent existence beyond the social. (Waksler, 1991, p. 146, in Mills, 2000, p. 9)

For theorists of childhood, the idea of innocence is accompanied by the presumed passivity of the Child and of development as something that nature does to children to turn them into adults. It follows from this objectification of the Child that correct development is expressed through a checklist of adult-defined needs and rights that adult-led institutions, in turn, underwrite (Stainton Rogers, 2009) – the approach to understanding this Child, as an object, has little difference to the scientific methodologies by which plants, animals and other biological phenomena were classified by Natural History; hence Stainton Rogers describes these approaches as *taxonomic*. It is surely ironic that despite the agency found at the heart of Rousseau's Enlightenment vision for the *Child* (as expressed in *Emile*), scientifically driven taxonomies of deterministic needs embody a theorization of the Child as passive, and thus frequently fail to express or embrace the actuality of real children's lives. There are many other areas in which people are not consulted about decisions that affect their lives, but almost uniquely, when children are not consulted it is because of an presumed incapacity to make sensible judgements and this is usually justified by developmental theories (this also applies, of course, to groups deemed to be *childlike* in the popular imagination – such as those with disabilities or psychiatric disorders). This presumed passivity implicitly constructs children as always requiring adult guidance and protection, thus denying their agency as people who co-construct their lives and identities with other people. However, drawing on post-structuralist feminist theory, MacNaughten demonstrates the active, agentic capacity of even young children to deploy a rich repertoire of identities to navigate the social world and their relationships with others – see the exchange with four-year-old Tom over the scent bottle and his adroit command of discourses of gender, sexuality and age (MacNaughten, 2000, pp. 30–3).

Developing this and allied themes, Stainton Rogers (2009) argues that we should be more concerned about the quality of real children's lives and that a starting point for this concern is to allow children a say in shaping their lives, which might include an extension of the suffrage in some form (see the work of the UK Youth Parliament, 2010).Attention to children as people means that there is a chance both to accommodate difference and diversity and to acknowledge and benefit from the active resilience that many young people show in the face of huge adversity. Stainton Rogers suggests that if we listen to children, we will be forced to acknowledge the resilience shown by many and particularly: 'those who somehow manage to grow up healthy, happy and "together" despite having to face major setbacks and difficulties…' (Stainton Rogers, 2009, p. 154). Thus the focus shifts from securing normative development in the child towards facilitating what children identify as leading to quality of life. The thrust of needs and rights discourses is that childhood must be congruent with those needs and rights if pathology in adulthood is to be avoided; however, the quality of life discourse:

> …helps individuals to challenge the assumption often made that a 'bad childhood' inevitably means growing up into an incompetent adult and, especially, a 'bad parent': 'history is not destiny. (Stainton Rogers, 2009, p. 155)

Although many vulnerable children and young people require serious help and support to navigate their lives, it is worth reflecting that many of them also exhibit extraordinary levels of resilience in just living and transacting their everyday lives; moreover, their resilience has to be as important in meeting the challenges of an unknown future as it has proved for humankind in the past. Stainton Rogers' proposal that we look at less quantifiable aspects of children's lives (like well-being, quality of life and resilience) is indicative of the direction in which social constructionism takes us; that is, away from an essentialist view of the child and childhood, towards one that is the product of shared and openly debated meanings – including those of the children themselves. Perhaps our schools and educational institutions should place the pursuit of greater resilience at the heart of their curricula and open their doors to the abundant and diverse capabilities our children and their communities possess.

Reflection:

Are there ways in which children's resilience is acknowledged and encouraged in the curriculum; is enough emphasis placed on this?

Both the UNCRC and critical Childhood Studies appeared at a time when globalization and post-colonial realities had become prominent features of children's education, care and welfare systems in wealthy countries such as Britain. Thus a changing cultural context gave an acute edge to discussions over the specific intellectual and cultural roots of the idea of the *Child* and debates over universal rights and cultural difference. Moves towards cultural relativism in academic circles were reflected in a growing rhetorical commitment to multiculturalism across government policy – although the extent to which rhetoric was translated into reality is debatable (see Parekh, 2000; Race, 2010). However, high profile, headline events may make this iconoclastic approach to understanding childhood difficult to apply in risk-averse practice. For many professionals an essentialist view of the child based on specific needs and rights is seen as both a solid point of anchorage, safeguarding children against abuse, and part of the commonsense of every-day practice. By suggesting that childhoods are socially constructed and that they must always be understood in relation to other sociological variables, such as ethnicity, gender and social class – in practice, this frequently means in relation to family norms – there is a perceived danger that the capacity to exercise judgement over cases of neglect, physical and psychological abuse and laborious exploitation may be compromised and those who abuse children may be handed a defence. It is one thing to engage in a philosophical debate about moral matters concerning childhood, it is another to be responsible for making judgements that affect real children and high-profile cases. For instance, the tragic murders of Victoria Climbie and baby Peter Connolly, have effectively put children's services and individual professionals on (very public) trial by media; under these conditions the avoidance of risk may be the prime concern, ruling out tolerance or concessions over difference (Ahmed, 2009).

For others there are concerns about where the New Sociology of Childhood's emphasis on the agency of the child could lead; Vanderbeck (2008) cites evidence from Ruddick (2006) suggesting that the presumed agency of the child may lead to unintended consequences by, for example, reinforcing deterministic arguments about how petty misdemeanours prefigure later youthful delinquency. Furthermore, he suggests that although the assertion of agency attempts to challenge the passivity and innocence found in the Enlightenment's construction of the Child, exponents of children's agency are not beyond using the Child's moral purity as a 'knock-down punch' when debating with those who are sceptical about children's entitlements in any number of areas, including voting reform, lower alcoholic drinking age limits, sexual consent, limits to media access and engagement with compulsory education (Vanderbeck, 2008). The difficulties this can lead to are evident in the recent ground-breaking BBC comedy 'Outnumbered' (BBC, 2010c), in which beleaguered parents walk an impossibly fine and conflicted line between their social duty to keep the family together and the imperative to ensure that the agency of each individual child is respected and not compromised in the process. The emphasis afforded agency may be yet another adult rhapsody on childhood, fuelled by adult memories and driven by yearning that can never be requited (Philo, 2003). That said, whereas, say, women's liberation can be pursued by feminists and equality in civil rights be advocated by the groups directly impacted, children are somewhat different and their liberation may necessarily always remain to a significant extent in the hands of adults.

> **Reflection:**
>
> Who best supports the interests of children – the family or the State? Can you identify any cases where it might be difficult to make the call between them?

Social exclusion and child poverty: Sure Start, Every Child Matters and the Children Act 2004

When New Labour swept to power in 1997, 25 per cent of the United Kingdom's children lived in households where the family income was less than 60 per cent of the median (i.e. the figure midway between the income of the richest and poorest) and were, thereby, considered to be living in poverty. In 1979 on the eve of Margaret Thatcher's Conservative Government this figure stood at 12 per cent, and therefore these years had seen the figure more than double (Stewart, 2009, p. 47). Although a relative measure, and higher than the income of the majority of those in poverty across the globe, this is considered significant because once a family's income falls below a certain level it will prove impossible to provide many of the things that become accepted as a cultural norm within a society and allow children to participate on roughly equal terms with their wealthier peers, for example, being able to partake in school visits and journeys, attending the cinema, enjoying at least one brief holiday each year; all of which are, arguably, no longer exceptional or luxuries in a wealthy country such as Britain. Besides the immediate material constraints:

> growing evidence emphasised the importance of childhood poverty for later outcomes. Children growing up poor appeared to have lower self-esteem, were less likely to be successful in education and employment and were at increased risk of early childbearing, low income, benefit dependency and homelessness. (from Hobcraft, 1998 and Ermisch et al., 2001, and cited in Stewart, 2009, p.47)

The analysis was supported by a concept of 'social exclusion' that was installed at the heart of New Labour's social policy and assault on poverty. This emphasized the existence of a growing body of the nation's population who due to economic poverty were effectively excluded from full participation in the cultural and social life of their neighbourhoods, communities and society at large. In response the government set up the Social Exclusion Unit (SEU) in 1997. Children and young people featured heavily in their first report (SEU, 1998) as in the SEU's four subsequent reports and the Treasury, under the stewardship of the future Prime Minister Gordon Brown, took an active role in formulating policy as well as paying for it.

Among the signs of social exclusion affecting children and young people identified by the SEU were:

- persistent, *low-level* youth crime and *anti-social behaviour*
- high levels of families led by a *lone-parent* with limited means to access quality child care (and hence work)
- a disturbingly high level of teenage pregnancy by western European standards
- long-term unemployment and the absence of working role models
- all-too-frequent cases of child abduction, sexual abuse and murder accompanied by a panic about the systems designed to prevent paedophile access to children and young people and more fundamental concerns about how endemic this criminal pathology might actually be
- fears about children's health and especially the effects of poor diet on levels of obesity among the young as well as growing levels of alcohol and other drug use by minors
- low academic achievements, including on-going questions about the standards and fitness of educational qualifications, and especially disturbingly low levels of achievement among *looked-after children*.

The New Labour government became particularly concerned with looked after children; perhaps because of the criticism within its own ranks that

New Labour economic and fiscal policy was largely indistinguishable from its Conservative predecessors. In consequence Blair's government:

> ... was keen to show its commitment to a more socially equitable and cohesive society that involved the efforts of all government departments... A range of policies, including Sure Start, the welfare to work programme, tax credits, national minimum wage and national strategy for neighbourhood renewal, were all intended to tackle social deprivation and poor health. (Hunter, 2007, pp. 8–22)

On child poverty, policy was propelled by ambitious targets that committed the government to reducing child poverty to three-quarters of the 1997 level by 2005 and for it to be halved by 2010. Although the figure did fall, it was only by 16 per cent and the first target was missed and thereafter, to huge disappointment, poverty actually increased (Stewart, 2009). Clearly, as the SEU had found, the problem of exclusion and child poverty were deep-seated and Stewart identifies a clear correlation between these missed targets and the failure to maintain initial rates of expenditure on the problem as a prerequisite for sustained improvements.

The New Labour government introduced a number of other measures that were trained on the geography of exclusion and decay. They included the establishment of the Neighbourhood Renewal Unit (NRU) (2001) to oversee urban regeneration, Health Action Zones (HAZs – 1997) and Education Action Zones (EAZs – 1998) (see Maguire et al., 2006; Pratt-Adams et al., 2010). As part of the drive to address the highly visible exclusion and disadvantage presenting itself in the late 1990s was a concern to seek sustainable change and so a very specific focus on the education, health, safety and well-being of the young emerged. Research evidence from the Head Start and High Scope preschool programmes in the United States suggested that socially targeted and appropriately resourced provision for very young children could be effective in breaking cycles of poverty and deprivation. This aspect suited the New Labour government since they had made a public commitment to using research evidence to frame social policy; therefore when the Treasury-led Cross Departmental Review of Provision for Young Children was set up by Norman Glass (overseen by Gordon Brown), the Sure Start programme described as an 'upstream intervention' was the result. Gidley explains:

> An upstream intervention is one that seeks to intervene in a social problem or a health problem early and deal with the causes rather than the symptoms. The

development of upstream interventions is linked to what is called refocusing, a shift in balance from heavy-end provision, the treatment of the results of social or health problems (such as acute or restorative services), to front-end provision, which is prevention and early intervention before problems develop. (Gidley, 2007, p. 144)

Sure Start was conceived spatially, but the geographically defined provision created problems. Drawing boundaries frequently leads to inequities, and many workers involved can tell a story about how families on one side of a street were included (irrespective of actual need) and others opposite were denied access. However, the geographical focus had the potential to resolve other difficulties, by offering a range of services and supports that were universal on the basis of location and the problems of stigmatization attaching to welfare provision for specific children and families were diminished. Furthermore, an emphasis on geography promoted localized responses that were sensitive to the needs and character of communities. As a key development, Sure Start brought together health, education (including agencies such as local library services) and social care under a single roof, but also encouraged the development of inter-professional working in ways that echo the work of Rachel and Margaret McMillan in Deptford in the decades up to the 1930s (see Chapter 3). In the United States a comparable, but earlier, phenomenon is that described as Full Service Schooling (see Maguire et al., 2006, p. 152, for more details).

Coincident with all this policy making, the sustained torture and murder of Victoria Climbie at the hands of her guardians in 2000 sent shockwaves through national consciousness about the condition of the UK's children – as had the deaths of Maria Colwell, Jasmine Beckford and James Bulger over the preceding 30 years and Peter Connolly has since. Victoria's tragic death led the government to commission a committee of enquiry, chaired by Lord Laming that published its findings in 2003.

The fact that the Climbie case had such an effect was not solely down to its intrinsic horrors, but it served as an emblem for widespread concerns about the quality of childhood within the United Kingdom. Action was instigated by the Home Office in 2003, and although this was largely a social services matter, education along with health became implicated in tackling what was seen as a wider, systemic malaise. Encouraged by the apparent achievements of Sure Start but chastened by the Climbie case, Margaret Hodge, the Minister for Children, introduced fundamental proposals for an integrated and inter-professional approach to provision for children in the Green Paper entitled

Every Child Matters (DfES, 2003) and that substantially passed into law as the Children Act 2004 (DfES, 2004b). The raft of developments this Act ushered in continued to be identified under the Every Child Matters (ECM) (DfES, 2004a) banner and was supplemented in 2005 by the publication of Youth Matters by the UK government that addressed provision for 13–19 year olds (DfES, 2005; see Jones, P., 2008, pp. 65–70). It is worth noting that there was precedent for legislation following on the heels of damaging reports on the abuse and death of specific children; the report (1974) into the death of Maria Colwell was followed by the 1975 Children Act and the 1989 Act followed the Jasmine Beckford, Kimberley Carlile and Cleveland abuse inquiries (Reder et al., 1993).

The general expectation was that Hodge's Green Paper would very largely address itself to the particular failings in child protection that the Climbie case and the Laming Report had exposed. However, the paper set out a much broader vision for childhood in the twenty-first century and sought to offer the best possible start for children through a combination of State provision and family support (including childcare that enables carers to work) that brought together children's health, social care and education – each of the major domains in which the State claimed a stake in children's lives (Horner and Krawczyk, 2006).

Such integrated provision was well established in countries such as Cuba or Sweden and historically we see similar provisions, for example, the work of Robert Owen at New Lanark, the Ragged School Movement that offered social welfare along with education and the McMillans who trained their efforts on the education, welfare, moral and spiritual well-being of the children of Deptford (see Chapter 3). Further, Plowden in 1967 was not merely interested in transforming the pedagogy of primary education, but sought to make inroads into the poverty and deprivation that conditioned educational underachievement. A near contemporary of the Plowden Report was the Seebohm Report published by the government department responsible for health in 1968. The report offers a view of education from its location within the health and welfare domain and is unequivocal about the need for generic, inter-professional service provision 'as the bedrock of services for all children, young people and their families' (Horner and Krawczyk, 2006, p. 12).

In surveying the main differences between childhoods at the beginning of the nineteenth century and its end, Hendrick (1997a, p. 34) cites what he calls an 'increasingly compulsory relationship between the child and the state'; with the passing of the Children Act in 2004 a comprehensive as well as compulsory relationship seems to have been made complete. Every Child Matters (DfES, 2003) sets out to end the fragmentation in services and the strict professional demarcations flowing from this, in favour of cooperative inter-professional work founded upon an integrated view of the child. It is worth reflecting that although much of Rachel McMillan's work was supported by wealthy philanthropists, as a socialist she endorsed the role of the State as guarantor of universal improvement in children's life chances; in this, the New Labour government not only confirmed her opinion, but also passed the legislation that most authentically expressed Old Labour values during this period of their office.

The provisions of the Children Act 2004

The Children Act 2004 set out a framework that would establish a raft of new professional roles and institutions. At a local level Children's Services Authorities were established with a number of new duties and roles that included convening Local Safeguarding Children Boards (LSCBs) to address child protection matters in an inter-agency approach. They were also responsible for the compilation and publication of local Children and Young People's Plans (CYPPs) to coordinate the work of Children's Centres, Extended Schools Services and local Youth Support Services (Horner and Krawczyk, 2006 p. 16). The Act also established the overall position of Children's Commissioner (England) to stand up for children's interests, canvass their views in matters that concern them and to align provision with the UNCRC (1989). Inter-professional working is underwritten by a Common Assessment Framework (CAF) through which health, education and social work professionals use a shared format and criteria for assessing children's needs.

The Children's Centre is intended to be the focus for this inter-agency and inter-professional working, and there is an aim that there should be one in every community throughout England. This development was intended to be transformative in its impact and could match the completist achievements of other landmark legislation, such as the 1870 Elementary Education Act. At the heart of the 2004 Act is also a particular vision for schools and a sense that they should be able to do much more than hitherto; indeed the National Foundation for Educational Research (NFER) described the aspirations of the Children Act as a 'quiet revolution' (Horner and Krawczyk, 2006, p. 20).

This enhanced agenda for schools embodies the idea of 'extended schools' and the provision of wraparound childcare – in the United States the expression 'full-service schooling' has been coined and expresses this re-imagination of the role of schools well (Maguire et al., 2006). The Act envisages a more complete utilization of the capital resources, with schools conceived as hubs in community networks that create the spaces for social regeneration through some or all of the following:

- before- and after-school care
- holiday childcare, play and sport provision
- family support and community-based education that enables carers to take on substantial paid employment.

It is also envisaged that armed with the CAF closer ties between professionals and service providers will facilitate referral of children for more comprehensive additional support. 'In short, it is anticipated that schools will be the epicentre for support systems for all children, and in particular for those in need' (Horner and Krawczyk, 2006, p. 20).

Smith and Barker (1999a, 1999b, 2000, 2002) in a series of papers report their research findings showing that After-School Clubs struggle with a number of contradictory factors; these include whether they are school- or home-related or neither, and what sorts of compulsion should be placed upon children attending them. Furthermore, their research suggests that children feel they have little say in designing or directing their After-School Club. Playworkers have also challenged the values and practices of these new childhood institutions on the grounds that they are frequently overly adult-directed with fun, free and flexible play curtailed by adult regulation of children's spatial range and timetable (Hughes, 2001; Brown, 2003). This seems to suggest that NFER's 'quiet revolution' has not been entirely welcomed by children, who may now spend the bulk of their waking lives in school and institutional settings.

Early Years Foundation Stage and One Children's Workforce

Alongside the emergence of new childhood institutions, such as the Children's Centre and After/Before-School Clubs, a transformation of the working lives and professionalism of those involved in the education and care of children was underway. At the heart of this was the erstwhile Children's Workforce Development Council's (CWDC) aspiration to construct a comprehensive, single body of workers addressing the whole child.

The most elaborated area for workforce development thus far is that for the early years and builds on the achievements of Sure Start; in academic terms it has boosted the emergence of Early Childhood Studies as a recognizable discipline in its own right as many universities and other higher education institutions have embraced a wide range of new degrees and professional qualifications. This comprehensive development was further catalysed by the UK government's Childcare Act 2006 intended to offer comprehensive regulation and direction for *all* childcare in the United Kingdom under an inspection regime managed by the Office for Standards in Education (OFSTED). For the first time all providers in receipt of State funding, whether formal nurseries or individual childminders, had to register in order to operate legally – indeed there were flurries of concern about whether friends who shared childcare between them would be subject to the force of legislation (see BBC News report from September 2009 concerning the case of two police officers who shared childcare in this way; BBC, 2009). A curriculum bringing together education, welfare provision and care was set out in the Early Years Foundation Stage (EYFS) providing an agenda for the professional development and regulation of child carers that led to a new post-graduate qualification – Early Years Professional Status (or EYPS). Although described by the erstwhile New Labour government's Department for Children, Schools and Families (DCSF) as a flexible document (DCSF, 2010), able to accommodate differences in approach and conviction concerning young children and their care and education, from inception the EYFS generated controversy, especially with regard to its educational expectations. There was a familiar ring to the controversy as it rehearsed debates found in the ideas of Locke, Rousseau, Pestalozzi et al., concerning the nature of the Child, the proper condition for childhood, and its relation to adulthood.

One instigator of critical opposition was the 'OpenEYE' campaign (2007), comprising a group of notable educationists who argued that the EYFS was too prescriptive in its educational expectations, runs against the development of children and therefore could be harmful and breaches the human rights of parents to educate their children according to their own philosophies. There were also objections from other quarters, notably those in the Steiner-Waldorf movement, who adhere to the educational philosophy of

Rudolf Steiner (SaveSteinerSchools, 2008; DCSF, 2009). Proponents of this system found themselves deeply opposed to those early educational targets set out in the EYFS that require rudimentary recognition and use of letters and numbers, because:

> In keeping with Steiner Waldorf philosophies, children in kindergarten are not presented with abstract concepts or symbols such as letters and numbers, nor – for much the same reasons – are they presented with information and communication technology or programmable toys.

Further,

> ...the EYFS requires that 'All the areas must be delivered through planned, purposeful play, with a balance of adult-led and child-initiated activities'. The Steiner philosophy does not recognise the concept of 'adult-led play', and particularly not as a vehicle for education. Play is not 'planned and purposeful'; it comes from within, is spontaneous, and is of value in and of itself. If an adult plans and prepares an activity, however enjoyable, for the purpose of advancing the child's learning, this is not play but a lesson. The Steiner view is that the time for lessons does not begin until the child leaves kindergarten at the age of 6-7 years. (Save Steiner Schools, 2008)

The Steinerians' argument concluded that 'the educational aspect of the Early Years Foundation Stage cannot in any way be incorporated into the Steiner system without one or both being seriously compromised'.

Clearly there are the very real challenges entailed in rolling out a nationwide programme that ensures equitable, intellectually informed and professionally accountable provision while attempting to avoid a 'one size fits all' reductionism. The apparent technical-rationalism and managerial character of the EYFS – including its inspection regime – as a *framework*, does not sit well with the Steinerians' romantically numinous conviction that education must be driven by developmental needs embedded in and emanating from the child (Steiner, 1948; Kraftl, 2006). Much of the dispute converges on the meaning of play and its place in relation to the purpose of education – on the one hand, as a medium for the acquisition of knowledge, skills and understanding and on the other as the outward spontaneous manifestation of a child's more spiritually rooted self-realization. (For more on play, see Holland, 2003; Manning-Morton and Thorp, 2003; Aitken and Powell, 2005; Moyles, 2010) The Steinerians' position is perhaps summed up by the aphorism usually ascribed to Froebel, 'play is the child's work' (Brehony, 2010) and is not to be enterprised for adult ends; moreover, their critique of the EYFS seems to echo McLuhan and Fiore (1967) that 'growing up' rather than play per se, has become the new work. As another variation on the being – becoming dualism, the dispute appears Manichaean and unbridgeable.

The whole project of constructing a national inter-disciplinary and inter-professional system is shot through with challenges and difficulties for practitioners that may resolve into a workable synthesis over time, but that always risks reinforcing professional differences. The creation of *multi-disciplinary* teams is not, in itself, sufficient to guarantee *inter-disciplinary* accommodation or understanding. It is, however, important not to presume that what the framework sets out is identical to what practitioners seek to do in the actuality of everyday working lives. Our account has been marked by a distinction between the rationally proposed, theory-laden grounds for the way children should be educated and a good childhood secured and the more complex actuality of what human beings do for, and give to, each other. The raw kindness, generosity and motivation to make things better that many workers channel through their working lives (and that frequently draws from the wellspring of personal biography) is not generally captured within, or expressible through, the managerial matrices of national frameworks. The difference between high-resolution national policies and the more intimate personal experience at their point of impact has been explored using the geographical concept of scale by Giesbrecht et al. (2010). It is surely also the case that whereas professional identities and cultures may not be congruent, team members can learn to accommodate difference in the interests of shared convictions about the whole child and in pursuit of what is agreed as best for children. Managerialist frameworks can embody a pessimistic outlook on human nature, wherein little is left to trust and just as the agency of the child can become *abandoned in theory* (echoing Jenks, 2005) so the agency of those who work with and for children, can be found *missing in policy*. We need to know more about the lives, beliefs and motivations of the grassroots army who selflessly seek to serve the best ends for our children.

Future?

Following the election of what turned out to be the Conservative-Liberal Democrat coalition government led by David Cameron on 6 May, 2010, the New Labour years came to an end. A priority for this government has been the reduction of the UK's budget deficit following the years of economic boom and the global banking crisis. In consequence public spending in education and children's services may be vulnerable. Within days of the Coalition taking power in the United Kingdom, the DCSF was re-branded as the Department for Education (DfE). The extent of the restructuring that must surely follow this is yet to be seen. However, there is an early intention to ensure that Sure Start, tax credits for working families, the hitherto universal Child Benefit and a new 'pupil premium' are better targeted at those seen as genuinely needy. Furthermore, school refurbishment and building programmes have either been halted or reduced, and the role of the LEAs has been curtailed through policies that encourage Free Schools and Academies. Moreover, most Conservatives and many Liberal Democrats have a visceral aversion to the sort of centralizing measures found in the Childcare Act 2006, meaning that a change of philosophy is likely.

The full picture has yet to emerge. However, beyond the relatively temporary currency of policy, three factors seem set to exert an enduring influence. One is the large and growing discrepancy between the quality of life and life chances of the wealthiest and the poorest people in the United Kingdom and the grinding reality of child poverty that is its direct corollary. The second is the challenges that come with globalization and the powerful insistence that voices other than those of white, male Europeans be heard. Third is the groundswell of demand for greater involvement of children and young people in decisions that affect their lives (e.g. the UK Youth Parliament) and a recognition of young people's political concerns (Hopkins and Alexander, 2010; Skelton, 2010). The emergence of Childhood Studies has bolstered this by insisting that research should not merely be undertaken *on* children, but that children's perspectives and voices are central in the design and transaction of research that concerns their lives (Lewis and Lindsay, 2000; Stainton Rogers, 2009, pp. 155–8). The extent to which this represents a movement directed by children and young people, or another example of adult advocacy, is not entirely clear. However, this does suggest that we might be witnessing a sea change in the way in which institutions transact their relations with children.

This book has explored the influence of Enlightenment constructions of the *Child* and of childhood to the educational experience of children. In demanding a dismantling of the universal *Child* and the dissolution of childhood into other sociological variables, James and Prout's (1997) New Paradigm seems to be of a piece with a wider post-modern critique of the

Enlightenment and its achievements. These critics contend that whereas the Enlightenment was driven by the conviction that humankind was perfectible and sought to liberate and promote equality, the evidence of dictatorship, racism, mass-murdering brutality and environmental degradation that litters the twentieth century suggests that it fell far short of its aspiration (Neiman, 2009, pp. 124–5). For children, these shortcomings have arguably been experienced as objectification, an overly taxonomic theorization that is at odds with their empirical life-circumstances, an excessive burden of expectation and a moral assessment that veers from the angelic to the demonic without much in between. Hence the apparent concern of the New Sociology to offer an antidote to the overbearing Enlightenment vision. However, there is gathering anxiety that we risk throwing the baby out with the bathwater if we abandon Enlightenment aspirations too readily, and fail to acknowledge that the moral and political imperatives motivating our desire for social justice also have their origins in that Enlightenment vision. Neiman suggests that we do not give up easily when technological development is at stake, so why abandon our aspiration to realize worthy, but more abstract ideals? Thus:

> You think that what failed in the past will fail in the future? Kant reminds us of how many sheer technological advances have disproved that old saw. His example? Air travel with balloons. If we don't abandon efforts where science hopes we may create technology, how dare we abandon them where morality demands we create justice? (Neiman, 2009, p. 153)

Furthermore, James and James (2004, p. 2) quote Kuper to suggest that far from rejecting the Enlightenment project, we should seek to enhance its prospects for success by enabling children to become part of the conversation and thereby '... confront the models current in the social sciences with experiences and models of our ... [children] ... insisting that this should be a two way process' (Kuper, 1994). That said, the realities of children's poverty, lack of social power and political subordination cannot solely be tackled through the installation of new ways of seeing children or smarter theories of childhood, especially if these distract from more basic demands for social justice and the mitigation of that poverty – impoverished children live with impoverished adults. The stakes are high; continued failure to embrace and release the resilience, energies and capabilities of the *whole* UK population – thereby catalysing a surge in optimism among our children and young people – must surely lead to further decline, division and discontent. We must seek to do better rather than give up because the going gets tougher.

> **Reflection:**
>
> Over to you – this book cannot predict the future, but you can reflect on how well it helps you to make sense of an emerging present.

Further reading

Buckingham, D. (2000), *After the Death of Childhood: Growing Up in the Age of Electronic Media*, Cambridge: Polity Press.

Corsaro, W. (1997), *The Sociology of Childhood*, Thousand Oaks, CA: Pine Forge.

James, A. and James, A. L. (2008), *Key Concepts in Childhood Studies*, London: Sage.

James, A., Jenks, C. and Prout, A. (1999), *Theorizing Childhood*, London: Polity Press.

Jenks, C. (2005), *Childhood*, London: Routledge.

Jones, L. Holmes, R. and Powell, J. (eds) (2005), *Early Childhood Studies: A Multi-Professional Perspective*, Buckingham: Open University Press.

Kehily, M. J. (2009), *An Introduction to Childhood Studies*, Maidenhead, UK: Open University Press.

Lewis, A. and Lindsay, G. (eds) (2002), *Researching Children's Perspectives*, Buckingham: Open University Press.

Philo, P. (2003), '"To go back up the side hill": memories, imaginations and reveries of childhood', *Children's Geographies*, 1(1), pp. 7–23.

Prout, A. and James, A. (1997), *Constructing and Reconstructing Childhood*, London: Routledge.

Robinson, K. and Jones Diaz, C. (2006), *Diversity and Difference in Early Childhood Education: Issues for Theory and Practice*, Maidenhead, UK: Open University Press.

Ruddick (2006), 'Abnormal, the "new normal," and destabilizing discourses of rights', *Public Culture*, 18(1), pp. 53–77.

Smith, F. and Barker, J. (1999), 'From "Ninja Turtles" to the "Spice Girls": children's participation in the development of Out of School play environments', *Built Environment*, 25(1).

Smith, F. and Barker, J. (2002), 'School's Out? Out of school clubs at the boundary of home and school', in Edwards, R. (ed.), *Children, Home and School: Regulation, Autonomy or Connection?* London: Routledge, pp. 57–74.

Vanderbeck, R. M. (2008), 'Reaching critical mass? Theory, politics, and the culture of debate in children's geographies', *Area*, 40(3), pp. 393–400.

Welch, S. (2008), 'Childhood: rights and realities', in Jones, P., Moss, D., Tomlinson, P. and Welch, S. (eds), Childhood: Services and Provision for Children, Harlow: Pearson.

Website

The Children's Rights Alliance: www.crae.org.uk/rights/uncrc20.html, last accessed 17 December 2010.

The UK Youth Parliament: www.ukyouthparliament.org.uk/, last accessed 17 December 2010.

Bibliography

Academic Dictionaries and Encyclopaedias (2004), 'Herbert Fisher', www.en.academic.ru/dic.nsf/enwiki/1015344, last accessed 3 November 2010.

Adelman, C. (2000), 'Over two years, what did Froebel say to Pestalozzi?', *History of Education*, 29(2), pp. 103–14.

Ahmed, M. (2009), 'Baby Peter case in Haringey', www.communitycare.co.uk/Articles/2009/08/11/109961/baby-peter-case-in-haringey.htm, last accessed 3 November 2010.

Aitken, S. and Powell, J. (2005), 'International perspectives', in Jones, L., Holmes, R. and Powell, J. (eds), *Early Childhood Studies*, Maidenhead, UK: Open University Press.

Aldrich, R. (1982), *An Introduction to the History of Education*, London: Hodder and Stoughton.

Alexander, R. (ed.) (2009), *Children, their World, their Education: Final Report and Recommendations of the Cambridge Primary Review*, London: Routledge.

Apperson, G. L. (ed.) (1993), *The Wordsworth Dictionary of Proverbs: A Lexicon of Folklore and Traditional Wisdom*, Ware: Wordsworth Editions.

Aries, P. (1962), *L'Enfant et la Familiale Sous l'Ancien Regime (Centuries of Childhood)*, New Jersey: Cape.

Ashley-Cooper, A. (seventh Earl of Shaftesbury) (1841), *A Narrative of the Experience and Sufferings of William Dodd, A Factory Cripple*.

— (seventh Earl of Shaftesbury) (1842), *The Factory System: Illustrated*.

Bannerjee, J. (2008), 'Edward Robert Robson, Pioneering Architect of State Schools', www.victorianweb.org/art/architecture/robson/index.html, last accessed 3 November 2010.

Barnard, H. C. (1971), *A History of English Education from 1760*, London: Unibooks.

Barnardos (2010), 'Children in trouble campaign film – Hunting', www.barnardos.org.uk/resources/resources_students_advertising/children_in_trouble_campaign/children_in_trouble_online_ads/children_in_trouble_hunting_campaign.htm, last accessed 3 November 2010.

Barnardos (2010), 'Barnardo's children in trouble campaign – Hunting film', www.youtube.com/watch?v=JNXUzEzZSXE, last accessed 3 November 2010.

Barron, C. (2007), 'The child in Mediaeval London: the legal evidence', in Rosenthal, J. T., (ed.), *Essays on Mediaeval Childhood: Responses to Recent Debates*, Donington: Shaun Tyas, pp. 40–53.

Bartlett, S. and Burton, D. (eds) (2007), *Introduction to Education Studies*, London: Sage.

BBC (2009), 'Review of babysitting ban ordered', www.news.bbc.co.uk/1/hi/uk/8277378.stm, last accessed 3 November 2010.

— (2010a), 'Olaudah Equiano' (c.1745 - 1797)', www.bbc.co.uk/history/historic_figures/equiano_olaudah.shtml, last accessed 3 November 2010.

— (2010b), 'The World's Strictest Parents', www.bbc.co.uk/iplayer/episode/b00wmjt1/The_Worlds_Strictest_Parents_Series_3_Chicago/, last accessed 16 December 2010.

— (2010c), 'Outnumbered', www.bbc.co.uk/programmes/b00fq31t, last accessed 3 November 2010.

Bennett, N. (1976), *Teaching Styles and Pupil Progress*, London: Open Books.

Birley, D. (1989), *The Willow Wand: Some Cricket Myths Explored*, London: Aurum.

Blackburn, R. (1988), 'Slavery – its special features and social role', in Archer, L. J. (ed.), *Slavery and Other Forms of Unfree Labour*, London: Routledge.

Board of Education (1870), *The Elementary Education Act*, London: HMSO.

— (1926), *The Hadow Report: The Education of the Adolescent*, London: HMSO.

— (1931), *The Hadow Report: The Primary School*, London: HMSO.

— (1933), *The Hadow Report: The Nursery School*, London: HMSO.

Boden, M. (1980), *Piaget*, New York: Viking, and London: Fontana.

Braudel, F. And Mayne, R. (1993), *A History of Civilizations*, Harmondsworth: Penguin.

Brehony, K. (2000), 'Montessori, individual work and individuality in the elementary school classroom', *History of Education*, 29(2), pp. 115–28.

— (2006), 'Early years education: some Froebelian contributions', *History of Education*, 35(2) March, pp. 166–72.

— (2010), 'Working at Play or Playing at Work? A Froebelian Paradox Re-examined', www.roehampton. ac.uk/staff/Kevin%20j.brehony/docs/inaugural%20.pdf, last accessed 19 November 2010.

The British Schools Museum, www.iguidez.com/Hitchin/british-schools-museum/, last accessed 17 December 2010.

Brown, F. (2003) (ed.), *Playwork: Theory and Practice*, Buckingham: Open University Press.

Bruce, T. (2006) (ed.), *Early Childhood Education: A Guide for Students*, London: Sage.

Buckingham, D. (2000), *After the Death of Childhood: Growing Up in the Age of Electronic Media*, Cambridge: Polity Press.

Bunyan, J. and Owens, W. R. (ed.) (1678 and 2008), *The Pilgrim's Progress*, Oxford: Oxford World Classics.

Burke, C. (2009), George Baines – Obituary, *The Guardian*, 28 October 2009.

Burman, E. (1994), *Deconstructing Developmental Psychology*, London: Routledge.

Burnett, J. (ed.) (1994), *Destiny Obscure: Autobiographies of Childhood, Education and Family from the 1820s to the 1920s*, London: Routledge.

Burr, V. (2003), *Social Constructionism*, London: Routledge.

CACE (1967), *Children and Their Primary Schools – The Plowden Report*, London: HMSO.

Callaghan, J., Speech at Ruskin College, Oxford, 18 October, *Times Educational Supplement*, 22 October, 1976.

Calvin College (2005), 'Creeds of Christendom, with a History and Critical notes. Volume I. The History of Creeds', www.ccel.org/ccel/schaff/creeds1.ix.vi.iv.html, last accessed 3 November 2010.

Castle, K. (1996), *Britannia's Children: Reading Colonialism through Children's Books and Magazines*, Manchester: Manchester University Press.

Chandos, J. (1985), *Boys Together: English Public Schools, 1800-64*, Oxford: Oxford Paperbacks.

Channel 4, (1989), *A Century of Childhood: School*, London: Domino.

— (1991), 'A Century of Childhood – School', Broadcast 6.8.91, The Children's Rights Alliance, www.crae.org.uk/rights/uncrc20.html, last accessed 17 December 2010.

The Children's Society (2009), *A Good Childhood*, London: Penguin.

Chinouya, M. and O'Keefe, E. (2003), 'Young African Londoners affected by HIV: making sense of rights', www.lshtm.ac.uk/publications/list.php?inpress=1&grouping=recent&filter=staff_id&value=105339, last accessed 2 October 2010.

Chitty, C. (2002), 'A national system, locally administered, 1944-79', *Understanding Schools and Schooling*, London: RoutledgeFalmer.

Claire, H. (2004), *Not Aliens: Primary School Children and the Citizenship/PSHE Curriculum*, Stoke: Trentham.

Coard, B. (1971), *How the West Indian Child is Made Educationally Subnormal in the British School System: The Scandal of the Black Child in Schools in Britain*, London: New Beacon.

— (2005), 'Why I wrote the SEN book', *The Guardian*.

Compass (2008), *The Commercialisation of Childhood*, London: Compass.

Connell, R. W. (1987), *Gender and Power: Society, the Person and Sexual Politics*, Cambridge: Polity Press.

Connolly, M. and Ennew, J. (eds) (1996), 'Children out of place', *Childhood: A Global Journal of Child Research*, 3(2), pp. 131–45.

Copeland, I. (1999), *The Making of the Backward Pupil in Education in England 1870–1914*, London: Woburn.

Corsaro, W. (1997), *The Sociology of Childhood*, Thousand Oaks, CA: Pine Forge.

Cox, C. B. and Dyson, A. E. (1972), *The Twentieth Century Mind: History, Ideas and Literature in Britain, 1:1900–1918*, Oxford: Oxford Classics.

Cox, C. B. and Dyson, A. E. (eds) (1970), *Black Paper Two: The Crisis in Education*, London: The Critical Quarterly Society.

Crosby, A. W. (1993), *Ecological Imperialism: The Biological Expansion of Europe, 900–1900*, Cambridge: Canto, pp. 2–3.

Cross Commission (1886), *Royal Commission on the Elementary Education Acts (RCEEA)*.

Cunningham, H. (1995), *Children and Childhood in Western Society since 1500*, London: Longman.

— (2006), *The Invention of Childhood*, London: BBC Books.

The Daily Telegraph, 12 December 2006, 'Childhood dying in spend, spend Britain', www.telegraph.co.uk/news/uknews/1536653/Childhood-dying-in-spend-spend-Britain.html, last accessed 25 September 2010.

Daniels, H. (2001), *Vygotsky and Pedagogy*, London: Routledge.

Daniels, H., Cole, M. and Wertsch, J. V. (2007), *The Cambridge Companion to Vygotsky*, Cambridge: Cambridge University Press.

David, T. (2004), 'Re-enchanting early childhood?', in Hayes, D. (ed.), *The Routledge Guide to Key Debates in Education*, London: Routledge.

Davis, P. and Hersh, R. (1981), *The Mathematical Experience*, Harmondsworth: Pelican.

DCSF (2006), *Childcare Act 2006*, London: HMSO.

— (2009), www.nationalstrategies.standards.dcsf.gov.uk/node/259359, last accessed 2 October 2010.

— (2010), www.nationalstrategies.standards.dcsf.gov.uk/node/84579, last accessed 2 October 2010.

Dearden, R. F. (1968), *The Philosophy of Primary Education: An Introduction*, London: Routledge & Kegan Paul.

De Boeck, F. and Honwara, A. (eds) (2005), 'Introduction: children and youth in Africa', *Makers and Breakers: Children and Youth in Post-Colonial Africa*, Oxford: James Currey.

De Groot (2000), '"Sex" and "race": the construction of language and image in the nineteenth century', in Thomas, C. (ed.), *Cultures of Empire: A Reader*, Manchester: Manchester University Press, pp. 37–60.

De Mause, L. (ed.) (1974), *The History of Childhood*, New Jersey: Jason Aronson.

DES (1963), *Half Our Future – The Newsom Report*, London: HMSO.

— (1978), *The Warnock Report*, London: HMSO.

— (1981), *West Indian Children – The Rampton Report*, London: HMSO.

— (1985), *Education for All: Report of the Committee of Enquiry into the Education of Children from Ethnic Minority Groups (The Swann Report)*, London: HMSO.

DfES (2003), *Every Child Matters – Green Paper*, London: HMSO.

— (2004a), *Every Child Matters: Change for Children*, London: HMSO.

— (2004b), *Children Act 2004*, London: HMSO.

— (2005), *Youth Matters – Green Paper*, London: HMSO.

Dewey, J. (1902), *The Child and the Curriculum: The School and Society*, Chicago: University of Chicago Press.

Dickens, C. (1861 and 1994), *Great Expectations*, London: Penguin Popular Classics.

Diptee, A. A. (2006), 'African Children in the British Slave Trade during the Late Eighteenth Century', *Slavery & Abolition*, 27(2) August, pp. 183–96.

— (2007), 'Imperial ideas, colonial realities: enslaved children in Jamaica, 1775–1834', in Marten, J. (ed.), *Children in Colonial America*, New York: New York University Press.

Donnachie, I. (2005), *Robert Owen: Owen of New Lanark and New Harmony*, London: John Donald.

Drummond, M. J. (2000), 'Susan Isaacs: pioneering work in understanding children's lives', in Hilton, M. and Hirsch, P. (eds), *Practical Visionaries: Women, Education and Social Progress, 1790–1930*, Harlow: Longman.

Dunn, J. (1984), *Locke*, Oxford: Oxford University Press.

— (2003), *Locke: A Very Short Introduction*, Oxford: Oxford University Press.

Electric Scotland, www.electricscotland.com/history/women/wh31.htm, last accessed 17 December 2010.

Eldred, J. (1955), *I Love the Brooks*, London: Skeffington.

Ellis, E. (1978), 'As It Was and Twenty One Today', Unpublished.

Engels, F. (1844), *The condition of the working-class in England in 1844 / translated (from German) by F. K. Wischne*, London: Allen & Unwin.

Ennew, J. (2002), 'Future generations and global standards: children's rights at the start of the millennium', in MacClancy, J. (ed.), *Exotic No More: Anthropology on the Front Lines*, Chicago and London: University of Chicago Press, pp. 305–15.

Ermisch, J., Francesconi, M. and Peralin, D. J. (2001), *Outcomes for Children of Poverty*, DWP Research Report no. 158, Leeds: Corporate Document Services.

Evans, B. (2010), 'Anticipating fatness: childhood, affect and the pre-emptive "war on obesity"', *Transactions of the Institute of British Geographers*, 35(1) January, pp. 21–38.

Evans, M. (1995), 'Culture and Class', in Blair, M., Holland, J. and Sheldon, S. (eds), *Identity and Diversity: Gender and the Experience of Education: A Reader*, Clevedon: Multilingual, pp. 61–73.

Faith, N. (1994), *The World the Railways Made*, London: Pimlico.

Floud, R. and Johnson, P. (eds) (2004), *The Cambridge Economic History of Modern Britain, Volume 1: Industrialisation, 1700–1860,* Cambridge: Cambridge University Press.

Foley, P. (2001), 'The development of child health and welfare services in England (1900–1948)', in Foley, P., Roche, J. and Tucker, S. (eds), *Children in Society: Contemporary Theory, Policy and Practice*, Basingstoke: Palgrave, pp. 6–20.

Ford, D. (1999), *Theology: A Very Short Introduction*, Oxford: Oxford University Press.

Froebel, J. F. (1826 and 1967), *The Education of Man (Die Menschenerziehung)*, selections in Lilley, I. M. (ed.), *Friedrich Froebel: A Selection from His Writings*, Cambridge: Cambridge University Press.

Galton, F., (1944 revised draft), *Autobiography*, Coll misc 315: Galton, British Library of Political and Economic Science.

Gammon, V. (2008), ' "Many useful lessons": Cecil Sharp, education and the folk dance revival, 1899–1924', *Cultural and Social History*, 5(1), pp. 75–97.

Gardener, D. (1969), *Susan Isaacs*, London: Methuen.

Gidley, B. (2007), 'Sure Start: an upstream approach to reducing health inequalities', in Scriven, A. and Garman, S. (eds), *Public Health: Social Context and Action*, London: McGraw Hill, pp. 144–53.

Giesbrecht, M., Crooks, V. and Williams, A. (2010), 'Scale as an explanatory concept: evaluating Canada's Compassionate Care Benefit', *Area*, 42(4), pp. 457–67.

Graham, P. (2009), *Susan Isaacs: A Life Freeing the Minds of Children*, London: Karnac.

Griffiths, H. B. and Howson, A. G. (1974), *Mathematics, Society and Curricula*, Cambridge: Cambridge University Press.

Grosvenor, I. (2005), ' "There's no place like home": education and the making of national identity', in McCulloch, G. (ed.), *The RoutledgeFalmer Reader in History of Education*, London: RoutledgeFalmer, pp. 273–85.

Hall, J. S. (2000), 'Psychology and schooling: the impact of Susan Isaacs and Jean Piaget on 1960s science education reform', *History of Education*, 29(2), pp. 153–70.

Hankins, J. (2007), *The Cambridge Companion to Renaissance Philosophy*, Cambridge: Cambridge University Press.

Hattersley, R. (2010), *David Lloyd George: The Great Outsider*, London: Little, Brown.

Heafford, M. (1967), *Pestalozzi: His Thought and Its Relevance Today*, London: Methuen.

Heaton, J. and Groves, J. (2005), *Introducing Wittgenstein*, Royston: Icon Books.

Hendrick, H. (1997a), 'Constructions and reconstructions of British childhood: an interpretive survey, 1800 to the present', in James, A. and Prout, A. (eds), *Constructing and Reconstructing Childhood: Contemporary Issues in the Sociological Study of Childhood*, London: Routledge, pp. 33–60.

— (1997b), *Children, Childhood and English Society 1880–1990*, Cambridge: Cambridge University Press.

Hennessy, P. (1993), *Never Again: Britain 1945–1951*, London: Vintage.

Heywood, C. (2001), *A History of Childhood*, London: Polity Press.

Higonnet, A. (1998) *Pictures of Innocence: The History and Crisis of Ideal Childhood*, London: Thames & Hudson.

Hilton, M. And Hirsch, P. (2000), *Practical Visionaries: Women, Education and Social Progress, 1790–1930*, Harlow: Longman.

HM Government (1988), *Education Reform Act 1988*, London: HMSO.

Hobcraft, J. (1998), *Intergenerational and Life-Course Transmission of Social Exclusion: Influences of Childhood Poverty, Family Disruption and Contact with the Police*, CASE paper 15, London: London School of Economics and Political Science.

Holland, P. (1992), *What is a Child? Popular Images of Childhood*, London: Virago.

— (2003), *We Don't Play With Guns Here*, Maidenhead: Open University Press.

— (2004), *Picturing Childhood: The Myth of the Child in Popular Imagery*, London: I. B. Tauris.

Hollindale, P. (ed.) (2008), *J. M. Barrie: Peter Pan and Other Plays*, Oxford: Oxford World Classics.

Holloway, S. L. and Valentine, G. (2000), *Children's Geographies: Playing, Living, Learning*, London: Routledge.

Hopkins, P. and Alexander, C. (2010), 'Politics, mobility and nationhood: upscaling young people's geographies', *Area*, 42(2) June, pp. 142–44.

Horner, N. and Krawczyk, S. (2006), *Social Work in Education and Children's Services*, Exeter: Learning Matters.

Huggins, M. (2004), *The Victorians and Sport*, London: Hambledon & London.

Hughes, B. (2001), *Evolutionary Playwork and Reflective Analytic Practice*, London: Routledge.

Hughes, T. (1857 and 2007), *Tom Brown's Schooldays & Tom Brown at Oxford*, London: Wordsworth Classics.

Hunter, D. (2007), 'Public health: historical context and current agenda', in Scriven, A. and Garman, S. (eds), *Public Health: Social Context and Action*, London: McGraw Hill, pp. 8–22.

Hymns for Little Children (1848), 'Once in Royal David's City', www.oremus.org/hymnal/o/o777.html, last accessed 2 October 2010.

Internet Encyclopaedia of Philosophy(IEP) (2005), 'Jean-Jacques Rousseau (1712–1778)', www.iep. utm.edu/rousseau/, last accessed 3 November 2010.

Isaacs, S. (1933), *Social Development in Young Children: A Study of Beginnings*, London: Routledge.

Jackson, B. and Marsden, D. (1962), *Education and the Working Class*, Harmondsworth: Penguin.

Jackson, S. (2004), 'Early childhood policy and services', in Maynard, T. and Thomas, N. (eds), *An Introduction to Early Childhood Studies*, London and Thousand Oaks, CA: Sage.

James, A. and James, A. L. (2004), *Constructing Childhood: Theory, Policy and Social Practice*, Basingstoke: Palgrave Macmillan.

— (2008), *Key Concepts in Childhood Studies*, London: Sage.

James, A. and Prout, A. (eds) (1990), *Constructing and Reconstructing Childhood: Contemporary Issues in the Sociological Study of Childhood*, (1st edn) London: Routledge.

— (eds) (1997), *Constructing and Reconstructing Childhood: Contemporary Issues in the Sociological Study of Childhood*, London: Routledge.

James, A., Jenks, C. and Prout, A. (1998), *Theorizing Childhood*, Cambridge: Polity Press.

James, C. L. R. (1963), *Beyond a Boundary*, London: Serpent's Tail.

JamieOliver.com (2010), 'Jamie's school dinners', www.jamieoliver.com/school-dinners, last accessed 3 November 2010.

Jenks, C. (2005), *Childhood* (2nd edn), London: Routledge.

— (2009), 'Constructing childhood sociologically', in Kehily, M. J. (ed.), *An Introduction to Childhood Studies*, Maidenhead, UK: Open University Press, pp. 93–111.

Jones, C. (2008), '"Suffer the little children": setting a research agenda for the study of enslaved children in the Caribbean colonial world', unpublished paper, courtesy of author.

Jones, K. (2003), *Education in Britain: 1944 to the Present*, London: Polity Press.

Jones, L., Holmes, R. and Powell, J. (eds) (2005), *Early Childhood Studies: A Multi-Professional Perspective*, Buckingham: Open University Press.

Jones, O. (2003), ' "Endlessly revisited and forever gone": on memory, reverie and emotional imagination in doing children's geographies. An "addendum" to "To go back up the side hill": memories, imaginations and reveries of childhood' by Chris Philo, *Children's Geographies*, 1(1), pp. 25–36.

Jones, P. (2008), 'Pictures of children: what are the attitudes behind services and provision?', in Jones, P., Moss, D., Tomlinson, P. and Welch, S. (eds), *Childhood: Services and Provision for Children*, Harlow: Pearson, pp. 269–79.

Jordanova, L. (1989), 'Children in history: concepts of nature and society', in Scarre, G. (ed.), *Children, Parents and Politics*, Cambridge: Cambridge University Press, pp. 3–24.

Judd, D. and Surridge, K. (2002), *The Boer War*, London: John Murray.

Judge, H. (2006), 'H.A.L. Fisher: scholar and minister', *Oxford Review of Education*, 32(1), pp. 5–21.

Kant, I. (1781 and 1787), *Kritik der reinen Vernunft*.

Keen, S. (1989), 'Original blessing, not original sin – Matthew Fox and creation spirituality', www.abuddhistlibrary.com, last accessed 5 November 2010.

Kehily, M. J. (2009), *An Introduction to Childhood Studies*, Maidenhead, UK: Open University Press.

Kehily, M. J. and Montgomery, H. (2009), 'Innocence and experience: a historical approach to childhood and sexuality', in Kehily, M. J. (ed.), *An Introduction to Childhood Studies*, Maidenhead, UK: Open University Press, pp. 70–92.

Key, E. (1909), *The Century of the Child*, New York: Putnam.

Kilpatrick, W. H. (1951), *The Education of Man – Aphorisms*, New York: Philosophical Library.

Kitzinger, J. (1997), 'Who are you kidding? Children, power and the struggle against sexual abuse', in James, A. and Prout, A. (eds), *Constructing and Reconstructing Childhood: Contemporary Issues in the Sociological Study of Childhood*, London: Routledge, pp. 161–86.

Korner, S. (1955), *Kant*, Harmondsworth: Pelican.

Kraftl, P. (2006), 'Building an idea: the material construction of an ideal childhood', *Transactions of the Institute of British Geographers*, 31, pp. 488–504.

Kramer, R. (1988), *Maria Montessori: A Biography*, Chicago: Da Capo.

Kuhn, A. (1995), 'Passing', *Family Secrets: Acts of Memory and Imagination*, London: Verso.

Kuper, A. (1994), 'Culture, identity and the project of a cosmopolitan anthropology', *Man*, 29, p. 551.

The Lancasterian Society (2006), 'The Lancasterian Monitorial System of Education', www.constitution. org/lanc/monitorial.htm, last accessed 3 November 2010.

Lave, J. and Wenger, E. (1991), *Situated Learning: Legitimate Peripheral Participation*, Cambridge: Cambridge University Press.

Lawton, D. and Gordon, P. (2002), *A History of Western Educational Ideas*, London: Batsford.

Lengborn, T. (1993), 'Ellen Key', *Prospects: The Quarterly Review of Comparative Education*, 23(3–4), pp. 825–37, Paris, UNESCO: International Bureau of Education.

Levine, R. A., Dixon, S., Levine, S., Richman, A., Leiderman, H. P., Keefer, C. H. and Brazelton, T. B. (1994), *Child Care and Culture: Lessons from Africa*, Cambridge: Cambridge University Press.

Lewis, A. and Lindsay, G. (eds) (2000), *Researching Children's Perspectives*, Buckingham: Open University Press.

Lewis, B. (1982), *The Muslim Discovery of Europe*, London: Phoenix.

Liebschner, J. (1991), *Foundations of Progressive Education: The History of the National Froebel Society*, Cambridge: Lutterworth.

— (2006), *A Child's Work: Freedom and Guidance in Froebel's Educational Theory and Practice*, Leicester: Lutterworth.

The Literature Network (2006), www.online-literature.com/dickens/miscellaneous-papers/3/, last accessed 2 October 2010.

Llewellyn-Jones, B. (2004), 'Early childhood education', in Maynard, T. and Thomas, N. (eds), *An Introduction to Early Childhood Studies*, London and Thousand Oaks, CA: Sage.

MacCulloch, D. (2009), *A History of Christianity*, London: Allen Lane.

MacLure, S. (1986), *Educational Documents: England and Wales, 1816 to the Present Day*, London: Methuen.

MacNaughten, G. (2000), *Rethinking Gender in Early Childhood*, London: Paul Chapman.

MacNaughten, G. And Smith, K. (2009), 'Children's rights in early childhood', in Kehily, M. J. (ed.), *An Introduction to Childhood Studies*, Maidenhead: Open University Press, pp. 161–76.

Magee, B. (1988), *The Great Philosophers*, Oxford: Oxford University Press.

Maguire, M., Wooldridge, T. and Pratt-Adams, S. (2006), *The Urban Primary School*, Maidenhead, UK: Open University Press.

Mahmood, S. (2009), *A History of English Education in India*, New York: BiblioBazaar.

Mangan, J. A. (2000), *Athleticism in the Victorian and Edwardian Public School: The Emergence and Consolidation of an Educational Ideology*, London: Frank Cass.

Mangan, J. A. (2005), 'Eton in India: the imperial diffusion of a Victorian educational ethic', in McCulloch, G. (ed.), *The RoutledgeFalmer Reader in History of Education*, London: RoutledgeFalmer, pp. 163–78.

Manning-Morton, J. and Thorp, M. (2003), *Key Times for Play: The First Three Years (Debating Play)*, Maidenhead, UK: Open University Press.

Matheson, D. (2004), *An Introduction to the Study of Education*, London: David Fulton.

Maynard, T. and Thomas, N. (2004), *An Introduction to Early Childhood Studies*, London and Thousand Oaks, CA: Sage.

McCulloch, G. (2005), *The RoutledgeFalmer Reader in History of Education*, London: RoutledgeFalmer.

McDowell Clark, R. (2010), *Childhood in Society for Early Childhood Studies*, Exeter: Learning Matters.

McLuhan, M. and Fiore, Q. (1967), *The Medium is the Massage*, Harmondsworth: Penguin.

Michaelis, E. and Keatley Moore, H. (2008), *Autobiography of Friedrich Froebel: Translated and Annotated*, Charleston: BiblioBazaar.

Miller, P. and Davey, I. (2005), 'Family formation, schooling and the patriarchal state', in McCulloch, G. (ed.), *The RoutledgeFalmer Reader in History of Education*, London: RoutledgeFalmer, pp. 83–99.

Mills, J. and Mills, R. (eds) (2000), *Childhood Studies: A Reader in Perspectives of Childhood*, London: Routledge.

Mills, R. (2000), 'Perspectives of childhood', in Mills, J. and Mills, R. (eds), *Childhood Studies: A Reader in Perspectives of Childhood*, London: Routledge, pp. 7–38.

Milner, D. (1975), *Children and Race*, Harmondsworth: Penguin.

Monk, R. (1991), *Ludwig Wittgenstein: The Duty of Genius*, London: Penguin.

— (2005), *How to Read Wittgenstein*, Cambridge: Granta.

Montessori, M. (1912), *The Montessori Method*, New York: Heinemann.

Morgan, J. (2007), 'The Key Concepts in Piaget's Theory of Learning', www.suite101.com/content/the-key-concepts-in-piagets-theory-of-learning-a237499, last accessed 3 November 2010.

Moriarty, V. (1998), *Margaret McMillan: 'I learn, to succour the helpless'*, London: Educational Heretics.

Moyles, J. (ed.) (2010), *The Excellence of Play*, Maidenhead, UK: Open University Press.

Mullard, C. (1985), *Race, Power and Resistance*, London: Routledge.

The National Society for Promoting Religious Education (2003), 'Joshua Watson and the National Society', www.natsoc.org.uk/society/history/jwatson.html, last accessed 3 November 2010.

Neill, A. S. (1972), *Neill! Neill! Orange Peel! A Personal View of Ninety Years*, London: Weidenfield & Nicholson.

Neiman, S. (2009), *Moral Clarity: A Guide for Grown-Up Idealists*, London: Bodley Head.

Newton, I. (1689 and 1729) (translated by Motte) *Philosophiæ naturalis principia mathematica*, London: Prometheus.

Opie, P. and Opie, I. (1959), *The Lore and Language of Schoolchildren*, Oxford: Oxford University Press.

Owen, R. (2007), in Claeys, G. (ed.), *A New View of Society and Other Writings*, London: Penguin.

Palmer, J. (ed.) (2001), *Fifty Major Thinkers on Education: From Confucius to Dewey*, London: Routledge.

Palmer, S. (2006), *Toxic Childhood: How the Modern World is Damaging Our Children and What We Can Do about It*, London: Orion.

Parekh, B. (2000), *The Future of Multi-Ethnic Britain: The Parekh Report*, London: Profile.

Pestalozzi, J. H. (1801), *How Gertrude Teaches Her Children*.

Petrie, P. and Moss, P. (2002), *From Children's Services to Children's Spaces: Public Policy, Children and Childhood*, London: Routledge.

Phillips, J. L. (1975), *The Origins of Intellect: Piaget's Theory*, San Francisco: Freeman.

Philo, P. (2003), ' "To go back up the side hill": memories, imaginations and reveries of childhood', *Children's Geographies*, 1(1), pp. 7–23.

Piaget, J. (1952), *The Origins of Intelligence in Children*, New York: Basic.

Pine-Coffin, R. S. (1961) (translated), *Saint Augustine: Confessions*, Harmondsworth: Penguin.

Pollock, L. (1983), *Forgotten Children: Parent-Child Relations from 1500–1900*, Cambridge: Cambridge University Press.

Ponting, C. (1991), *A Green History of the World*, London: Sinclair Stevenson.

Porter, R. (2001), *Enlightenment: Britain and the Creation of the Modern World*, London: Penguin.

Pratt-Adams, S., Maguire, M. and Burn, E. (2010), *Changing Urban Education*, London: Continuum.

Prince, H. C. (1976), 'England circa 1800', in Darby, H. C. (ed.), *A New Historical Geography of England after 1600*, Cambridge: Cambridge University Press.

Pring, R. (2007), *John Dewey: A Philosopher of Education for Our Time*, London: Continuum.

Project Canterbury (1999), 'The Clapham Sect', www.anglicanhistory.org/misc/clapham.html, last accessed 3 November 2010.

Prout, A. and James, A. (1997) (2nd edn), 'A new paradigm for the sociology of childhood? provenance, promise and problems', in James, A. and Prout, A. (eds), *Constructing and Reconstructing Childhood: Contemporary Issues in the Sociological Study of Childhood*, London: Routledge, pp. 7–32.

Race, R. (2001), 'Bureaucratic rationality, flux or neutrality? Analysing the relationship between civil servants and politicians affecting education policy, 1970–74', PhD Thesis, (Keele University), United Kingdom.

— (2010), *Multiculturalism and Education*, London: Continuum.

The Ragged School Museum, www.raggedschoolmuseum.org.uk/nextgen/, last accessed 17 December 2010.

Reder, P., Duncan, S. and Gray, M. (1993), *Beyond Blame: Child Abuse Tragedies Revisited*, London: Routledge.

Rice, M. (2009), *Rice's Architectural Primer*, London: Bloomsbury.

Richards, M. and Light, P. (1987), *Children of Social Worlds: Development in a Social Context*, Cambridge: Polity Press.

The Robert Owen Museum, www.robert-owen-museum.org.uk/, last accessed 17 December 2010.

Robinson, D. and Groves, J. (1998), *Introducing Philosophy*, London: Icon.

Robinson, K. and Jones Diaz, C. (2006), *Diversity and Difference in Early Childhood Education: Issues for Theory and Practice*, Maidenhead, UK: Open University Press.

Ronge, B. (1854), *A Practical Account of the Kindergarten*.

Rorty, R. (1980), *Philosophy and the Mirror of Nature*, Oxford: Blackwell.

— (1999), *Philosophy and Social Hope*, London: Penguin.

Rose, J. (2001), *The Intellectual Life of the British Working Classes*, New Haven: Yale University Press.

Rosenthal, J. T. (ed.) (2007), *Essays on Mediaeval Childhood: Responses to Recent Debates*, Donington: Shaun Tyas.

Ross, A. (2000), *Curriculum Construction and Critique*, London: Routledge.

— (2009), *The Rest is Noise: Listening to the Twentieth Century*, London: Harper Perennial.

Rouse, W. H. D. (1898), *A History of Rugby School*, London: Duckworth.

Rousseau, J. J. (1762 and 2005), 'Emile', *Jean-Jacques Rousseau: Selected Writings*, London: The Collector's Library of Essential Thinkers, pp. 229–469.

Rowling, J. K. (1999), *Harry Potter and the Philosopher's Stone*, London: Bloomsbury.

Ruddick (2006), 'Abnormal, the "new normal," and destabilizing discourses of rights', *Public Culture*, 18(1), pp. 53–77.

Russell, B. (1979), *A History of Western Philosophy*, London: Counterpoint.

Sandiford, K. P. and Newton, E. H. (1995), *Combermere School and the Barbadian Society*, Mona: University of West Indies Press.

Sargant, W. L. (2005), *Robert Owen and His Social Philosophy*, London: Elibron Classics.

Sarup, M. (1986), *The Politics of Multiracial Education*, London: Routledge & Kegan Paul.

Save Steiner Schools (2008), 'The "early learning goals and educational programmes" of the EYFS framework requirements: areas of conflict with the Steiner system', www.savesteinerschools.org/wp-content/uploads/file/EYFS_SW_conflict.pdf, last accessed 3 November 2010.

Schmidt, J. (ed.) (1996), *What is Enlightenment? Eighteenth Century Answers an[d] Twentieth Century Questions*, Berkeley: University of California Press.

Scraton, P. (1997) (ed.), *'Childhood' in 'Crisis'*, London: University College London.

Scriven, A. and Garman, S. (eds) (2007), *Public Health: Social Context and Action*, London: McGraw Hill.

Seecharan, C. (2006), *Muscular Learning: Cricket and Education in the Making o[f] the British West Indies at the End of the 19th Century*, Kingston, Jamaica: Ian Randle.

Selleck, R. J. W. (1972), *English Primary Education and the Progressives, 1914–1939*, London: Routledge.

Simon, B. (1965), *Education and the Labour Movement, 1870–1920*, London: Lawrence & Wishart.

Skelton, T. (2010), 'Taking young people as political actors seriously: opening the borders of political geography', *Area*, 42(3) June, pp. 145–51.

Smith, F. and Barker, J. (1999a), 'From "Ninja Turtles" to the "Spice Girls": children's participation in the development of Out of School play environments', *Built Environment*, 25(1).

— (1999b), 'Learning to Listen: involving children in the development of out of school care', *Youth and Policy: The Journal of Critical Analysis*, Spring.

— (2000), 'Contested spaces: children's experiences of out of school care in England and Wales', *Childhood: A Global Journal of Child Research*, 73, February.

— (2001), 'Commodifying the countryside: the impact of out-of-school care on rural landscapes of children's play', *Area*, 33(2), pp. 169–76.

— 'School's Out? Out of school clubs at the boundary of home and school', in Edwards, R. (ed.), *Children, Home and School: Regulation, Autonomy or Connection?* London: Routledge, pp. 57–74.

Smith, M. K. (1997), 'Johann Heinrich Pestalozzi', www.infed.org/thinkers/et-pest.htm, last accessed 25 September 2010.

— (2009), 'Ragged schools and the development of youth work and informal education', www.infed. org/youthwork/ragged_schools.htm, last accessed 10 April 2009.

Social Exclusion Unit (SEU) (1998), *Bringing Britain Together: A National Strategy for Neighbourhood Renewal*, London: HMSO.

Spartacus Educational (2006), 'Rev. Andrew Bell', www.spartacus.schoolnet.co.uk/EDbell.htm, last accessed 3 November 2010.

Spartacusnet (2005), 'Herbert Fisher', www.spartacus.schoolnet.co.uk/EDfisher.htm, last accessed 3 November 2010.

— (2006), 'Joseph Lancaster', www.spartacus.schoolnet.co.uk/RElancaster.htm, last accessed 2 October 2010.

Stainton Rogers, W. (2001), 'Theories of child development', in Foley, P., Roche, J. and Tucker, S. (eds), *Children in Society: Contemporary Theory, Policy and Practice*, Basingstoke: Palgrave, pp. 202–14.

— (2009), 'Promoting better childhoods: constructions of child concern', in Kehily, M. J. (ed.), *An Introduction to Childhood Studies*, Maidenhead, UK: Open University Press.

Stanley, A. P. (2009) (facsimile edn), *The Life and Correspondence of Thomas Arnold, D. D., Late Head master of Rugby School, and Regius Professor of History at Oxford University*, London: BiblioBazaar.

Steiner, R. (1907 and 1948), *Die Erziehung des Kindes vom Gesichtspunkte der Geisteswissenschaft*, Stuttgart: Verlag Freies Geistesleben.

Stewart, K. (2009), ' "A scar on the soul of Britain": child poverty and disadvantage under New Labour', in Hills, J., Sefton, T. and Stewart, K. (eds), *Towards a More Equal Society? Poverty, Inequality and Policy since 1997*, London: Policy, pp. 47–70.

Stone, M. (1981), *The Education of the Black Child: The Myth of Multiracial Education*, London: Fontana.

Stott, A. (2002), 'Hannah More', www.victorianweb.org/authors/more/bio.html, last accessed 2 October 2010.

Tarnas, R. (1991), *The Passion of the Western Mind*, London: Pimlico.

Lord Taylor of Mansfield (1977), *Uphill All the Way: A Miner's Struggle*, London: Sidgwick & Jackson.

Taylor, J. (1996), *Joseph Lancaster: The Poor Child's Friend*, West Wickham: Campanile.

Thomas, N. (2000), *Children, Family and State: Decision Making and Child Participation*, Basingstoke: Macmillan.

Thompson, F. (1981), *Lark Rise to Candleford*, Harmondsworth: Penguin.

Thurschwell, P. (2000), *Sigmund Freud*, London: Routledge.

Tomes, N. (1985), 'From useful to useless: the changing social value of children', in Zelizer, V. (ed.), *Pricing the Priceless Child: The Changing Social Value of Children*, New York: Basic, pp. 50–4.

Troyna, B. and Williams, J. (1986), *Racism, Education and the State*, London: Croom Helm.

Trueman, H., Adlington, E., Marriott, F. and Steele, J.(ed.) (1999), *The Children Can't Wait: The McMillan Sisters and the Birth of Nursery Education*, London: Deptford Forum.

UNICEF (2007), 'Child Poverty in Perspective: A comprehensive assessment of the lives and well-being of children and adolescents in the economically advanced nations', www.unicef-irc.org/publications/pdf/rc7_eng.pdf, last accessed 3 November 2010.

United Kingdom Youth Parliament (2010), www.ukyouthparliament.org.uk/, last accessed 2 October 2010.

United Nations Convention on the Rights of the Child (UNCRC) (1989), www.unicef.org/crc/, last accessed 3 November 2010.

Valkonova, Y. and Brehony, K. (2006), 'The Gifts and "contributions": Friedrich Froebel and Russian education (1850–1929)', *History of Education*, 35(2) March, pp. 189–207.

Vanderbeck, R. M. (2008), 'Reaching critical mass? Theory, politics, and the culture of debate in children's geographies', *Area*, 40(3), pp. 393–400.

Vaughan Williams, U. (1988), *RVW: A Biography of Ralph Vaughan Williams*, London: Clarendon.

Victoria & Albert Museum of Childhood, www.vam.ac.uk/moc/, last accessed 17 December 2010.

Waksler, F. C. (ed.) (1991), *Studying the Social Worlds of Children: Sociological Readings*, London: Falmer.

Walford, R. (2001), *Geography in British Schools 1850–2000*, London: Woburn Press.

Walkerdine, V. (1984), 'Developmental psychology and the child-centred pedagogy: the insertion of Piaget into early education', in Henriques, J., Hollway, W., Urwin, C., Venn, C. and Walkerdine, V. (eds), *Changing the Subject: Psychology, Social Regulation and Subjectivity*, London: Routledge, pp. 148–98.

— (2009), 'Developmental psychology and the study of childhood', in Kehily, M. J. (ed.), *An Introduction to Childhood Studies*, Maidenhead, UK: Open University Press, pp. 112–23.

Walkup, V., Hughes, M. and Woolfolk, A. E. (2007), *Psychology in Education*, Harlow: Longman.

Welch, S. (2008), 'Childhood: rights and realities', in Jones, P., Moss, D., Tomlinson, P. and Welch, S. (eds), *Childhood: Services and Provision for Children*, Harlow: Pearson, pp. 7–21.

Weston, P. (2000), *Friedrich Froebel: His life, Times and Significance*, London: University of Surrey Roehampton.

Whitbread, N. (1972), *The Evolution of the Nursery-Infant School: A History of Infant and Nursery Education, 1800–1970*, London: Routledge & Kegan Paul.

Wiggin, K. D. (1895 and 2009), *Froebel's Gifts*, London: BiblioBazaar.

Williams, A. E. (1953), 'Thomas John Barnardo ("the doctor")', www.infed.org/thinkers/barnardo.htm, last accessed 3 November 2010.

Williams, J. (2001), *Cricket and Race*, London: Berg.

Wittgenstein, L. (1952), *Philosophical Investigations*, Oxford: Blackwell.

— (2001), *Tractatus Logico-Philosophicus*, London: Routledge.

The Women's Library, www.londonmet.ac.uk/thewomenslibrary/, last accessed 17 December 2010.

Young, R. (2010), *Electric Eden: Unearthing Britain's Visionary Music*, London: Faber and Faber.

Zuma, P. (2009), 'Approaches to the Education of Traveller Children', unpublished undergraduate dissertation (London Metropolitan University) – courtesy of the author.

Discography

Ornette Coleman (1959), *The Shape of Jazz to Come*, Atlantic Records, 1317.

Bob Dylan (1964), *The Times They Are A-changin'*, CBS Records, BPG 62251.

Joni Mitchell (1969), 'Woodstock', *Ladies of the Canyon*, Reprise Records.

Igor Stravinsky (1913), *Le Sacre de Printemps (The Rite of Spring)*, London Philharmonic Orchestra, Bernard Haitink, Decca, 438 350-2 (1993).

Index